MW01490434

POWER *and*
IDEAS

SUNY Series in Global Politics

James N. Rosenau, Editor

POWER *and* IDEAS

*North-South Politics of
Intellectual Property
and Antitrust*

Susan K. Sell

State University of New York Press

Chapter 6, "Intellectual Property Protection and Antitrust in the Developing World: Crisis, Coercion and Choice" is reprinted with permission from *International Organization* 49:2 (Spring 1995), pp. 315–349. © 1995 by the IO Foundation and the Massachusetts Institute of Technology.

Published by
State University of New York Press

© 1998 State University of New York

All rights reserved

Printed in the United States of America

No part of this book may be used or reproduced in any manner whatsoever without written permission. No part of this book may be stored in a retrieval system or transmitted in any form or by any means including electronic, electrostatic, magnetic tape, mechanical, photocopying, recording, or otherwise without the prior permission in writing of the publisher.

For information, address the State University of New York Press,
State University Plaza, Albany, NY 12246

Marketing by Patrick Durocher
Production by Bernadine Dawes

Library of Congress Cataloging-in-Publication Data

Sell, Susan K.
    Power and ideas : North-South politics of intellectual property and antitrust / Susan K. Sell.
        p.   cm. — (SUNY series in global politics)
    Includes bibliographical references and index.
    ISBN 0-7914-3575-X (alk. paper). — ISBN 0-7914-3576-8 (pbk. : alk. paper)
    1. Intellectual property (International law)   2. Antitrust law (International law)   3. Technology transfer—Law and legislation. 4. Developing countries—Foreign economic relations.   I. Title. II. Series.
    K1401.S455   1998
    341.7'58—dc21   97-31486
                                                              CIP

1 2 3 4 5 6 7 8 9 10

Contents

Preface

Once considered arcane issues, intellectual property and antitrust have emerged in the last decade as central items on national and international agendas. Governments recently negotiated intellectual property rules in a trade context in the Uruguay Round of General Agreement on Tariffs and Trade (GATT) talks. The United States and China repeatedly have engaged in trade brinkmanship over intellectual property rights. The North American Free Trade Agreement incorporated new rules covering both intellectual property and antitrust policies for the United States, Mexico, and Canada. Many observers believe that competition (antitrust) policy will be the centerpiece of the next round of multilateral trade negotiations. While these issues have just begun to make headlines, conference diplomacy of the 1970s and 1980s began to address these issues, which have become ever more central to the politics of technology transfer in the 1990s.

This book analyzes the North-South politics and diplomacy of technology transfer, antitrust, and intellectual property in two eras—from the early 1970s to 1985 and from 1985 to the present. For the first era, the book focuses on the United Nations Conference on Trade and Development (UNCTAD) negotiations over codes of conduct for the international transfer of technology, the World Intellectual Property Organization (WIPO) conference on revising its intellectual property code, and the United Nations' 1980 rules on restrictive business practices (antitrust). These cases illustrate the changes from the New International Economic Order debates of the 1970s and early 1980s to the new global emphasis on economic liberalization in the 1980s and 1990s. For the second era, the book analyzes the spreading debate over antitrust policies in developing countries and the efforts of the United States to get developing countries to protect U.S.-held intellectual property. The book concludes with the Uruguay Round of trade negotiations and the implications for technology transfer, antitrust, and intellectual property protection.

I am grateful for the many people and organizations who assisted me in developing this project. I am particularly thankful for the support, encouragement, and criticism that I received from Ernst Haas, who has been an invaluable mentor. His inspired teaching sparked my initial interest in international relations, and his conscientious and patient guidance helped make my graduate experience at University of California–Berkeley wonderful. He set a splendid example. Richard Buxbaum also provided tough criticism and priceless advice on early drafts. I wish to thank Alasdair Bowie, James Lebovic, and Wayne Sandholtz for their friendship, unflagging moral support, and helpful comments on numerous drafts. I thank Lee Sigelman, who prepared the figures for chapter 1. James Alverson provided outstanding research assistance.

I am grateful for the cooperation and candor of all those whom I interviewed in Geneva, at UNCTAD, WIPO, GATT, and the national missions. The librarians at WIPO were particularly helpful. The Licensing Executives Society USA and Canada, the Gallatin grant program, the Institute of International Studies at University of California–Berkeley, and the MacArthur Foundation provided financial assistance that made this research possible. An earlier version of chapter 6 first appeared in *International Organization*, vol. #49, no. 2 (Spring 1995).

I owe a great debt to my parents, Donald and Estelle Sell, whose example inspired a lifetime love of learning. I treasure the many hours spent discussing intellectual property issues with my father, who generously shared his insights and experience. Ellen and George Sell were always available with encouragement, and at crucial times, a place to write. I thank Doug Abrahms for his support and genuine partnership, and Nicholas Quinn, for making the home stretch much more fun and interesting.

Figures and Tables

Figures

Tables

Introduction

Technology has always been important to states. Technological evolution renders some industries obsolete while creating new ones. States seek to harness technology for wealth and power; state responses to technological change can determine decline or prosperity. Nations are increasingly preoccupied with economic competition and either maintaining or developing an edge in technology-intensive industries. Technology and trade policies have become so intertwined that domestic regulatory policies for intellectual property and competition are the object of negotiation between states, and market access has become the rallying cry of the 1990s.

The pace of change is rapid and prompts new thinking by economic and legal scholars. New breakthroughs in the economics of innovation have forced governments and firms to rethink the old proposition that invention of new products and processes is paramount. Commercialization has replaced invention as the best catch-up strategy. Economic competition among the United States, Japan, the European Community, and the Newly Industrializing Countries (NICs) of East Asia has raised the stakes of staying at the forefront of technological change. Japanese and East Asian success has prompted policymakers in the United States to rethink traditional approaches and seriously consider industrial policy along Japanese lines. The rising costs of research and development (R & D), short product life cycles, and nontariff barriers have all altered the strategies of firms. The old intrafirm paradigm of innovation has given way to the pursuit of strategic corporate alliances among competitors in high-technology fields such as semiconductors, commercial aircraft, and telecommunications. These trends pose new dilemmas and are forcing states to rethink the relationship between domestic policy and international commerce.

Previously arcane issues, such as intellectual property protection, antitrust, and competition policy have suddenly emerged as central items on everyone's political agendas. The North American Free Trade Agreement (NAFTA) incorporated new rules governing intellectual property protection and competition policy between the United States, Mexico, and Canada. In the spring and summer of 1996, the United States and China narrowly averted a trade war over China's failure to enforce intellectual property rights. The United States and Japan's Structural Impediments Initiative incorporated antitrust law in the United States' quest to limit Japan's oligopolies *(keiretsu)*, which the United States argues are barriers to market access. Therefore, governments increasingly are motivated to coordinate their domestic regulatory environments. Finally, for the first time, governments negotiated intellectual property rules in a trade context in the recently concluded Uruguay Round of General Agreement on Tariffs and Trade (GATT) talks. Many observers speculate that competition policy will be the central topic of the next round of multilateral trade negotiations.[1] Thus, these topics are important and will not go away. While the pace of change has accelerated in the last decade, conference diplomacy of the 1970s and 1980s began to address these issues, which have become ever more central to the politics of technology transfer in the 1990s.

In the early 1970s, national policies had come into conflict with predominant modes of international technology transfer. By the mid-1970s both the developing and industrialized countries began multilateral negotiations over technology transfer, intellectual property protection, and competition policy. The international dialogue that began in the 1970s deeply informs currrent conflicts between developing and industrialized countries over intellectual property rights, market access, and competition policy.

While the issues may seem new, they highlight enduring concerns about economic development. What strategies for development are open to the South? What constraints and opportunities exist for technological "latecomers" as opposed to pioneers? How do rich countries use their wealth and power to structure constraints for the poor? Do the rules and practices governing international technology transfer favor the "haves" over the "have-nots"? Is the international economy structured in a way that disadvantages developing countries? By examining power asymmetries, intersubjective dimensions of politics, and globalization as complicating domestic regulatory policy, this book sheds light on these enduring questions.

This book examines the politics and diplomacy of intellectual property rights and antitrust between developed and developing countries in two eras. The first, beginning in the 1970s and lasting until the mid-1980s, was dominated by negotiations over a New International Economic Order (NIEO). This era presented opportunities for developing countries, linked to the commodity power demonstrated by the Organization of Petroleum Exporting Countries (OPEC). The developing countries, negotiating as a bloc, articulated an alternative vision for the organization of technology transfer. This vision presented a critique of the existing international order. The negotiations on technology transfer, intellectual property protection, and competition policy (antitrust) reflected a clash between competing ideas about the international economic order. Developed countries resisted this challenge.

The second era, beginning in the early 1980s, was marked by an economic crisis that left developing countries particularly vulnerable. This was an era of constraints, and it prompted both developed and developing countries to rethink their policies for the transfer of technology, and in some cases to wholly redefine their interests. Developed countries went beyond their previous policies of damage control in the NIEO context and used bilateral pressure to attempt to change the domestic laws of developing countries. This era culminated in a new round of multilateral negotiations, the Uruguay Round of GATT, in which the developed countries set the agenda.

While the NIEO has rapidly slipped from memory, it is in this set of negotiations that one finds the roots of the current conflicts between the North and South over technology transfer. This book reconsiders the traditional power-based interpretations of North-South relations and argues that these standard treatments obscure important aspects of the politics surrounding intellectual property and antitrust. If North-South relations were only about power, we would see a different world today. What states believe is as important as what they can get away with. Nowhere is this more evident than in intellectual property protection. Even though power shifted, ideas did not. Despite their glaring vulnerability to trade threats, developing countries have not enforced intellectual property protection. They do not believe in it at this point. The most egregious violators of intellectual property rights continue to violate them, threats of trade sanctions notwithstanding.

Furthermore, in antitrust policy the negotiations of the 1970s still resonate. Indeed, an intergovernmental institution, the Intergovernmental Group of Experts on Restrictive Business Practices established in the United Nations Conference on Trade and Development (UNCTAD) in 1980, as a result of these negotiations has come to play an important role in expediting the adoption of antitrust policy in the developing world. This institution has become a source of detailed, substantive information about the rationale for and operation of antitrust policies. Developing countries have changed their minds about the merits of antitrust policies and have accepted the idea prior to adopting such policies. Developing countries voluntarily have consulted with this international institution, which has helped them devise domestic policies in a way that does not compromise their legitimacy.

The evolution of the international transfer of technology is also a story of increasing restrictions on the primary agents of transfer, transnational corporations. In the two decades following World War II, American transnational corporations were relatively unfettered in their activities and faced little competition. By the mid-1960s they confronted more restrictive government policies and new competitors based primarily in Japan and Western Europe. By the late 1970s and 1980s they faced new competitors from the NICs of East Asia. Over time, transnational corporations have had to change their strategies in response to nontariff barriers and intensifying competition. Barriers to entry abroad and the rising costs of R & D have led former competitors to participate in research consortia and, more recently, in strategic corporate alliances in which proprietrary technology is shared for the purpose of rapid commercialization of innovation.

New thinking about the economics of innovation has produced tension between traditional approaches to intellectual property and competition and the pressure to prevail in a rapidly changing economic and technological landscape. Just as developing countries are adopting policies consistent with economic liberalism, policymakers in the industrialized countries are redefining the purposes of these policies, reflecting new concerns about market access and competitiveness.

This book addresses three questions: (1) How and why did the industrialized and developing countries come together to negotiate an international regulatory framework for the transfer of technology in the 1970s? (2) Why did these efforts ultimately fail? (3) In the wake of these failed multilateral efforts, how and why have the parties redefined their interests? Using insights from both neorealist and neoliberal theories of international relations, this study examines the role of both power and ideas in explaining the genesis and failure of these efforts, as well as emerging trends in the wake of the negotiations.

This study argues that both neorealist and neoliberal theories are needed to explain these cases. The role of ideas is most important in accounting for the *demand* for negotiations. Interpretivist neoliberalism addresses the origin of states' preferences and provides important insights into the perceived legitimacy of new ideas. The role of power is most important for explaining the *results* of the negotiations. Neorealist analysis provides powerful insights into factors such as asymmetrical power relations and international constraints. However, examining the changes in states' policies in the wake of the negotiations reveals a more nuanced pattern and requires an analysis of both power and ideas. Changing power configurations present both constraints and opportunities, providing the context for the politics of technology transfer. Realist theories focus on constraints. Interpretivist theories focus on responses to constraints and opportunities. Choices are not preordained, and the way that actors frame the problem and

perceive those constraints matters. Both industrialized and developing
countries have radically redefined their interests in technology transfer
and have revised their ideas about cause-effect relationships in intellectual property, antitrust, and technology policy. The combination of
the new context and new thinking will shape the politics of technology
transfer for decades to come.

The formal negotiation process of the NIEO agenda ended in
1985. Since then developing countries have been adopting policies in
both intellectual property protection and antitrust that the industrialized countries have long desired. Developing countries have now begun
to offer stronger protection of intellectual property. I argue that these
policies have been adopted under duress, or pressure from more powerful states. Developing countries have changed their policies, not
their minds. Still unconvinced of the intrinsic merits of intellectual
property protection, policymakers in these countries have neither implemented nor vigorously enforced these policies. By contrast, in antitrust, developing countries *have* changed their minds. There has been
no discrepancy between the adoption of antitrust policies and their
enforcement. Developing countries' governments have been adopting
these new policies voluntarily and have sought the counsel of international institutions to learn more about the role of antitrust policies.

Furthermore, even though both types of policy change embrace
a market orientation and integration into the global economy, the different mechanisms by which they have been adopted suggest different
prospects for the sustainability of these new policies. Based on my
analysis of these processes I argue that the prognosis for antitrust is
much better than it is for intellectual property protection.

Organization of the Book

Chapter 1 presents the analytic argument. Chapter 2 provides a historical perspective on the issues leading up to the multilateral negotiations
of the NIEO. Chapters 3 through 6 provide the empirical core of the
book. Chapter 3 covers negotiations on an international code of conduct for technology transfer (under the auspices of the United Nations
Conference on Trade and Development [UNCTAD]). Chapter 4 dis-

cusses negotiations on the revision of the Paris Convention for the Protection of Intellectual Property (under the auspices of the World Intellectual Property Organization [WIPO]). Chapter 5 examines the negotiations on the Restrictive Business Practices Code of Conduct (under UNCTAD). Chapter 6 provides a comparison of trends in intellectual property protection and antitrust in developing countries from the mid-1980s to the present. Finally, chapter 7 discusses the recently concluded GATT agreement on intellectual property protection (the TRIPs [Trade-Related Aspects of Intellectual Property, Including Trade in Counterfeit Goods] accord) and provides a summary of both power and ideas as explanations for two eras of North-South technology transfer—from the mid-1970s to the mid-1980s and from 1985 to the present.

1 ❖
POWER AND IDEAS

This book is about power and ideas. It begins by presenting an historical perspective on economic development and examining the origins of the "Third World," answering the question of how a disparate group of countries spanning three continents, Latin America, Asia, and Africa, came to see themselves as part of a whole. Chapters 3 through 5 examine the politics and diplomacy of intellectual property rights, antitrust, and technology transfer between developed and developing countries during the 1970s and 1980s, when developing countries as a bloc confronted industrialized countries with a critique of the existing international economic order. Chapter 6 is an account of what happened in the ten years following the multilateral negotiations over these issues. Therefore, this study seeks to explain the genesis and failure of these efforts, as well as emerging trends in the wake of the negotiations.

The book addresses three questions: (1) How and why did industrialized and developing countries come together to negotiate an international regulatory framework for the transfer of technology in the 1970s? (2) Why did these efforts ultimately fail? (3) In the wake of these multilateral efforts, how and why have the parties redefined their interests?

The three multilateral negotiations discussed are: (1) Negotiations on an International Code of Conduct for the Transfer of Technology (TOT Code); (2) Diplomatic Conference for the Revision of the Paris Convention (intellectual property); and (3) Negotiations on a Restrictive Business Practice (RBP) Code (antitrust). The issues at stake—intellectual property protection, antitrust, and technology transfer—all reflect a broader concern for the proper role of the state in economic development. These issues are embedded in a larger context that includes industrial policies, development strategies, and state policies vis-à-vis foreign investment.

National policymakers gradually came to see the predominant arrangements for international technology transfer as impediments to achieving the goals of economic development and competitiveness. The developing countries, especially in Latin America, became dissatisfied with their programs of import-substituting industrialization (ISI). By the early 1970s, Mexico, Argentina, Brazil, and the Andean Pact countries felt they had exhausted the possibilities of this strategy. They determined that they could go no further placing so much emphasis upon ISI and were eager to hasten the pace of nondependent economic development. They blamed prevailing modes of technology transfer as the source of their problems. The developed countries, especially Western European countries, became concerned with prevailing modes of technology transfer when their economic recovery was in full swing. They had benefited from the United States' largesse after World War II, but upon recovery they faced a new dilemma— how to become effective economic competitors in a world dominated by the United States and, increasingly, Japan.

The fact that countries of both the North and South came together to negotiate new international rules for the transfer of technology reveals that by the early 1970s, while the two groups had different goals, they settled upon a common means to achieve them. In the ensuing negotiations, they sought to construct an international cooperative framework to establish minimum ground rules for international technology transactions. They wanted to increase the benefits of international technology transfers while reducing the costs (namely, impediments to economic development for the South, and limits on competitiveness for the North). In short, the negotiations on the Code of Conduct for the Transfer of Technology, the Restrictive Business Practice Code, and revisions of the Paris Convention constituted a concerted effort at multilateral cooperation.

In the cases of the Code of Conduct for the Transfer of Technology and the Paris Convention revisions, the developing countries set the agenda and pressed for rules that would maximize their development goals. In contrast, the United States, seeking to devise international rules that would prohibit practices that hindered fair competition, pushed for the Restrictive Business Practice Code. The three negotiations were related in the sense that both the RBP and TOT Codes were designed to provide guidelines for contracts for international technology transfers, while the Paris Convention revisions dealt with the international system of intellectual property protection that shapes the transfer process.

Prior to the negotiations, developing countries came to see the state as the primary engine of economic development. In the past decade, these same countries have redefined their interests and increasingly have come to accept a reduced role for the state and a larger role for the private sector. What accounts for this change?

Mainstream analyses of international politics, neorealism and neoliberal institutionalism, are ill-equipped to address the questions raised here. Both approaches treat interests as exogenous. These analyses, by design, assume away some of the more interesting questions in international politics such as: Where do interests come from? What is the relationship between ideas and interests? How and why are they redefined? To the extent that they consider the role of ideas at all, they either assume that ideas are a product of the structure of the system,[1] or that ideas must be viewed in opposition to interests.[2] Neorealism focuses on power and constraints. Its theories, while weak on examining the origin of interests, are stronger in explaining success or failure in the conclusion of agreements. Neoliberal institutionalism shares many of the assumptions of neorealism, yet accords a stronger role for institutions in solving collective action problems. Neoliberal institutionalism emphasizes how institutions can make cooperation possible and robust, even in an anarchic world comprised of rational egoists.

By contrast, interpretivist neoliberal theories[3] focus on the role of ideas and learning. I call it "interpretivist" because it addresses the intersubjective dimension of international politics and treats interests as endogenous. In other words, these theories pay attention to how the actors themselves interpret their circumstances. Power and interests are not "given" but rather must be interpreted and are periodically redefined. I retain the label "neoliberal" to indicate this type of theorizing's roots in idealism and nineteenth-century liberalism. As E. H. Carr emphasized in his discussion of the "utopians,"[4] what I call "interpretivist neoliberalism" retains a concept of human agency; international relations is not the product of some abstract structural puppetmaster but of people making choices and trying to alter their circumstances. People learn, change their minds, and redefine their interests in ways that make a difference in international politics.

My analysis of intellectual property protection and antitrust constitutes a critique of both instrumentalist/rationalist (neoliberal institutionalist) and structural (neorealist) theories of international politics. These perspectives certainly do not exhaust the range of possible alternative explanations. I chose to address these perspectives because they currently dominate the contemporary debate in American international relations scholarship. Other theories, such as world systems theory and structural Marxism, also have offered explanations of North-South relations. However, for purposes of my argument these two approaches suffer from the same deficiencies as do neorealist theories; they emphasize structure over agency, neglect the role of ideas, and are indeterminate. For example, the analytic similarities between structural Marxism and neorealism have been well-documented by Stephen Krasner.[5] Therefore, these approaches do not provide analytic leverage that would override my assessment of neorealism or structural analyses in general.

Two important alternative theoretical traditions are structuration theory and Gramscian analysis.[6] While both types of theorizing take intersubjective aspects of politics seriously, both privilege structure in favor of agents. In particular, Gramscian approaches may be considered relevant because they take the role of ideas seriously and stress the close relationship between power structures and ideas. However, in these approaches it is not clear what "ideas" explain that structural factors do not. My analysis contributes insights into the role of ideas as disentangled from structure and power. For example, in the antitrust case, power shifted and ideas did too; developing countries became more receptive to antitrust policy, albeit without overt coercion. This outcome is consistent with a Gramscian perspective that rejects a sharp distinction between overt coercion and persuasion, or the power of ideas. By contrast, in the intellectual property case, power shifted but the ideas did not. This case demonstrates the usefulness of examining ideas as an independent force. Both structuration theory and Gramscian analyses are pitched at a very high level of abstraction that obscures significant variations between both issues (intellectual property and antitrust) and regions (e.g., Latin America versus East Asia). Interpretivist neoliberalism, emphasizing voluntarism and choice, can explain important aspects of international politics that are obscured by other perspectives.

For purposes of this analysis I adopt the following definition of learning: "to learn is to alter one's beliefs as a result of new information; to develop knowledge or skill by study or experience."[7] Learning, by definition, is a process of change. These cases demonstrate that developing countries learned over time. At the end of World War II, developing countries passively accepted market mechanisms. With the emergence of new economic ideas, Latin American structuralism and antidependency, these countries came to believe that market mechanisms were not in their best interests and championed a much larger role for the state in economic development. They institutionalized these ideas in their domestic and regional economic policies. When they confronted the industrialized countries with their alternative conception in multilateral negotiations, they were unable to prevail. As the negotiations wound down, developing countries were in the process of redefining their interests yet again and began to accept market mechanisms and the logic of neoclassical economics.

The analysis presented here examines the interaction between power and ideas. It seeks to combine explanations pitched at the level of the international system with those pitched at the domestic level. While the scope of this study prohibited an in-depth examination of the domestic politics of each of the countries involved, I have incorporated domestic, or unit-level, variables in my discussion. I generally use the term the "state" as a shorthand for elites or policymakers, although in several instances my "unit-level" factors also include domestic processes such as interest-group lobbying and bureaucratic considerations.[8] I use domestic legislation and regulatory policy as indicators of the institutionalization of specific economic ideas. For example, developing countries' dissatisfaction with predominant modes of technology transfer and the slow pace of economic development led them to adopt novel domestic laws and to press for a multilateral approach to the management of technology transfer. Additionally, domestic developments in the United States contributed to its push for a multilateral approach to restrictive business practices and, later, its trade-based approach to intellectual property protection.

The politics of international technology transfer is as much about contested beliefs as it is about power. To assert that ideas "matter" in international relations says very little; I seek to demonstrate how, when, and why they matter, and when they do not. I argue that: (1) new economic ideas can create group identities and cohesion; (2) unit-level learning leads states to redefine their interests; (3) unit-level learning can account for the substance of multilateral demands, and it plays an agenda-setting role; (4) if unit-level learning does not become consensual knowledge, it will not affect diplomatic outcomes; diplomatic outcomes will be those predicted by a neorealist structural analysis; (5) in international relations, ideas matter when they are institutionalized in the domestic practices of states, and the practices come into conflict with those of other states. Figures 1.1 and 1.2 summarize the overall argument of this book.

Neorealism

Neorealism has dominated postwar American international relations scholarship. Its strengths are well known; it is parsimonious, elegant, and generates powerful explanations. It is "rationalist" in its basis in rational choice theory,[9] which takes an "outside-in" approach to its objects of study. The power, simplicity, and wide applicability of this approach derive from the fact that it eschews the intersubjective dimension of politics in favor of strategic interaction and treats actors' preferences and interests as exogenous. Its main incarnation is structural.

Structural neorealist theories derive nations' interests from the structure of the anarchic international system, based on the distribution of

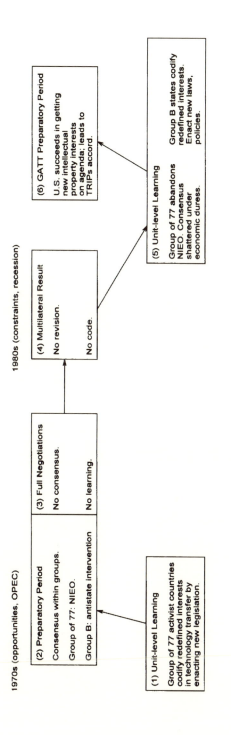

Figure 1.1

The Restrictive Business Practices Code

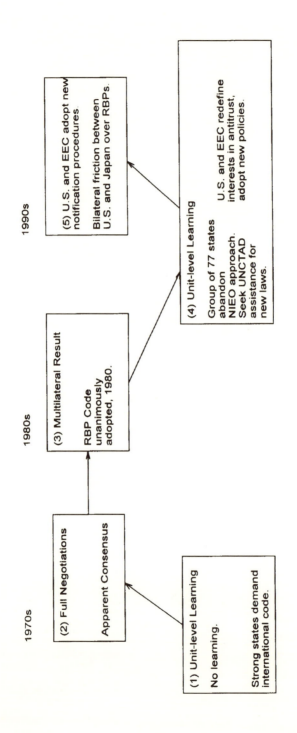

1970s

1980s

1990s

(1) Unit-Level Learning

No learning.

Strong states demand international code.

(2) Full Negotiations

Apparent Consensus

(3) Multilateral Result

RBP Code unanimously adopted, 1980.

(4) Unit-level Learning

Group of 77 states abandon NIEO approach. Seek UNCTAD assistance for new laws.

U.S. and EEC redefine interests in antitrust, adopt new policies.

(5) U.S. and EEC adopt new notification procedures.

Bilateral friction between U.S. and Japan over RBPs.

Figure 1.2

power throughout the system. These theories predict that the more powerful states will prevail over weaker states, and that the powerful states make the rules. In this perspective, states are defensive positionalists, concerned with their relative positions in the system. The structure of the system imposes constraints upon states' freedom of action.

However, deriving interests from structure leaves much unexplained. States do not respond in identical ways to structural constraints. For instance, in the North-South context, structure provides a misleading picture of interests. To argue, as does Stephen Krasner,[10] that developing countries' interest in the NIEO was a product of their weakness in the international system overemphasizes similarities at the expense of critical differences between the overwhelmingly "weak" states. The NIEO clearly was not the only choice that weak states had available to them. The fact that the East Asian countries declined to participate in any meaningful way underscores this point. At that time they were "weak" too, but did not believe that they needed an NIEO. They had an altogether different philosophical view about the relationship between governments and markets. Structure tells us nothing about either the national policies of participants or the characteristics of the desired multilateral regime. The NIEO movement was a product of a handful of states whose leaders agreed with the views of influential development economists and based quite specific domestic legislation on these ideas. These states took a leadership role in the multilateral effort, and the substance of the NIEO platform for technology transfer was a product of their domestic legislation. In short, structural neorealism is too indeterminate and diffuse to provide satisfactory explanations of the cases at issue here.

Strategic Interaction and Neoliberal Institutionalism

Theorists of strategic interaction represent a second prominent mainstream approach. Arguments based on this approach assume that, rather than acting as defensive positionalists, states are rational egoists pursuing their self-interests. Given a specified constellation of preferences, cooperation in this sense is a matter of overcoming collective action problems based on dilemmas of common interest or common aversion. For example, Arthur Stein argues that:

> the same forces of autonomously calculated self-interest that lie
> at the root of the anarchic international system also lay the foun-
> dation for international regimes as a form of international order. . . .
> There are times when rational self-interested calculation leads
> actors to abandon independent decision-making in favor of joint
> decision-making.[11]

As straightforward and sensible as this sounds, this logic begs the
question—where do interests come from? At what point does business
as usual become a dilemma requiring joint action? In any case, why
were prevailing modes of international technology transfer universally
accepted at one time and perceived as highly contentious and requiring immediate attention at another? While the analysis of strategic
interaction captures an important part of the picture, without a fuller
explanation of interests and how those interests change, Stein's explanation is too spare to be of much help in providing an in-depth understanding of either the process of attempted regime creation or the
redefinitions of states' interests that occurred in the wake of the failed
multilateral efforts. As I will demonstrate, state perceptions, overlooked
by both structural neorealism and theories based on rational choice,
have important consequences.

Keohane, a leading proponent of neoliberal institutionalism, raises
the question of "why self-interested actors in world politics should
seek, under certain circumstances, to establish international regimes
through mutual agreement."[12] Keohane relies upon the notion of
efficiency and suggests that regimes may provide benefits such as
reducing transaction costs, facilitating information exchange, and establishing mechanisms to determine liability and monitor compliance
with agreements. For Keohane, international cooperation can help
correct political market failure. As Keohane states, "insofar as international regimes can correct institutional defects in world politics, along
with any of these three dimensions (liability, information, transaction
costs), they may become efficient devices for the achievement of state
purposes."[13] Yet states may not evaluate efficiency the same way. As
John Ruggie argues, "what constitutes institutional inefficiences or
costs is not entirely independent of the attributes of the states making
the calculation."[14] This underscores the limits of the "outside-in"
approach.

Keohane assumes that preferences are given and fixed. Keohane's functional approach is limited by its lack of attention to the formulation and redefinition of interests. An analysis of the nature and compatibility (or lack thereof) of states' interests in an issue would help to explain why some efforts at regime creation succeed and some fail. As Roger Smith points out, "the functional theory does not explain the creation and simultaneous convergence of a new interest by a host of states differing widely in history, politics, culture, and capability. . . . It does not get at why there was a redefinition of egoistic self-interest."[15]

Keohane argues that we see greater demands for international regimes as issues become more complicated and interlinked. As issues compound around concepts once conceived of as simple and isolated, states may seek to create regimes. As relationships between various issues are discovered, and the interdependence between the resolution of x aspect with y aspect is recognized, the issue can be said to be more dense. For example, in terms of technology transfer, policymakers used to consider issues such as patents, market access, foreign investment, and technology purchases as separate and isolated. But these issues did not become "more dense" by themselves. Policymakers began to link these issues as they discovered that if they did not treat the issues as interrelated, they might be working at cross-purposes. As the developing countries linked technology transfer to economic development, they began to see the advantages of a multilateral approach.

Substantive issue linkage is crucial for understanding cooperation. As Ernst Haas argues:

> Experts in developing countries have come to think of technology transfer as an overarching concept, instead of worrying separately about such matters as foreign capital inflows, obtaining patents for specific products, finding markets for their products, or building a certain type of factory. . . . Instead of being ends in themselves, they become means toward a more complicated end—the achievement of technological self-reliance. Instead of being effects, they are reconceived as causes leading to more basic effects such as wealth, prestige, status, autonomy.[16]

For example, in many Latin American states policymakers linked issues under the umbrella concept of technology transfer and altered their institutions to reflect this new, more comprehensive approach. These new institutions reflected their new interests in technology transfer. Without examining unit-level processes, such as the gradual consolidation of technology-related tasks into as few as one or two governmental agencies in many Latin American states, we cannot understand how issues become more "dense" and what form this density takes.

As Friedrich Kratochwil points out: "theoretical frameworks distort by two means, either by marginalizing a set of interesting problems or by making it impossible to raise certain questions at all."[17] Both neorealism and neoliberal institutionalism have important limitations; both neglect the question of where interests come from.[18] Yet addressing the formulation and redefinition of interests is essential for a satisfactory explanation of the demand for multilateral cooperation. Both structural and functional theories of cooperation marginalize the domestic level of analysis.

Indeed, domestic, or unit-level, factors were crucial in the demand for a regime for the transfer of technology and the NIEO. New economic ideas provided an identity for developing countries and facilitated group cohesion. These ideas helped constitute a negotiating group and provided a substantive agenda. The origins of this effort were rooted in domestic politics of states that took leadership roles in seeking multilateral solutions to their perceived problems. The way that these states framed the problem provided the substance of the issues for negotiation. Changes in perceptions about the prevailing pattern of international technology transfer led to the realization among policymakers in Latin America that the costs of going it alone had become too high, and that joint action along their desired lines might be preferable.

Therefore, by ignoring unit-level processes, neorealism, neoliberal institutionalism, and theories of strategic interaction fall far short of a satisfactory explanation of the demand for a technology transfer regime. Moreover, by overlooking the unit-level, or domestic, factors, these theories tell us little about the process of change—the question of how countries come together to negotiate regimes in lieu of conducting business as usual. Furthermore, they are ill-suited for explaining redefinitions of interests in the wake of the negotiations.

The most obvious starting point for an explanation of the demand for a regime for technology transfer would be the success of OPEC. While the OPEC story provides a partial explanation, especially for the North's willingness to negotiate, we need to know more about the parties' interests. We may think about the significance of OPEC for creating the demand for a technology transfer regime in causal terms; the first obvious point is that OPEC's rise preceded the negotiations by several years. OPEC's first major price hike was in 1971, followed by a second, sharper increase in 1973. The negotiations followed an apparent shift in the distribution of capabilities in favor of the South as a result of OPEC. Before the negotiations began, both the North and South shared this perception and acted on it. It was highly significant because OPEC's success led to a flurry of multilateral negotiations. These North-South negotiations created an unprecedented opportunity for the demands of the South to be taken seriously in multilateral forums. In short, OPEC's success created favorable conditions for new interests to be heard at the international level. The perceived shift in the structure of the system created an opportunity for changes in interests to be influential in the international arena. However, we need to understand what these interests were and from where they came. As James Caporaso points out: "mainstream international relations theory relies heavily on power, interest, and anarchy for its explanatory foundation. . . . The concentration of power may make it easier to solve collective action problems, but it tells us nothing about the content of the regime. For this, we must introduce ideas, norms, and social purposes."[19] Therefore, we now turn to nonstructural explanations, which provide a guide to such an understanding.

Interpretivist Neoliberalism

While neorealist and neoliberal institutionalist theories explain the demand for cooperation in terms of the variables of power and interest, interpretivist neoliberal theories adopt a different approach. Unlike neorealism and neoliberal institutionalism, interpretivist neoliberalism adopts an "inside out" approach to analysis; it focuses on the intersubjective dimension of politics. It also assumes that actors are rational in the sense that they are purposeful goal seekers. However, interpretivist scholars inquire critically about the origin of preferences and the substance and redefinitions of interests. While neorealism concentrates on the structure of international politics, neoliberalism focuses on processes. Some of the central questions in interpretivist neoliberalism include: (1) What is the relationship between the unit level and systemic level of analysis? (2) How are states' preferences formed? (3) How are states' interests redefined in response to systemic level changes? (4) When does learning matter: "when has it led to the development of new institutions, such as international regimes, and when has it not?"[20]

One of the core differences between interpretivist neoliberalism and the mainstream approaches discussed earlier is that it examines the relationship between ideas and interests. Here, its roots in idealism are apparent in the sense of privileging the force of ideas, as opposed to materialism.[21] Haas suggests that much of what is taken for granted in structural theories—such as the notions of fixed interests, given preferences, and the structural derivation of interests—should not be. Haas states that "whether states really calculate their participation in a regime on the basis of a concern for their overall rank in some international pecking order is a matter for empirical investigation, not definition."[22] It is not enough to assert that a state's interests are x because it is a weak state. One needs to know how states form interests, why particular ideas (and not others) shape policy, and how states interpret their options—their constraints and opportunities. In this perspective, interests are understood as social constructions. Ideas and values play a constitutive role in interest formation. As Audie Klotz suggests, "interpretive scholars allow for the possibility of conceptual change (be it in the realm of norms, cultures, ideas or knowledge) for policy choice, rather than presenting norms as either an alternative to interests in motivating action or a source of ethical constraint on interest driven behavior."[23]

One prominent approach to the role of ideas in international politics insists upon ideas as an alternative to interests. Judith Goldstein and Robert Keohane have classified ideas as world views, principled beliefs, and causal beliefs.[24] World views are most encompassing, reflected, for example, in world religions and the scientific rationality of the Enlightenment. Principled beliefs are normative ideas that provide yardsticks of right and wrong. Causal beliefs imply strategies for goal attainment, which are embedded in both world views and principled beliefs. Goldstein and Keohane argue that ideas can have such political effects as: road maps, focal points to identify cooperative solutions or coalitional glue to promote group cohesion, or being embedded in institutions that specify policy. The economic ideas, primarily Latin American structuralism and antidependency, that animated the NIEO quest reflected all three types of ideas and had all three types of effects. However, this formulation is not satisfactory for this discussion insofar as the Goldstein and Keohane approach tells us nothing about which ideas might be persuasive or why ideas are originally adopted. The authors cling to a distinction between ideas, on the one hand, and interests, on the other, and then proceed to examine the effects of given ideas on political outcomes.[25] By insisting on this distinction, their approach obscures the relationship between ideas and interests[26] and ignores the origin of preferences.

In fact, interests do not exist outside of cognitive and social contexts. The cognitive context, ideas, defines how the world works, and therefore what is possible to do. The social context consists of norms and rules, and shape actors' beliefs about what should be done. According to Ngaire Woods, "ideas and ideologies play a critical role in defining social categories and social expectations."[27] These contexts and expectations are not static. As John Jacobsen points out: "actors and coalitions also devise their 'interpretations' of changing economic circumstances. . . . If the circumstances change dramatically, the notion of what is pragmatic widens and may even be up for grabs."[28] The very notion of what constitutes a pragmatic option must be understood in its cognitive context. For instance, in the fifteenth century, a "pragmatic" navigation strategy would look very different for one who believed that the earth was flat, and another who believed it was round.

One variant of interpretivist neoliberalism focuses on the ideational variables of consensual knowledge and learning to explain international cooperation. Two of the early proponents of this variant of neoliberalism are Ernst Haas and Robert Rothstein. Haas and Rothstein both examine the role of knowledge and learning in international cooperation. However, their approaches to the issue are slightly different.

Haas defines consensual knowledge as "the sum of technical information and of theories about that information which commands sufficient agreement at a given time among interested actors to serve as a guide to public policy."[29] Haas's requirement for knowledge to be considered *consensual* is that it must transcend group cleavages and be transideological. Haas hypothesizes that consensual knowledge can provide the basis for international transformation, or the construction of new international regimes.[30]

In contrast to Haas, Rothstein relaxes the requirement for consensual knowledge, and instead suggests that learning and knowledge can play significant roles in cooperative efforts even when the consensus exists only *within* a particular group. Thus Rothstein's argument is more useful for examining the period prior to the full intergroup negotiations, such as when the Group of 77 reached a consensus on their package of demands under the rubric of the NIEO. Haas's argument is better suited for examining the negotiating process between the Group of 77 and Group B.

Rothstein examines consensus *within* groups. He points out that consensus within a particular group can impede the building of consensus across groups. He underscores the point, suggested by Haas, that consensual knowledge between groups is a relatively rare phenomenon. Rothstein argues that it is easier to build consensus within each group than between groups because "at the intergroup level . . . conflicts in values and interests are likely to be sharpest . . . and the need of each group to maintain unity may . . . mean that the resulting group position is impervious to knowledge and learning, [and] genuine bargaining."[31]

In the negotiations over an international technology transfer regime, learning and new knowledge played a significant role in both the construction of the identity of the "Third World" and in the development of an intragroup consensus on the part of the Group of 77. New economic ideas created a sense of community and identity.[32] The community and identity of the "Third World" was formed before these countries settled upon their particular demand package in these negotiations. The consensual knowledge within the Group of 77 created a package of demands built upon the concept of technological self-reliance to promote economic development. The Group of 77 sought to achieve the goal of reduced dependence on the North, facilitated by greater state intervention in technology transactions and an international regime supportive of the increased role of the state. However, consensus at the Group of 77 level impeded consensus at the inter-group level.

Learning and redefinition of states' interests, especially on the part of the Group of 77, provided the context for these negotiations. In these cases learning was both a unit-level and intragroup (or coalitional) phenomenon. This learning never became consensual knowledge across groups.

Using the concepts of consensual knowledge and learning as variables to explain the demand for multilateral cooperation transcends some of the shortcomings of structural analyses based on power and interest. Ideational concepts focus squarely on the *content* of interests, how those interests are perceived and defined, and how they change over time. If one accepts the premise that the system does not exist independently of the perceptions of the actors, or in Alexander Wendt's terms, if "anarchy is what states make it,"[33] then what matters for understanding their behavior is the actors' perceptions of the constraints and opportunities facing them.

According to Haas, "if and when states perceive that they cannot be secure or prosper without new principles, norms, and rules the time is ripe for designing organizations to reflect the need. The particular character of the demands, however, still dictates the design to be chosen."[34] The negotiations on the Code of Conduct for the Transfer of Technology, the Restrictive Business Practices Code, and the Paris Convention revisions all focused on the proposed mode of resource allocation. At issue was the debate between a market-oriented regime, emphasizing the private allocation of resources, and a regime based upon the authoritative allocation of resources.[35] The strength of states' commitments to competing values will shape the bargaining process and set the terms of the debate. As Kratochwil points out, most disputes over policy are not so much about "the likely result, given a certain distribution of 'preferences,' as they are debates over which preferences deserve priority over others, . . . and which judgements deserve our assent. Here the overall persuasive 'weight' of claims rather than their logical necessity or aggregation is at issue."[36] In the multilateral negotiations over international technology transfer, nations clashed over competing ideological views about the role of the state in allocating resources. The developing countries were committed to the authoritative allocation of resources, whereas the North was committed to a more market-oriented system. This opposition was a reflection of each group's primary interest in the multilateral endeavor—namely, development for South, competitiveness for the North.

However, despite the fact that interpretivist neoliberalism, in its ideational incarnation, corrects for some of the shortcomings in structural analysis, it presents problems of its own. According to Haggard and Simmons, the most difficult problem for ideational theorists is to isolate the autonomous influence of knowledge and ideology when ideology and structural position are congruent.[37] However, sophisticated variants of interpretivist neoliberalism, as presented by Rothstein and Haas, do not claim that knowledge is an autonomous variable. Both Haas and Rothstein's work focuses on the intersection between knowledge and power. Knowledge must be consistent with the perceived interests of powerful actors if it is to have a significant impact. If the learning is confined to the weak actors, it will not be decisive in shaping negotiating outcomes. The task for interpretivists is to trace the path of learning and its relationship to power in international negotiations.

Events in the wake of the negotiations underscore the importance of ideas and beliefs. The economic crisis of the early 1980s exposed developing countries as especially vulnerable, and the North reasserted its power to set the agenda. Yet even though power shifted in favor of the North and developing countries began to adopt policies that the North desired, it is clear that in some issues developing countries have changed their policies and not their minds. For example, they appear to have embraced the norm of competition by promoting and enforcing antitrust policies but have not embraced the norm of protecting intellectual property. Despite quite credible threats of trade sanctions and palpable vulnerability, these countries have neither rigorously enforced nor complied with Northern demands for intellectual property protection. Therefore, structure, in this context, is a poor predictor of the responses of the "weak."

When interpretivist neoliberals concentrate on the interests of the actors and on who holds the relevant knowledge (i.e., weak or powerful actors), they sharpen the focus on the interaction between knowledge and power. However, ideational analysis "cannot predict at what point consensual values or knowledge will produce cooperation."[38]

The following discussion addresses the core issues of this study: the origin of the demand for multilateral cooperation; diplomatic outcomes; and redefinitions of states' interests in the wake of the failed multilateral efforts.

The Origins of the Demand for Cooperation: An Interpretivist Analysis

The attempt to achieve multilateral cooperation can be an effort to codify changes that have already taken place in international relations or to establish forums to press for change in international relations. The push for international cooperation and the nature of the demands resulted from three main factors: (1) new economic ideas that played a constitutive role in forming the identity of the "Third World," which later acted as a coherent negotiating bloc; (2) unit-level learning (national consensus on dependency reduction in selected Latin American countries) and its institutionalization in domestic practices; these new ideas became the basis of specific regulatory policies, institutionalized in domestic and regional legislation; and (3) unit-level perceptions shared by both the North and South that the structure of the international system had changed. I will discuss each of these variables in turn.

New economic ideas—primarily Latin American structuralism and, later, dependency theory—played a crucial role in creating an identity for developing countries. These ideas exposed underlying inequalities in the structure of the global economy that hindered economic development and helped explain the gap between the rich and poor states. Placing the blame on unfair terms of trade with the rich states, and offering a strategy to overcome structural disadvantages, these ideas identified an important source of difference between the rich and the poor, the powerful and the exploited, and offered the hope of autonomous development by advocating a different path. These ideas helped unite a large number of countries that widely differed in culture, historical experience, economic circumstances, and geography. Both Latin American structuralism and dependency theory pinpointed the common concerns of this disparate group of countries and promoted a sense of "us" (the poor) versus "them" (the rich). Developing countries embraced these ideas as both a reassuring diagnosis of their situations as well as a blueprint for overcoming obstacles to their economic development. These ideas helped to forge Third World unity and provided persuasive substantive arguments in favor of a new and different way of conducting business.

The key states that led the movement to establish an international regulatory framework for the transfer of technology redefined their interests in this issue area. Originally, the developing countries passively accepted market-oriented mechanisms for the transfer of technology. Later, they redefined their interests in technology transfer as a result of learning through new information (i.e., the analyses of influential Latin American economists of the dependency school) and experience (feeling disadvantaged by the old market-oriented rules). They came to believe that market-oriented mechanisms were not in their best interests, since they were not reaching their economic development goals rapidly enough, and adopted an approach sanctioning increased state intervention in the technology transfer process. They created new state institutions to screen technology contracts to ensure that the transactions would meet their national and regional development goals. Their new interests were reflected in their adoption of national legislation that challenged the old ways of conducting technology transactions.

These new interests found expression in the Declaration of the Establishment of a New International Economic Order. The NIEO expressed developing countries' dissatisfaction with an international system that seemed to leave them out in the cold. It presented a sweeping critique of global inequality. In this declaration, developing countries called for resource transfers from North to South as well as for the restructuring of global economic relations to redress the balance. They argued that a new international scientific and technological order was a crucial component of the NIEO.

Developing countries complained that technology was overpriced and that technology suppliers engaged in unfair practices that severely limited the recipients' control over the process. These countries sought greater national control over the transfer of technology and took measures to reduce their dependence on foreign suppliers.

While the evolution of development strategies reflected developing countries' reevaluation of their relationship to foreign private enterprises, and the NIEO packaged a variety of their demands, the more immediate impetus for the international regulation of the transfer of technology came from key national and regional experiments in legislative control over technology transfer. In the late 1960s and early 1970s, Argentina, Brazil, Mexico, India, and the Andean Pact countries had all enacted laws that codified their dissatisfaction with market principles governing technology transactions.[39] These legislative measures institutionalized their redefined interests with respect to technology transfer and were designed to enhance recipient countries' bargaining power and to reduce dependency on foreign suppliers.

These developing countries took the lead in pressing for multilateral codes of conduct and the Paris Convention revision (with the sole exception of the Restrictive Business Practice Code). The developing countries wanted greater access to modern science and technology on more favorable terms. The purpose of each of these efforts was to incorporate the specific concerns of the developing countries into an international framework for technology transfer. In a nutshell, the developing countries felt that acceptance of their proposed measures would significantly tip the scale in their favor and redress past inequities.

The appearance of these redefined interests on the international agenda cannot be explained without reference to an important variable that created the opportunity for the new demands to be heard. This variable—unit-level perceptions—had important consequences. In effect, unit-level perceptions in the wake of OPEC's success led to multilateralism. Developed and developing countries perceived that the tide had turned in the South's favor. In short, leaders from both the North and South acted on the basis of their perceptions that commodity power had given the South new power, and that the South would have to be taken more seriously.

At first glance, the most obvious explanation for why these multilateral efforts ever got off the ground despite the parties' different objectives is the success of OPEC. The importance of the oil producers' cartel in the early 1970s cannot be overestimated. The fact that OPEC was able to extract important concessions from the North, and the fear that its power generated among highly dependent oil-importing states, goes a long way toward explaining why the South suddenly was taken very seriously. The OPEC example raised the possibility that developing countries might cartelize other commodities in order to extract resources from a resource-dependent North. As Bhagwati points out, by 1973 "the South entered, with a perception of new strength, the negotiations phase, for negotiations cannot occur meaningfully between grossly unequal partners. . . . The South's perception of new power was largely shared by the North at that time. OPEC's demonstrated strength made commodity power seem credible."[40] The sense of Southern solidarity, forged by OPEC, led to a unified Southern challenge in multilateral forums, culminating in the South's call for a NIEO. Since the South promoted a New International Scientific and Technological Order as an integral part of a NIEO, the TOT Code and Paris Convention revision negotiations were a product of oil.

In the early 1970s, it seemed that the distribution of capabilities *had*, in fact, changed. Both the South and the North were convinced that the tide had turned in the South's favor, and they acted on that assumption. In the autumn of 1975 the U.S. Secretary of State, Henry Kissinger, addressed the Seventh Special Session of the United Nations and indicated that the United States was willing to "turn away from confrontation" and was ready to take the needs of developing countries more seriously.[41] The South pushed for sweeping international changes to rectify past inequities, while the North granted concessions to the South that were previously unimaginable.

The political ramifications of OPEC's success were extensive; among the most important was the weakening of Western political unity regarding Israel. Most of the Western European countries and Japan were highly dependent on oil from the Middle East and wavered in their backing of the United States' position of support for Israel during the Arab-Israeli War of 1973. "Many Northern states either were very cautious in giving any form of support to Israel during and immediately after the war or quickly became decidedly pro-Arab in their public pronouncements."[42] Furthermore, the OPEC success led to a brief competitive scramble for special bilateral relationships that threatened Northern cohesion, and "demonstrated a very limited Northern capacity to take coordinated actions of a nonmilitary nature to deal with the energy problem."[43]

In addition, the OPEC states were able to capitalize on their newfound power to bring the Northern states to negotiate broader development interests in Paris. OPEC linked the North's willingness to negotiate with a credible threat to increase oil prices again in 1975. As a result, multilateral negotiations were held under the auspices of a specially created Council on International Economic Cooperation between 1975 and 1977. This example illustrates that, whether truly chimerical or not, states were behaving as if the distribution of global power resources had shifted toward the South.

Fueled by the success of OPEC, the early 1970s ushered in an era of conference diplomacy, particularly in various UN forums. This presented unprecedented opportunities for the voice of the South to be heard, and North-South issues took center stage. The combination of these auspicious factors—a vigorous multilateralism fueled by national perceptions that the distribution of capabilities had shifted in the South's favor—turned events into opportunities for the developing countries to press their demands and be taken seriously.

Unit-level learning helps to explain the origins and substance of the developing countries' demands. Consensus within the Group of 77 on a demand package (NIEO) explains their negotiating position. The changed perception that there was a shift in the distribution of capabilities, and the vigorous multilateralism as a result of this apparent structural change, explain the North's willingness to negotiate and the appearance of the South's redefined interests in international negotiations over a regime for technology transfer.

During the full negotiations, the Group of 77 and Group B (industrialized country bloc) made conflicting knowledge-based claims and fundamentally disagreed about cause and effect relationships. The Group of 77's dependency-influenced arguments called for strong state intervention in technology transfer transactions. Group B's neoclassical arguments advocated minimal state interference and reliance upon market mechanisms for the transfer of technology. There was no consensual knowledge bridging the groups. The fragmentary consensus, especially one firmly rooted in a discrete ideological position, was not sufficient to create a mutually acceptable compromise. In fact, the consensus within the Group of 77 made *inter*group consensus more difficult to achieve, since it represented a maximalist bargaining position that left little room for compromise.

Diplomatic Outcomes: Interpretivist and Neorealist Explanations

All three of the multilateral efforts to construct an international regime for technology transfer fared badly from the point of view of developing countries. The TOT Code effort ran out of steam. Many participants on all sides either lost interest or gave up. The RBP Code was moribund for the decade following its unanimous adoption in 1980. Some developed countries defiantly rejected it (in deed, not in word); many developing countries had serious doubts about having agreed to it in the first place, and some felt they were duped. In the case of the Paris Convention revision conference, what began as an NIEO-inspired revision attempt took a rather dramatic turn by the mid-1980s. Several developed countries went beyond merely resisting the developing countries' proposals to balance private rights and public interests. They changed from holding a status-quo (antirevision) stance to actively seeking stronger patent protection (prorevision, but in the opposite direction from that desired by developing countries). Not convinced that WIPO was even the appropriate forum for such changes, some developed countries, led by the United States, succeeded in getting intellectual property protection included in the agenda of the Uruguay Round of GATT negotiations.

Since unit-level learning cannot explain diplomatic outcomes because that learning never became consensual knowledge, one must look elsewhere to explain the causes of failure. Clearly the NIEO's "moment" has passed. In the mid-1970s the developing countries were able to set the international agenda in multilateral forums. However, by the early 1980s the developed countries were setting the international agenda once again. The world that existed in the early and mid-1970s, when preparations for the conferences were in full swing, changed dramatically by the early 1980s. The buoyant optimism of the developing countries gave way to fierce efforts to stay competitive in a rapidly changing world economy.

Both perceptual and structural factors explain the diplomatic outcomes. The failure of efforts to establish an international regulatory framework for technology transfer can be explained by: (1) a shift in unit-level perceptions—that the South's power had peaked and waned—and (2) the world economic situation of the early 1980s. Both of these factors had important consequences for the fate of the multilateral efforts.

First of all, unit-level perceptions changed. By the early 1980s the parties to the negotiations realized that the perceived shift in the distribution of capabilities in the wake of OPEC's success had been a mirage. Both the North and South came to realize that oil was the exception, and both fears and hopes of commodity power were unjustified. Both sides had overestimated the promise or peril of commodity power. The promise of Southern commodity power was discovered to have been merely a temporary illusion. Furthermore, OPEC's crucial solidarity fell apart as member countries cheated by overproducing, causing oil prices to fall. Even OPEC was unable to sustain its concerted approach. This was indicative of the death of the NIEO; it was another nail in the coffin. The fact that the chimera of Southern power had vanished in everyone's eyes led to the reassertion of the North's power to call the shots in the North-South arena with renewed confidence and vigor.

A direct consequence of these perceptions was a retreat from the multilateralism of the 1970s and the ushering in of a new era emphasizing bilateralism over multilateralism in technology transfer issues. Of course, even during the height of the NIEO movement, bilateralism never entirely disappeared. Yet there was a shift in emphasis—a decline in the use of multilateral channels in this issue area until 1986, when the United States succeeded in including intellectual property protection in the new GATT Round. The developing countries, in effect, lost their platform since the developed countries no longer felt compelled to take them as seriously as they had in the early stages of the NIEO movement.

However, the main causal factor explaining the failure of these negotiations is the world economic situation of the early 1980s. The

economic slump that began in the late 1970s and progressively worsened in the 1980s forced many countries to reconsider their interests.
Power differentials between the North and South were heightened by
economic problems, and the consensus that had been so crucial to the
developing countries' multilateral agenda setting shattered under economic pressure. These changed circumstances led developing countries to reconsider the pragmatism of earlier strategies. The development
and transfer of technology requires external financing and foreign
investment. In these areas the situation became more bleak for developing countries. Bank lending to developing countries dropped sharply
in the early 1980s. The resulting scarcity of external financing in the
forum of private bank loans was accompanied by a sharp drop in
foreign direct investment (FDI) in developing countries. Between 1981
and 1986 inflows of FDI dropped by nearly 25 percent.[44] In addition,
many developing countries were saddled with huge foreign debts. This
situation was exacerbated by a resurgence in protectionism in Northern trade policies and a drop in commodity prices. All these developments led to depressed economic conditions in developing countries
and presented new constraints, which in turn led to changes in developing countries' policies and, in large part, an abandoning of the NIEO
program. Developing countries began to liberalize their economies in
an effort to attract foreign investment.

Aftermath: Redefining Interests

What effects has the reassertion of Northern power—facilitated by the
perceptions of actual Southern weakness, reflected in bilateralism, and
heightened by a drop in the levels of world economic activity—had on
the states that led the charge for the international regulation of the
transfer of technology? At the outset of the negotiations, the activist
developing countries were convinced that strong state intervention in
the economy, as dictated by ISI, was the best recipe for growth. From
the late 1970s onward, developing countries revised their earlier approaches. Most significantly, the activist developing countries who
helped galvanize developing country opinion to support an NIEO
program revised their national policies in a more liberal direction.

Development economics began to fall out of favor. The logic of dependency theory began to crumble under the weight of inexplicable empirical anomalies such as East Asian success. Faith in autonomous development gave way to renewed hope in invigorated economic engagement. Industrialized countries had always advocated free market principles, so Northern dominance alone cannot account for the fact that developing countries finally began to accept them in the mid-1980s. As Woods points out, "the political context and available alternative ideas most likely affected the demise of dependency theory."[45] Salient elements of the political context included: the external shock of the early 1980s recession; the perceived failure of past statist economic policies; the deterioration of the multilateral challenge to global liberalism; the political ascendance of economic technocrats advocating neoclassical economic policy strategies; and the international institutional backing of these ideas. These elements provided the context and opportunity for a redefinition of interests. As Thomas Biersteker suggests, during the 1980s "there was a growing sense of failure, a belief that the policies of the past had failed in some way, and that something new should be considered. . . . There was, therefore, a crucial opening for new ideas."[46] Neoclassical economics was resurgent in both academic and policy circles. The Thatcher and Reagan revolutions in the United States and the United Kingdom embraced an anti-Keynesian approach to economic policy.

The pressing problems faced by developing countries forced them to sacrifice many of the premises that animated the effort to establish a New International Economic Order. The activist developing countries' own lawmakers called into question legislation that had inspired numerous provisions for the restructuring of international relations in technology transfer, and they subsequently amended legislation to reflect new economic realities. For example, throughout the 1980s, more and more developing countries joined the "privatization" bandwagon. They increasingly denationalized public sector companies and subjected the public sector to competitive market pressures.[47] Mexico, Argentina, India, and the Andean Pact states revised their laws to make them less restrictive and more attractive to potential suppliers and investors. These trends, evident by the early 1980s, led many developing countries to lose interest in the code efforts. Apart from the fact that the developing countries had made so many concessions that the draft versions were a far cry from what they had originally hoped for, in the 1980s the whole enterprise seemed marginal at best. It seemed fruitless to pursue efforts to restrict and regulate the activities of foreign suppliers and investors when foreign suppliers and investments were so badly needed. Additionally, since private bank lending dried up in the face of the debt crisis, many developing countries had to actively court international agencies such as the International Monetary Fund (IMF) to overcome liquidity crises.[48] The IMF imposed lending conditions that reflected neoclassical economic prescriptions.

While the failure of the multilateral efforts to establish an international regulatory framework for the transfer of technology was due to changes in unit-level perceptions about the distribution of capabilities, the economic slump of the early 1980s was the strongest shock to the optimism of the Group of 77's member states. Not only did it take the wind out of their sails, but it led them to abandon the whole ship.

The economic crisis of the early 1980s presented constraints to which developing countries had to respond. In two subjects of the NIEO negotiations (intellectual property protection and restrictive business practices), they changed their policies. Neorealism can explain the power shift neatly; yet developing countries' responses to these constraints have varied according to issue area in a way not captured by neorealism. While power differentials between the industrialized and developing countries were accentuated by the economic downturn, and the economic crisis was an important causal factor in the shift toward more market-oriented policies, this change did not have the same effects in both issue areas.

In intellectual property protection, the more proximate cause for policy change was coercion by more powerful states. The United States pursued a vigorous bilateral effort to secure stronger guarantees of intellectual property protection. By linking intellectual property protection to trade, the United States posed a credible threat to developing countries through Section 301 of the U.S. Trade Act. However, targeted countries have not responded the way that neorealists would predict. Although they have adopted new and stiffer policies on paper, they have resisted implementing and enforcing the new policies with few exceptions. They have not embraced the norm of intellectual property protection. Since states do not accept this value, they do not comply with Northern wishes. While they may have redrafted domestic policies along the United States' desired lines, they have not redefined their interests in this area since the Paris Convention negotiations. Even though power shifted, the ideas did not.

In antitrust, the more proximate explanations for changes in policy also have a normative and ideational component. Overt coercive threats have been absent in this policy shift. Liberalization, in response to the economic crisis, has led developing countries to recognize the connection between liberalization policies and antitrust. Ten years after these countries unanimously adopted the Restrictive Business Practices Code, with which they initially were disappointed, the institutional mechanisms established by the agreement have played an important role in expediting the adoption of new antitrust policies. Beyond the neoliberal institutionalist emphasis on the efficiency of international institutions in overcoming "institutional defects" in world politics, the attendant institutions have been engaged in normative persuasion in which developing countries have learned more about and accepted the idea of restrictive business practice control prior to adopting policies. Developing countries voluntarily have sought the assistance of the Intergovernmental Group of Experts (IGE) for help in drafting their new policies. The IGE has been an important venue for socialization, information exchange, and education. Developing countries redefined their interests and have institutionalized them in their domestic practices. This supports a more interpretivist view that international institutions do not merely render the conduct of international relations more efficient but can play an important transformative role in changing substantive, versus instrumental, interests.

These trends have not been limited to developing countries alone. While advocating market-oriented policies to developing countries, industrialized countries have been redefining their interests, as reflected in domestic practices. They also felt the impact of the economic downturn, but in a different way. During the 1980s, industrialized countries and firms became increasingly preoccupied with competitiveness and market access. New constraints and challenges emerged in the forms of a resurgent Japan and the increasing success of the export-led growth strategies of the "fast seconds" (those that commercialize rather than pioneer new technologies), the NICs of East Asia.

In the United States, private sector actors pressed for a trade-based approach to intellectual property protection. These actors were well poised to have a domestic impact, given the facts that their industries enjoyed positive trade balances and their exports had a high intellectual property content. Pressure from these private sector actors coincided with the government's concern over U.S. trade deficits and led to the institutionalization of their interests in a trade-based approach. Initially codified in U.S. domestic legislation, these efforts culminated in the recently concluded GATT intellectual property (TRIPs) accord.

In antitrust, the origin of the United States' redefined interests was the new "Chicago school" economic approach. Institutionalized throughout the late 1960s and 1970s, the Chicago school perspective recast earlier U.S. approaches to antitrust. By the time the Reagan administration came to power, this new conception already was deeply entrenched in antitrust agencies and was reinforced by the administration's preoccupation with competitiveness. Therefore, when the Reagan administration advocated radical policy changes, these changes encountered no resistance and were implemented quickly.

In the European Community, competition from Japan heightened competitiveness concerns. The European Community also adopted newly relaxed antitrust policies for high-technology sectors, due to ideational shifts regarding the former national champions strategy and the policy entrepreneurship of the European Commission under the leadership of Etienne Davignon. The intersection of trade and technology policies became increasingly apparent, and even domestic regulatory environments were suddenly targeted for change, producing friction between the United States and Japan, and the United States and the European Community.

Summary

Nonstructural variables (especially unit-level learning and unit-level perceptions that the South was newly powerful) explain the push for international cooperation, as well as the substance of the demand for multilateral action. While in the 1970s, OPEC's success provided opportunities, this shift in bargaining power alone tells us little about the precise form of multilateral demands. New economic ideas played a constitutive role in the emergence of the "Third World" and the forging of a cohesive negotiating bloc. Activist developing countries institutionalized these ideas in their domestic regulatory policies and sought to achieve agreement on multilateral rules mirroring their own legislation. These states redefined their interests and seized opportunities to present their agenda at the international level.

However, unit-level learning cannot account for diplomatic outcomes; those lessons never became consensual knowledge. Developing and industrialized countries clashed over fundamental issues throughout the multilateral negotiating process. As the negotiations wore on, both developing and industrialized countries' perceptions about commodity power changed. The hopes and fears generated by OPEC's initial success disappeared, and states' commitment to the multilateral process diminished. Unit-level perceptions and the world economic situation explain diplomatic outcomes. While the shift from multilateralism to bilateralism reduced prospects for a successful conclusion to the negotiations, the drop in levels of world economic activity in the early 1980s was the main factor behind the failure. These cases provide a vivid example of how states redefined their interests in response to perceived shifts in power positions after 1980.

The fact that the activist developing countries substantially revised their policies in the face of severe economic pressure demonstrates that changed perceptions of the distribution of capabilities can provoke a redefinition of states' interests. Yet that is not the whole story, and developing countries, with very few exceptions, have resisted the United States' coercive trade-based efforts in intellectual property protection. They have yet to accept the norm of protecting these property rights. Furthermore, power and coercion had very little to do with antitrust reform in developing countries. As illustrated by the RBP case, the developing countries were not alone in redefining their interests. Economic pressure to remain competitive led the United States to redefine its interests in intellectual property, and both the United States and the European Economic Community to redefine their approaches to antitrust.

The chapters that follow highlight the relationship between power and ideas, and demonstrate that analyses that focus solely on power considerations or instrumental calculations of interests obscure as much as they reveal.

2 ❖

HISTORICAL PERSPECTIVES ON INDUSTRIAL DEVELOPMENT, TECHNOLOGY ACQUISITION, AND THE ROLE OF GOVERNMENTS

The transfer of technology has generated sharp controversy between nations. During the 1970s the developing and industrialized countries clashed repeatedly over issues surrounding technology transfer. At stake were competing conceptions of the role of the state in industrial policy, economic development, trade, and investment policies. Developing countries called for a NIEO and launched a vigorous multilateral assault of the technology transfer and foreign investment practices of multinational corporations (MNCs). The NIEO presented a sweeping critique of global liberalism and asserted a strong role for the state as an agent of industrial development. In contrast, industrialized countries insisted on the benefits of market transactions and the positive contributions made by MNCs.

As long as technology transfer was driven by the market, acquiring technology was a relatively simple matter. If you wanted it, you bought it. However, as the value of technology increased, buyers and sellers took steps to control it much more tightly. As a result governments have become more involved in the generation, acquisition, and diffusion of technology, and technology transfer has become a salient political, rather than purely economic, issue.

One of the earliest references to the transfer of technology comes from the myth of Prometheus, who stole fire from Olympus and brought it down to man. The importance of technology in the modern world has assumed near-mythological proportions. It is a measure of power, prestige, wealth, and autonomy. Over time, both the nature of the technology transferred and the nature of the transfer mechanisms have become increasingly complex. Technology is a valuable national resource and a crucial ingredient in industrial development.

The complex system of technology transfer that exists today is a result of the interplay of technology's increasing value and the efforts of both buyers and sellers to control the process of transfer. The main difference between the market-led technology transfers of the nineteenth century and the twentieth century is the role of the state. As states became more involved in the transfer of technology, the process of transfer became an international issue. Differences in prevailing economic doctrines and attendant regulatory policies surrounding foreign investment, economic development, and technology transfer gave rise to friction between states.

Specifically, states increasingly recognized the central importance of the acquisition of technology and technological capabilities to economic development and the ability to compete effectively. For developing countries, technology acquisition and the terms of its transfer were deemed absolutely critical political issues that held the key to economic development. In their view they had to achieve a high degree of technological independence or else they would remain economically backward. Ultimately they wanted to become economically effective global competitors, but since development must occur before competition makes sense, they were preoccupied with development. By contrast, the developed countries were more concerned with economic competition. Since they already had solid scientific and technological infrastructures and significant technological capabilities, the question of development was not so pressing. Thus, at the international level, on the North-South dimension development was the central concern, whereas on the North-North dimension the issue of competition was central.

This chapter provides a historical background to the issue of technology transfer, focusing on how developing countries came to see the state as an agent of technology acquisition and economic development, and why this changed several decades later. How did nineteenth-century economic liberalism shape the process of technological diffusion? How did countries originally acquire technology and technological capabilities? In what ways has the process of technological generation and diffusion changed since the nineteenth century? How did technology transfer become an important international political issue? What kind of international tension has the issue of technology transfer produced?

Technology Transfer—Nineteenth Century

Technology is essentially applied knowledge. Technology consists of more than artifacts, such as spinning-jennys or computers. An important component of technology is know-how, or the science and the knowledge behind the artifact. According to Jack Baranson and Robin Roark, high technology refers to a sophisticated range of products, components, management, and production techniques.[1] Technological innovation refers to the extension of this know-how by creating new products or processes or finding new applications of existing technologies. In the context of this discussion, the "transfer of technology" refers to horizontal transfers between multinational corporations and nations. This historical discussion addresses the international transfer of technology across national borders.

Technology transfer consists of three types: material, design, and capacity. These types correspond to operational, duplicative, and innovative capabilities respectively.[2] While they often overlap in practice, the distinctions are useful because these types of transfer lie on a continuum from maximum dependence on suppliers (in material transfers) to minimum dependence on suppliers (in capacity transfers). Material transfer is the simplest form; capacity transfer is the most complex.

A material transfer is one in which the artifact itself is transferred. The recipient country obtains the actual machine or equipment but is essentially a consumer in a passive sense. Design transfer refers to the transfer of items such as blueprints, formulas, books, and other items related to the process of design. Design transfers can expand the capacity of recipients to reproduce the technology domestically; in design transfers, while the recipient nation can produce the artifacts, it still depends upon technological knowledge produced elsewhere.[3]

Finally, for nations seeking technological independence, capacity transfer is the most desirable. Capacity transfer involves the transfer of scientific knowledge and technical expertise. This creates the capacity both for producing locally adapted technology from foreign prototypes and for achieving self-sustained industrial development because of the transfer of an active knowledge.[4] Before the industrial revolution, technology was craft based, and its transfer was simple. The industrial revolution changed that, and in the second half of the nineteenth century the relationship of technology to science was fundamentally different; people began to sense that the transfer of technology had ramifications beyond the hardware transferred.

Technology was becoming rapidly diffused via foreign investment and trade, and governments began to take an interest in protecting nationally generated technology. Change in technology's relationship to science went hand in hand with a growing realization that the transfer of technology required new forms of social organization.

As long as technology was craft based, "the skill and technical capacity embodied in the hands and minds of the skilled workman,"[5] the transfer of technological capacity was a simple matter. A craftsman taught his craft to his apprentices; a person could easily be taught to build a canoe, shoe a horse, or construct a barn. But as the role of scientific discovery became more important to the development of technology, the process of technological diffusion became less simple. As David Landes observes, before the mid-nineteenth century, "industrial change affected scientific exploration far more than scientific discovery influenced industrial innovation. . . . Thereafter, . . . scientific discoveries began to play an increasingly significant role in industry."[6] This meant that by the second half of the nineteenth century the successful transfer of technology depended upon innovative capacity rather than simple imitation. For example, the American's ability to adapt British steam engines for transportation depended on American science. The development of high pressure and expansion engines required scientific and engineering capacity.

Therefore the successful transfer was far more complex than merely acquiring the desired artifacts. Societies had to be organized in ways that would induce and encourage innovation and scientific discovery and would permit the fruits of science to be translated into applicable and useful technologies. Even though nineteenth-century Russia had achieved important scientific breakthroughs in both steam engine technology and wireless telegraphy, the Russians could not capitalize on these inventions due to "a political climate inimical to industrial growth, a low level of education, the lack of a free labor force and a strong entrepreneurial group."[7]

Furthermore, as a result of technology's increasing dependence on scientific discovery, more and more technology was of a "disembodied" nature, meaning that it would be either less obvious or entirely absent in the finished product (e.g., patents, know-how, techniques for processing or assembly). It was important to develop protection of new inventions. While the system of modern patent protection began with national legislation adopted by countries such as Britain in the late eighteenth century, this system expanded in the late nineteenth century. The commercial value of inventions and the growing importance of disembodied technology led to the creation of intellectual property rights. The legal protection of intellectual property (patents, know-how) was developed in the interest of economic efficiency. The economic justification was that increasing returns on innovative activity would create incentives to continue and expand such activity. The legal protection of intellectual property granted inventors monopoly rights over their inventions so that inventors could use, sell, or transfer these rights.

In the latter half of the nineteenth century, governments, persuaded by the economic efficiency rationale for intellectual property protection, created an international union for the protection of intellectual property. Adam Smith had argued that the only two limits to economic growth were the state of the arts (technology) and the size of the market.[8] From the point of view of technology owners and suppliers, what could be better than expanding markets through liberal trade conditions and ensuring a good economic return on commercially viable technology?

Technology supplying nations joined together in 1883 and established the Paris Union for the Protection of Industrial Property (including patents and know-how) through the Paris Convention. The convention was designed to ease the flow of technology between nations by creating common standards for the granting of patent rights, and ensuring national treatment of foreigners. The Paris Convention established principles of nondiscrimination in international trade in industrial property (patents, trademarks, industrial designs) among signatory countries. The convention protected inventors by affirming their monopoly rights over their inventions, and established minimum guidelines for national patent legislation to encourage and promote the diffusion of internationally new technology.

This international system of intellectual property protection fit well into Adam Smith's prescription for economic growth. As Curzon points out, in the second half of the nineteenth century,

> a quest for wider markets led the new manufacturing classes to press for more liberal trade conditions and to a rapid growth of trade. And the development of . . . commercially useful innovations and of patentable inventions by individual firms, led . . . to the establishment of manufacturing subsidiaries in foreign countries.[9]

The international diffusion of technology accelerated rapidly in the fifty years preceding the First World War. In 1867 the American-based Singer Sewing Machine Company was the first company to build its own factory abroad;[10] British firms rapidly fanned out into the British Empire.

Thus between the mid-nineteenth century and the First World War the diffusion of internationally new technology expanded rapidly. This was facilitated by an increasingly liberal economic order that allowed for the relatively unfettered flow of capital and technology across borders. The creation of the Paris Union contributed to the promotion of economic liberalism in the area of technology. On the eve of World War I, economic interpenetration based on trade, direct, and indirect investment had reached unprecedented levels.

Yet the increasing importance of scientific discovery in the process of technological innovation reduced the possibility that technology transfers would be automatically successful. The nature of the technology recipients' political and social organization were key determinants of their ability to successfully develop technological *capabilities*. Technology transfers can impart operational, duplicative, or innovative capabilities.[11] Operational capabilities refer to the ability to operate the technology transferred, such as a turnkey plant, in order to produce a good. Duplicative transfer implies design and engineering know-how so that the recipient can reproduce a plant or its components. Innovative capabilities are those in which the recipient is able to go beyond the technology transferred to alter products or processes to improve applications. As Baranson and Roark emphasize, passive recipients will not reap the full benefits; each of these capabilities "requires an increasing level effort."[12]

The historical experiences of America, Japan, and Russia illuminate the role of material, design, and capacity transfers of technology. Although it was not until 1867 that Singer Sewing Machines set up its first factory abroad, the international transfer of technology preceded factories by several hundred years. The transfer of technology existed long before the industrial revolution. For example, Britain began transferring technology to the Jamestown Settlement in America in 1607. At this time the transfer of technology was a very simple matter, consisting of craft-based technology. Handicraft technologies easily led to capacity transfer.

With the advent of the British industrial revolution the picture became more complex. The newly independent United States eagerly sought to acquire British industrial technology. Yet the Americans had to adapt British technologies to American conditions. Furthermore, to compensate for an American shortage of skilled workers, New England machine toolmakers developed a system composed of

> specialized, precision machine tools to make interchangeable parts, [that built] . . . the skill into the machine itself. Out of this grew America's mass-production capacities, . . . [its] industrial primacy and . . . [late-nineteenth-century transformation] from a borrower to an initiator of technology, from transferee to transferor.[13]

The United States thus acquired technological capabilities by first buying British technology and then adapting it to local needs. American capacity was further enhanced by skilled workers and managers who emigrated from Europe. The transfer of equipment and people from Europe helped to build America's technological prowess. All three types of technology transfer—material, design, and capacity—were important in the American case.

Latecomers: Japan and Russia

Countries that industrialize later can be expected to pursue different routes than their predecessors. The role of the state as an active participant in development looms larger for latecomers. The historical experiences of both Japan and Russia exemplify this difference and depart from the prior model of laissez-faire liberalism that characterized both the British and American experiences. These latecomers also provided important alternatives to liberal capitalism for future industrializers. In both countries, the state became an engine of industrialization and an agent of technology acquisition. As Alexander Gerschenkron suggests, "industrialization always seemed the more promising the greater backlog of technological innovations which the backward country could take over from the more advanced country."[14] Countries eager to hasten their entrance into the industrialization phase heavily relied upon borrowed technology.

Japan began industrializing during the Meiji Restoration in 1868. Japan's leaders, former feudal samurai warriors, made a conscious effort to develop technological *capabilities*. In Japan, the government played an active and central role in technology transfer. Beginning in the late 1860s, the Japanese emphasized the "people exchange" by sending its students abroad to learn new skills and by importing foreign technicians. They soon mastered design transfer and could imitate Western industrial products; but their focus on the people exchange helped them to develop "the capacity for 'creative imitation,' which enabled them to adapt imported technology and eventually produce their own."[15] The development of capacity transfer in Japan, as in the American case, grew out of the "people exchange" as well as the challenge of local conditions. For example, after World War II the Japanese sought to further mechanize agricultural production by importing small tractors from abroad. These tractors were not put into use but rather were used as models to copy—or design transfer— for the production of Japanese tractors. They successfully reverse engineered the imported tractors and were able to produce their own. This was an example of what Nathan Rosenberg calls "learning by doing," or learning by producing the product.[16] However, the Japanese quickly discovered that these imported tractors were poorly suited to waterlogged rice paddies, so they adapted them to the requirements of

Japanese farming. Here the Japanese were "learning by using,"[17] in which they improved the application of the technology in light of their conditions of use.

In the late nineteenth century, Russia relied upon European investors—imported technology and capital. Before the Bolshevik Revolution in 1917, Russia lagged well behind the West in industrialization. After the revolution the new leaders were anxious to accelerate the process, and the acquisition of foreign technology was critical to these efforts. According to Kranzberg, "while the Bolshevik regime bitterly denounced foreign imperialists . . . [it] welcomed capitalist technology, importing foreign technicians to teach them how to do things and imitating Western products, plans and processes."[18] This was a combination of material and design transfer.

In the 1920 and 1930s the Soviets invited American engineering firms to build dams and industrial complexes in the Soviet Union. However, the Soviets took steps to avoid becoming too dependent on American technology. For example, in 1929 the Ford Motor Company constructed a car and truck factory at Gorky. The Soviets sent their engineers to Detroit to observe Ford's production methods, while American engineers were sent to Russia to set up the plant and oversee its initial operation. As Kranzberg notes, "once the factory began producing Model A Fords under a Russian name, the connection with Ford ended and everybody went home."[19]

The Russians' acquisition of tractor technology from the United States was also a combination of material and design transfer. Between 1924 and 1934 the Soviets imported approximately one hundred thousand tractors from the United States. As in the case of automobiles, the Soviets achieved design transfer through arrangements with American tractor producers such as International Harvester and Fordson. Again, Soviet technical teams visited the American production plants, and American foremen came to the Soviet Union to train Soviets and start up Soviet tractor plants. As a result of these exchanges and considerable American assistance by the mid-1930s the Russians were successfully producing tractors copied from American designs. The Russians succeeded in material and design transfers in automobiles and tractors. However, the Soviets were less successful in capacity transfers. For example, the Ford-built car factory at Gorky continued to produce Russian Model A's until 1949.

The Japanese and Russian cases of acquiring foreign technology and developing indigenous technological capacity differed from the American case in important respects. The most important difference was that Japan and Russia were latecomers to industrialization compared to Britain and the United States, and for this reason the Japanese and Russian governments took a markedly more active role in technology transfer. The government's role in both Japan and Russia was to promote the rapid acquisition of foreign technology.

After World War I and the disintegration of the Ottoman and Austro-Hungarian Empires, economic nationalism gradually began to assert itself against the predominantly market-led prewar international economic environment. Especially after the Great Depression, which hit with full force in 1929, governments began to intervene much more vigorously in economic affairs and erected new barriers to the entry of foreign goods and investment. Many nations blamed the liberal global economic order for the Depression and sought to cushion themselves from the global shockwaves it generated by pursuing national economic autonomy. Even nations that recognized the futility of beggar-thy-neighbor policies felt unable to do anything else. Governments adopted policies of import substitution to reduce the influx of competing imports, and tax incentives to induce local innovation.

When the Great Depression hit in 1929, big business became a natural scapegoat for unemployment. International businesses were viewed with suspicion and were seen to represent foreign interests at the expense of local needs. For example, in the United States, France, and Germany, "foreign firms were discouraged and existing firms were occasionally obliged to sell out to local interests."[20]

This atmosphere led to an era of greater governmental involvement in economic affairs and the vigorous assertion of economic nationalism in the interwar period. It spelled an end to the relatively open international economy that existed until the Depression. The interwar period was an important precursor to post–World War II developments due to the rise of greater state intervention in economic affairs and a distrust of unfettered liberalism. In the industrialized world, a lasting legacy of the era was the erection of the welfare state as advocated by the influential economic theories of John Maynard Keynes.

The postwar economic order as negotiated by the industrialized countries at Bretton Woods did not signal a return to the liberalism of the late nineteenth century. The fear of the 1930s, that liberalism was the cause of the Depression, had not disappeared altogether. Thus the Bretton Woods arrangements reflected what John Ruggie has called "embedded liberalism," combining a commitment to multilateralism and a liberal trade and payments system with state intervention consistent with a Keynesian welfare state.[21] Despite its penchant for liberalism, the United States was content with this mixed formula because it was eager for its Allies to recover quickly; an economically strong and politically stable Western Europe and Japan would help to prevent a further extension of Soviet influence. Security considerations were an important factor in the construction of the postwar economic order. Nonetheless, for the purposes of this discussion the most salient point is the industrialized countries' shared commitment to global liberalism.

Post–World War II

The Expansion of Global Liberalism

The end of World War II ushered in an unprecedented expansion of global liberalism. The United States assumed leadership of the world economy and was committed to the establishment of liberal trade and investment policies.[22] The post-1945 world was much more market oriented than anything seen before. This system facilitated the rapid and extensive penetration of international businesses in the global economy, and the ascendance of multinational corporations as primary agents of foreign investment and technology transfer.

World War II left the economies of Western Europe and Japan shattered. The United States was the predominant economic and technological power after 1945. Not surprisingly at the end of the war the Western European countries and Japan agreed "that the rapid and free flow of American technology was a good and necessary policy."[23] Initially governments were eager for American multinational corporations' involvement in their economies. Devastated by the ravages of a long, destructive world war, countries were anxious to rebuild their economic strength, and multinational corporations were welcomed with open arms everywhere but Japan.

In the 1950s, American multinational corporations and foreign direct investment played a much larger role in international economic transactions. Much of this investment was in Western Europe: "From the early 1950s to the early 1960s, outstanding direct U.S. investment in the world increased three-fold, but direct investment in Europe increased more than ten times."[24] The rapid growth and expansion of American multinationals in Western Europe in the 1950s was the result of several factors: the increasingly robust and attractive European market; a politically more stable Europe; "the return to convertibility of European currencies, which made possible unrestricted repatriation of earnings and capital; . . . and the formation of the EEC, with its promise of a large market and its discrimination against third-party imports."[25] Western Europe and Canada welcomed the entry of American multinational corporations, "which transferred most of their technologies into their wholly-owned subsidiaries."[26]

The transfer of technology via wholly-owned subsidiaries represented an important change in the process of technological diffusion. Many technological transactions "were no longer conducted as exchanges between independent sellers and buyers in different countries. Rather they [became] captive exchanges, exchanges internalized by TNEs [transnational enterprises]."[27] American TNEs faced little economic competition, and their technological prowess was built on a model of intrafirm innovation and a penchant for strictly keeping proprietary technology in-house. The expansion of American MNCs proceeded through direct foreign investment in wholly U.S.-owned subsidiaries and market entry through outright acquisition of foreign enterprises to produce for protected local markets. While such exchanges represented a significant loss of control for the host countries, there were advantages to this type of technology transfer. As Helman suggests, the case for admitting wholly-owned foreign affiliates of foreign multinational corporations to their territories "is especially good for manufacturing industries because there is no better way to profit by the continuous flow of know-how produced inside multinationals than to have their affiliates inside your border."[28] Initially the Western Europeans and Canadians were willing to pay the price of powerlessness in order to attract much-needed foreign investment.

The Japanese were not. Since the Meiji Restoration in 1868 the Japanese pursued a policy of government involvement in the acquisition of technology. The leadership self-consciously developed technological *capabilities* rather than merely welcoming the fruits of foreign technology. The Japanese devoted considerable effort to the development of human resources, by training scores of engineers and investing in technical education. In the postwar era they continued to take steps to enhance their capabilities. The Japanese were cautious about how they spent their postwar foreign exchange and were wary of becoming dependent on foreign firms for their technology.[29] Thus, the Japanese did not permit takeovers or wholly-owned subsidiaries but rather favored joint ventures and technology purchases instead. By restricting foreign investment in this manner, the Japanese posed a dilemma for American managers. While the Japanese market seemed limited and remote, an American company could make quick and easy money by selling its technology. As Meeks points out, "the Japanese were eager to buy what has been estimated at between 25,000 to 30,000 technology contracts over a 30-year period for some $6 to $10 billion."[30]

Japan's Ministry of International Trade and Industry (MITI) controlled access to foreign exchange and "used this control both to keep foreign products out of markets in which it wanted to encourage Japanese industry and determine which Japanese industries could import machinery and raw materials."[31] The government controlled market entry, and MITI negotiated licensing terms with foreign innovators. According to David Mowrey and Nathan Rosenberg, "MITI was able to exercise monopsony power, gaining more favorable terms for the import of technology via licensing and other mechanisms."[32] As Dennis Encarnation points out: "early on . . . the licensing of products and processes represented almost the only way for foreigners to share in the Japanese market, since foreigners could neither export manufactured goods to Japan nor invest directly there."[33] Sharing proprietary technology on favorable terms was the price that American TNEs had to pay in exchange for access to Japan's market. For example after a four-year struggle Texas Instruments finally won the right to establish a wholly-owned subsidiary in Japan in 1968, but only after agreeing to make its proprietary technology available to its Japanese competitors for an unusually low licensing fee.[34] At the same time, MITI made foreign technologies available to numerous domestic firms, which ensured a competitive domestic environment and accelerated the diffusion of foreign technology within Japan.

Furthermore, during the 1960s the government sponsored a number of engineering research associations for small- and medium-sized firms that undertook research collaboration focusing on applied research.[35] Japanese firms concentrated on "intensive analysis of product features, consumer preferences, and process technology, striving to integrate the manufacturing and development processes as closely as possible."[36] They excelled at the strategy of what Mowrey and Rosenberg call "the fast second": "monitoring developments outside the firm and moving quickly to introduce high-quality, lower-cost modifications of designs of products or technologies introduced elsewhere."[37] In the quest to catch up to foreign technological leaders, the Japanese devoted themselves to improvements and commercialization of existing technologies rather than invention of wholly new ones. For example, Japanese firms commercialized American inventions—the transistor and the integrated circuit—and by the late 1960s came to dominate the global consumer electronics market. Thus Japan's conscious policies to restrict foreign investment and the entry of foreign multinational corporations preserved its autonomy and enhanced Japan's technological capacity.

Latecomers: The Developing World

American multinationals had long been involved in extractive industries, such as mining and petroleum, in resource-rich developing countries. American corporations dominated oil drilling and copper mining. Long before World War II, these corporations enjoyed enormous advantages insofar as host countries had no bargaining power, few skills, little knowledge of the market, and no capacity to exploit the resources on their own. Host countries routinely granted foreign corporations fifty- to one-hundred-year concessions that granted access to huge tracts of land in exchange for modest royalties based upon "the amount, not the price or profit, of extracted materials."[38] Many of these countries, especially in Africa, were colonies. Multinationals were relatively unfettered in their pursuit of valuable raw materials. This situation remained basically unchanged in the immediate postwar years.

American corporations enjoyed wide latitude in the developing world, benefiting from a lack of competition from the still-recovering Europeans and Japanese. Furthermore, "because the foreign companies could not be removed, replaced, or even threatened without great risk to the local economy, they tended to exercise de facto sovereignty over the pricing and marketing of output."[39] For example, "in the 1950 the United States treated Chile no differently than Belgium treated the Congo (which was then its colony) when it failed to invite Chile to meetings where the Allies set the price for the output of Chilean miles. But it did invite Anaconda and Kennecott."[40] This latitude was not limited to raw materials investments.

American corporations also had begun to invest in manufacturing during the Depression and the Second World War. These investors had been invited

> to move behind local tariff walls to aid the process of import-substituting industrialization. . . . They began by opening plants to assemble components imported from the parent or from traditional suppliers in the United States. There were few specifications as to local value added and little supervision of transfer pricing, technology sharing, or other inter-affiliate transactions.[41]

Postwar decolonization created numerous newly independent states in Asia and Africa. While the bulk of direct foreign investment from MNCs was concentrated in the developed world, many of the newly independent states were also the recipients of multinational investment. Until about 1960, "foreign corporations were virtually the sole source of capital, technology, and managerial expertise for the developing world."[42]

Initially, the policies of countries in the developing world were quite similar. Throughout Latin America, Asia, and Africa, countries embraced import-substituting industrialization. As Anne Krueger points out, in the first decades following World War II, development policies were based on "a deep-seated distrust of markets and a strong commitment to governments as the lead agent in economic activity."[43] These views were reflected in the plethora of licensing regulations covering imports, exports, and foreign investment, as well as the establishment of state-owned enterprises and marketing boards. With a few notable exceptions (India and, later, Korea) developing countries welcomed foreign investment to establish local manufacturing capacities. Latin America adopted relatively liberal policies toward foreign direct investment, and throughout the 1950s and 1960s American multinationals established numerous manufacturing facilities in automotive, electrical machinery, and electronics industries to produce for protected Latin American markets.

The predominant pattern of multinational investment in manufacturing in developing countries was the establishment of wholly foreign-owned or majority foreign-owned subsidiaries, and acquisition of local enterprises. Typically a multinational corporation would establish an enterprise in a developing country with its own capital and technology, "use cheap local labor and raw materials, control the firm with imported management and technical expertise, [would] not share technical know-how or invest in local R&D, and [would] sell the product mostly in the domestic markets, and finally repatriate huge profits back home."[44] Under this pattern of multinational corporate investment, the corporation maximized its control over its operations.

Foreign suppliers tightly controlled their technology. A 1971 UNCTAD study found that nearly 80 percent of the licensing agreements for manufacturing in the Andean Pact countries "forbade the local company the use of the technology of the foreign parent to produce exports."[45] As in the case of natural resources, host governments desired foreign investment but lacked bargaining strength to set their own terms. Thus foreign investors enjoyed relatively free rein to set terms that served their interests of closely controlling technology. The multinational corporations' penchant for holding technology within their own networks made sound economic sense from their perspective. As Vernon points out, technology owners prefer not to sell it if they can exploit the technology some other way, such as setting up their own foreign subsidiaries; in this way, "multinational enterprises can hope to capture the rents that are associated with the technology."[46] Multinationals preferred to transfer their technology through interaffiliate transactions.

In important respects the technology transfer pattern in developing countries in the 1950s and early 1960s was similar to that in Western Europe and Canada. As noted earlier, Japan was the exception because the postwar Japanese leadership adopted self-conscious policies to prevent undue dependence on foreign technology.

The Role of Ideas and the "Third World"

United States leadership also supported a second important postwar development—decolonization, which created many new nation-states. Most of these new nation-states emerged after the rules governing the global economy had been devised and implemented. In time, these nation-states began to question the benefits of the system into which they had been delivered and to think about economic development in a way that challenged the prevailing economic order. Liberal economic bromides such as "trickle-down" and "a rising tide lifts all boats" began to ring hollow as leaders in developing countries faced the daunting task of rapid industrialization. According to Gerschenkron, in order to mobilize people in the service of economic development, mere promises of better resource allocation or cheaper bread are not enough; "what is needed to remove the mountains of routine and prejudice is faith . . . that the golden age lies not behind but ahead of mankind."[47] The promise of the golden age came in the form of a new thinking about the role of the state in economic development, a new ideology, and a new identity.

The new economic thinking was Latin American structuralism, which advocated active state intervention to spur economic development. Initially developed as an attempt to understand Latin American development, this school of thought galvanized the bulk of the developing world. For a time, it became part blueprint, part ideology, and part source of a potent political identity—"the Third World."

But all economic ideas are not equal. In order to understand the political appeal of particular economic ideas over others one must examine how economic ideas resonate with political interests. Economic nationalism was fueled by the arguments of influential economists such as the Argentine Raul Prebisch, head of the United Nations Economic Commission for Latin America (ECLA) in the late 1940s.

As Ngaire Woods argues, economic ideas perform four basic functions: a cathartic function, a morale function, a solidarity function, and an advocatory function.[48] Her framework is not designed to predict which ideas will prevail but rather to help explain why one set of ideas is adopted rather than another. Latin American structuralism's cathartic component, apportioning blame for lack of economic performance, focused on unfair terms of trade between the center (industrialized world) and periphery (developing world). Developing countries' elites readily accepted Prebisch's arguments because his analysis shifted the blame for underdevelopment away from less-developed country (LDC) elites and their policy choices and instead pointed to the structure of the world economy as the primary culprit behind their problems. The morale function, or the inspirational aspect raised by Gerschenkron, provides the vision of a better future. The new economic ideas promised emancipation from the debilitating effects of dependency in favor of an autonomous future. Perhaps the most important effect of these economic ideas was the solidarity that they helped to engender. Structuralism helped to forge a powerful new sense of identity among a disparate group of countries—some long-independent, some newly created—spanning three continents. These countries became the "Third World." The Third World, an identity constructed around new economic ideas and a shared sense of the inequities of the existing international system, sharply defined an "us" pitted against "them." It became a focal point, a rallying device, and a basis for coalitional politics pressing a radical critique of the order of world political and economic power. As Harris points out, "it identified not just a group of new states . . . , nor the majority of the world's poor, but a political alternative other than that presented by Washington and Moscow."[49] It provided an indictment against the rich and powerful. Finally, these economic ideas provided an appealing advocacy function, one that stressed empowerment. Rather than wait idly until free trade and market mechanisms solved the problem of underdevelopment, Prebisch's ideas advocated taking the bull by the horns. Harness state power to restructure the national economy in more self-reliant form.

Thus, the new economic ideas held powerful appeal in economic, political, and even psychological dimensions. They more directly spoke to the dilemmas and aspirations of the developing world and appealed to its interests in a way that classical economic theory could not.

Structuralism offered an alternative to the prevailing commitment to the global liberalism underwritten by the United States. Developing countries had traditionally relied on their export of primary products, or raw materials, for foreign exchange. However, Prebisch warned that under the prevailing pattern of exporting primary products, the prospects for successful industrialization were bleak. He argued that the terms of trade for Latin American primary exports were falling because the prices of these exports did not keep pace with the steady increases in the costs of imported manufactured goods.

As the price of manufactured goods from the industrialized world steadily rose and the price of primary products from the developing countries fell, the Latin American countries faced worsening terms of trade. According to this line of argument, it would be increasingly costly to import goods necessary for industrialization, especially as the amount of available foreign exchange for their purchase would steadily diminish. The dilemma articulated by Prebisch would only get worse.

A UN economist, H. H. Singer, echoed Prebisch's arguments. Singer pointed an accusing finger at foreign investors in particular and argued that, "since much of the investment in primary products was foreign, and since foreign investors repatriated both high rates of profit, the secondary effects of the investment process would be lost. The 'spread effects' or 'linkage effects' of specialization in primary products were thus likely to be lost."[50]

How, then, were developing countries to escape this dilemma? The answer was rapid industrialization through an accelerated program of import substitution. Valuable foreign exchange could be saved by prohibiting imports of consumer goods, which would free up resources to import capital goods necessary for industrialization. New domestic industries would then supply consumer goods. Through adopting this strategy of state-directed development, developing countries would presumably begin to produce manufactured goods for both domestic consumption and for export. Thus they would free themselves from their old dependence on the center for such goods and break out of the primary products dilemma.

The elites in developing countries found the strategy of importing-substituting industrialization appealing on many fronts. Economically, it seemed wise since the price of primary products had indeed dropped sharply from the highs attained during the Korean War. But

the strategy's political and psychological appeal was even more compelling in the postcolonial era. As Harris points out, ISI

> seemed to be the natural complement to national political libera-
> tion. This might not be the liberation of people, but of states and
> local capital, and not a liberation from oppressive colonial gov-
> ernment, but from what was seen as the domination of the nine-
> teenth-century world division of labour, forcing particular countries
> into roles which both guaranteed their poverty and frustrated the
> possibility of economic development.[51]

Latin American elites' "export pessimism" was a legacy of the
First World War and the Great Depression and an important reason
why they preferred ISI. The First World War had curtailed the supply
of exports from the combatants to Latin America, which stimulated
local manufacturing in consumer goods. This ushered in a spontaneous
shift toward inward-oriented growth (ISI), which was a product of
changed market conditions rather than a well-developed economic
doctrine. The Great Depression of the 1930s also accelerated this trend,
as the economic crisis reduced both the volume and prices of Latin
America's raw materials exports. The drop in income and rise in debt
precipitated a foreign exchange crisis throughout the region. According to Charles Oman and Ganeshan Wignaraja, governments began to
curtail imports to save foreign exchange, which gave another spontaneous impulse to ISI, "'spontaneous' because government policies did
not seek to promote ISI but simply to deal with the foreign exchange
crisis."[52] Thus Latin America had already traveled a considerable distance toward ISI before Prebisch had articulated the economic rationale behind it as a conscious policy.

The ascendance of economic structuralism created new sources
of tension in the global economy. Throughout the developing world
the role of the state in economic affairs increased sharply. This served
to complicate the old market-led process of technological diffusion as
host countries erected new barriers for potential investors and established new terms governing host country/foreign investor relations.
The attendant regulatory policies in developing countries directly
clashed with the liberal economic policies pursued and advocated by
the industrialized world. As Harris states, "paradoxically, the liberal-

ism of national self-determination collided with the economics of liberalism."[53]

This new ISI orthodoxy, especially in Latin America, had important consequences for multinational corporations and the transfer of technology. Given the importance of technology to the process of industrialization, gaining access to technology became a central objective of developing countries. Since technology suppliers were predominantly multinational corporations, it was only natural that MNCs would be the targets of the developing countries' quest for technology.

The prevailing pattern of technology transfer in Latin America was material transfer (imports of finished goods, or product-embodied technology) and foreign direct investment in wholly-owned subsidiaries or the acquisition of existing local enterprises; the more desirable design and capacity transfers were nearly absent. The pattern of transfer gave rise to tensions, as Perlmutter suggests: "the high degree of significance attached to the role of technology in the development process has been coupled with the fact that MNCs have at their disposal a great deal of technology in both proprietary and non-proprietary form."[54] Thus, developing countries' quest for more and better technologies to promote economic growth led to conflict and debate. Developing countries were eager to build technological capabilities, which they viewed as the key to self-sustained economic growth and industrial development. Mexico was the first developing country after the war to challenge foreign investors in its quest to develop technological capabilities. In 1955 Mexico, "revised its basic investment law to favor foreigners who produced locally, rather than those who imported and assembled."[55] By the 1960s this challenge was extended by other Latin American countries as well. As Bergsten, Horst, and Moran point out: "American companies experienced mounting pressure to make more of a contribution to host-country goals. Once foreign investments were sunk, markets explored, and projects producing, local authorities found that they could use the subsidiary as a hostage to levy new requirements on the parent."[56]

In the extractive industries, such as minerals and petroleum, developing countries were especially successful in wresting control from foreign investors. In what has come to be known as the obscolescing bargain, once foreign investors had committed huge investments to discover and develop extractive industries, bargaining power shifted to host countries. Due to the large sunk costs and location of the resources, investors found it difficult to exit. During the 1960s numerous developing countries succeeded in forcing foreign investors engaged in extractive industries to dance to the host countries' tunes. For example, in 1968 the president of Zambia, Kenneth Kaunda, brought to an end to the ability of the Anglo-America Corporation of South Africa and Roan Selection Trust (42 percent owned by American Metal Climax) to freely remit all profits from their exploitation of Zambian copper; he imposed a 50 percent limit on after-tax profits that could be remitted abroad and required that the rest be reinvested locally.[57] In 1969 Zambia passed its first Mines and Minerals Act, and the state assumed all mineral rights. In Chile in 1964, "Kennecott . . . agreed to sell 51 percent of its shares to the government to escape a tax burden above 80 percent. However, chileanization speeded the entry of nationals into areas that were previously the monopoly of foreigners."[58] Between 1960 and 1969 a total of seventy-two foreign enterprises in mining (thirty-two) and petroleum (forty) were taken over by host governments.[59]

This rising host country assertiveness vis-à-vis foreign investors was not limited to extractive industries. Increasingly concerned with developing internal capabilities, host countries sought to force foreign investors to increase local participation in manufacturing enterprises as well. Host country policymakers blamed American companies for the limited success of the ISI strategy. "With a combination of threats, tax incentives, and harassment for noncompliance, they [the corporations] were required to buy more inputs locally, train supervisory personnel, take on local partners, and fill export quotas."[60]

The governments provided the manufacturing industries with subsidies, protection from foreign competition, and foreign capital in the form of loans and direct investment. Exchange rates were overvalued, and interest rates were kept low or negative. One of the goals of ISI was to reduce importation of goods from abroad in order to reduce foreign exchange outflows. However, the continued ISI strategy had the unintended effect of creating inefficiencies that discouraged transnational corporations from producing for export. As Douglas Bennett and Kenneth Sharpe have argued:

the manufacturing sector tended to be inefficient: oligopolistic market structures displaced domestic competition in a number of industries, and the import barriers which encouraged industrialization shielded these industries from foreign competition. Unused capacity and high prices were the consequences. Not only did this situation stifle manufactured exports; it also hindered exports of primary products whose process were affected by expensive industrial inputs.[61]

Transnational corporations invested in many of the Latin American manufacturing sectors through acquistion of existing local enterprises, which tended to increase economic concentration.[62] Their investments particularly dominated capital-intensive, higher technology sectors such as rubber, chemicals, fabricated metals, electrical and nonelectrical machinery, and transportation.[63]

Mexico, Argentina, and Brazil insisted on local content requirements as a condition for foreign investors. For example, between 1957 and 1967 the estimated local content of automobile production in Latin America rose from 30 percent to 70 percent.[64] These policies were facilitated by the entry of new foreign competitors—namely Volkswagen, Fiat, Toyota, and Datsun. However, with the sole exception of the Volkswagen facility in Brazil, all of these facilities were high-cost, inefficient, and did not produce enough volume to take advantage of economies of scale.[65] Furthermore, in Mexico, for example, these policies had the unintended effect of denationalizing the Mexican auto industry; by the mid-1960s private Mexican capital was completely driven out of the terminal industry.[66] The Mexican government increasingly insisted upon "Mexicanization" and required that firms be majority-Mexican owned, with foreign capital allowed only as a minority partner in a joint venture.[67] Latin American policymakers employed similar strategies in the electronics, electrical machinery, office equipment, food processing, rubber, chemical, petrochemical, pharmaceutical, and household goods industries.[68]

Host countries took advantage of competition between foreign investors to increase the incidence of joint ventures. By persuading MNCs to participate as partners in joint ventures, the host countries sought to make decisions about which technologies to import and which economic sectors they wanted to develop. A Harvard Business School study of 187 American MNCs found that between 1958 and 1968, American MNCs formed 487 joint ventures in manufacturing (27 percent of new manufacturing subsidiaries) in the developing countries and significantly decreased the share of ownership in 81 established operations. These totals show a marked increase from the previous decade in which American MNCs formed 147 joint ventures (16 percent of new manufacturing subsidiaries) and significantly decreased the share of ownership in 16 more.[69]

The emergence of economic nationalism, in part inspired by the arguments of Prebisch and the increasing competition between foreign investors (due in large part to the spectacular economic recovery of Western Europe and Japan), revealed a clash between host countries' interests and international business activity.

East Asia: The Beginning of a Different Path

Developing country strategies began to diverge sharply, however, by the early 1960s. Specifically, the small, natural-resource-poor nations of East Asia began to move out of the ISI phase and adopt development strategies that resembled Japan's in important respects.[70] Having saturated their domestic markets with light manufactures, they sought markets elsewhere. Like Japan they invested heavily in human resources with an emphasis on technical education, which increased their absorptive capacity of technologies from abroad. Like Japan, these East Asian countries have been quite successful in developing technological infrastructure, and in the past several years the United States has targeted these countries in its quest for greater market access. These Asian countries did not participate in the NIEO negotiations in any meaningful way, but given the fact that their policies have come to be widely emulated since the mid-1980s, a brief examination of their strategy is warranted.

As early as the late 1950s, Taiwan entered into technical cooperation agreements with foreign firms in the chemicals, basic metals, metal products, machinery, and electrical appliances industries.[71] The government of Taiwan, with the help of USAID, adopted a number of policies to coax foreign investors into its market. "Taiwan offered 100 percent foreign ownership and management and guarantees against expropriation, . . . a five year tax holiday or accelerated depreciation,"[72] and permitted profit repatriation. As early as 1963 the government invited Singer Sewing Machines to open a plant over the objections of local assemblers.[73] The government used a combination of significant incentives, yet also adopted a proactive stance toward the transfer of foreign-held technology to reduce the enclave nature of foreign investment. The government imposed local content conditions for foreign investors in order to maximize the benefits of those investments to the local economy.

South Korea's export-led push into light manufacturing began as early as 1961. As Shafer suggests, "the ISI effort had not become so entrenched that [South] Korea was stuck with a large, inefficient industrial sector able to demand protection by virtue of its size and weakness."[74] The emergence of East Asia as an attractive export platform, with a highly skilled yet low-wage labor force, fueled the increase in foreign investment. Originally American multinationals invested in East Asia for the same reasons they invested in Latin America—to get behind high tariff walls and supply local markets. By the late 1960s, however, investment increasingly became geared to labor-intensive, low-wage labor for the purpose of exporting back to the United States. High-technology firms such as General Electric, responding to increasing competition from Japanese firms in consumer electronics, opened an off-shore TV parts plant in Singapore to assemble American-made components.[75] General Electric was followed by RCA, Zenith, and then by semiconductor suppliers such as Fairchild, National Semiconductor, and Motorola.

Governments in South Korea and Taiwan provided substantial support to local firms seeking to produce for export. To shift producers' incentives from ISI to exporting, the governments granted would-be exporters favorable access to capital, tariff exemptions for imports of equipment and raw materials, tax breaks, and a variety of support services (including government-sponsored research centers that focused on production technologies, and management consulting services). These government policies helped to launch the impressive economic growth now widely referred to as the "miracle."

As these countries moved toward export-led growth, overvalued exchange rates—a common syndrome of ISI to discourage the purchase of imports—were abandoned in favor of competitive exchange rates. This was essential "to ensure that market signals reached firms undistorted."[76] Exporters had to compete in international markets and had to

> identify, adapt, and internalize the necessary foreign technology more efficiently. The stimulus and information which exporters must get from foreign markets have been critical for the continuous improvement of their absorptive capacities which helps to shift the comparative advantage toward higher skill and technology intensive products.[77]

David Yoffie has dramatically demonstrated the positive effects of market signals in his analysis of how U.S. protectionism prompted East Asian manufacturers to produce more technology-intensive, higher value-added products to circumvent protectionist barriers.[78] Again, like the Japanese, most of the growth in manufacturing productivity in these countries was a result of their mastering of existing foreign technologies and translating them into efficient production.[79]

MNCs under Fire and the Emerging Quest for a Multilateral Approach

By the early 1970s the activities of multinational corporations were under fire on several fronts. The Western Europeans and Canadians became alarmed by the degree of foreign penetration in their economies. For their part, the developing countries launched an energetic denunciation of the entire postwar economic order. On the North-North dimension, the debate focused on the issue of competition. On the North-South dimension, development issues dominated the debate.

Economic issues became increasingly politicized at the international level. Among the factors commonly cited for this trend were: East-West detente; the solidarity of developing countries; the actions of OPEC; and the willingness of the developing countries to use the multilateral channels of the United Nations system to press their demands. By the mid-1970s the North and South were engaged in multilateral negotiations to construct an international regulatory framework for the transfer of technology. These negotiations included deliberations to revise the Paris Convention for the Protection of Intellectual Property and to establish codes of conduct for restrictive business practices and the transfer of technology.

The developing countries voiced their concern with the transfer of technology in the 1960s and turned to the United Nations system for help. In 1963 the United Nations held a Conference on the Application of Science and Technology for Development in Geneva. This conference affirmed the developing countries' belief that the United Nations could help them in their quest for greater access to technology. According to Standke, the conference's most important outcome was the conviction that the United Nations had a central role to play "to facilitate the transfer of science and technology to developing countries and to help developing countries overcome obstacles in their access to necessary knowledge and its effective application."[80]

The UN Economic and Social Council (ECOSOC) was charged with the responsibility of following up on the conference, and ECOSOC set up an Advisory Committee for the Application of Science and Technology for Development (ACAST) in 1964. ACAST advocated a new and vigorous incorporation of issues surrounding the application of science and technology in the programs and activities of all relevant UN agencies' efforts in this field. ACAST's major concerns included the problems of research and application, and the need to build up and expand the scientific and technical service and institutions that the developing countries needed in order to effectively utilize science and technology. ACAST sharply emphasized the development of indigenous technological capacities.

In 1964 the United Nations' Conference on Trade and Development (UNCTAD) was created in response to pressure from the developing countries. UNCTAD reflected the developing world's changing views about its place in the international economic system. Raul Prebisch was the first secretary-general of UNCTAD, and his views continue to be influential. Through UNCTAD the developing countries sought improvements in their trading position. The Group of 77, the developing countries' negotiating bloc, adopted a strategy of unanimity in an effort to maximize their bargaining leverage. Prebisch stressed the need for developing countries to expand their manufactured and semimanufactured exports. The Group of 77 sought guaranteed markets for their exports and pressed for a preferential system under which the developed countries would remove restrictions on LDC imports (such as high tariffs and quantitative restrictions) while the LDCs could continue to restrict the importation of developed countries' goods. This "reverse system of protection in favor of the LDCs directly contradicted the efforts of the industrial countries to move toward a more liberal trading order"[81] in the GATT framework.

The Group of 77's arguments at UNCTAD I generated sharp criticism from Northern economists, and the developing countries were initially unsuccessful in their quest. Yet developing countries were taking their quest for greater equality vis-à-vis the developed world to the United Nations, and the politicization of economic issues in this multilateral forum gained momentum.

The Group of 77 continued to express its growing concern with the transfer of technology. In 1967, a Ministerial Meeting of the Group of 77 produced the Charter of Algiers, which emphasized the importance of acquiring technology from the North but at the same time intimated that existing terms of transfer were unfair and that the situation should be rectified. Specifically the charter stated that "developed countries should encourage the transfer of knowledge and technology to developing countries by permitting the use of industrial patents on the best possible terms and eliminate restrictions on the granting of licenses and the use of patents and trademarks."[82]

Two subsequent meetings, one in Lima, the second in Manila, expanded upon this theme. The Lima Declaration stated that the international community should promote the massive transfer of operative technology to developing countries on favorable terms to contribute to their industrialization.[83] Section Five of the Manila Declaration addressed the issues of technology transfer, strengthening the technological capacity of developing countries, cooperation among developing countries, and cooperation from developed countries, and called for a code of conduct for the transfer of technology and the revision of the international patents system. In 1973, the Fourth Conference of Heads of State or Government of Non-Aligned Countries produced an Economic Declaration and Action Programme for Economic Cooperation. The declaration stressed the need for the developing countries to bridge the gap in science and technology, to intensify their own research, and to obtain easier and less costly access to modern technology. This historic conference "witnessed a dramatic shift of interest and emphasis toward UNCTAD's economic agenda. And with that shift both organizational embodiments of 'Southern unity,' the Non-Aligned Countries and the Group of 77, coalesced in support of a single set of economic reforms that would become the touchstone of Southern unity."[84]

While pursuing their goals in the United Nations, the developing countries were not idle at the national and regional levels. In the context of new foreign investment policies, a number of developing countries introduced legislative measures to increase state intervention in the screening and control of technology transactions. The evolution of development strategies in the postwar era reflected developing countries' reevaluation of their relationship to private foreign enterprise. Key developing countries, influenced by the arguments of the dependentistas, experimented with national and regional legislation in technology transfer. In the late 1960s and early 1970s Argentina, Brazil, India, Mexico, and the Andean Pact countries each enacted laws that codified their dissatisfaction with market principles governing technology transactions.[85] Hereafter I will refer to these countries as the "activist developing countries," because they took the lead in pressing their demands in international forums. In the deliberations under investigation the East Asian countries were generally spectators and, with the exceptions of Tanzania and Algeria, the African and Carribean countries were joiners or followers of the activist program.

These legislative measures were all designed to enhance the recipient country's bargaining power and to reduce dependency on foreign suppliers. The laws all shared basic features that provided the basis for the developing countries' subsequent proposals at the international level. These laws included provisions for screening agreements and contracts with technology suppliers, prohibiting certain restrictive practices, and limiting payments to foreigners. The most prominent underpinnings of these legislative measures were the themes of technological self-reliance and dependency reduction. These laws were particularly important because they influenced the drafting of codes of conduct and proposals for revising the Paris Convention. For example, the United Nations' Group of Experts on a draft code of conduct for the transfer of technology used the Andean, Brazilian, and Mexican investment codes as models for the transfer of technology draft code.[86]

The impetus for the codes of conduct and the Paris Convention revision came from the developing countries. They wanted greater access to modern science and technology on more favorable terms. All these efforts were aimed at incorporating the specific concerns of developing countries into an international framework. In brief, the developing countries felt that the acceptance of their proposed measures would significantly tip the scale in their favor and redress past inequities.

In the postwar era, beginning in the late 1940s with Prebisch's influential economic analysis, the developing world launched efforts to challenge the relatively liberal postwar economic order erected by developed states. The challenge began gradually—first with Prebisch, then with the more activist developing countries' efforts to gain bargaining leverage vis-à-vis foreign investors in both raw materials and manufacturing industries, and the creation of UNCTAD. The Latin American countries and India led the charge. The developing countries' challenge intensified with the passage of novel national and regional legislation that codified their dissatisfaction with prevailing modes of foreign investment and technology transfer. As their efforts expanded, they gained greater ideological coherence with the help of a new generation of Latin American economists, such as Constantine Vaitsos and other dependentistas, who went further than Prebisch in placing the blame for underdevelopment on the international economic system.

While the dependency school of thought has had numerous incarnations, two in particular were relevant to the NIEO challenge: structural antidependency and pragmatic antidependency. As Emmanuel Adler points out, proponents of structural antidependency argued that "the expansion of capitalism places the developing countries in the periphery of world economic relations, thus causing them to be underdeveloped and poor; [and that] . . . technological knowledge is the main instrument in the maintenance of relations of domination."[87] The remedy for this state of affairs was to create autonomous scientific capacities that were appropriate for local conditions. Constantine Vaitsos embraced this approach in his analysis of the patent system. The means for achieving this goal included an enhanced role for the state in economic affairs, the abandonment of ISI technology transfer policies in which technology is overwhelmingly supplied by foreigners, and the adoption of a suspicious attitude towards private foreign investment.

The second prominent variant of dependency, pragmatic antidependency, implied a less hostile approach to the center. According to this perspective, state intervention was necessary to improve host countries' bargaining positions with foreign investors and technology suppliers. Foreign technology would be welcomed, but the state would need to ensure that it acquired only the most appropriate new technology that served national development goals.

Structural antidependency proponents and pragmatists both agreed that local technology is preferable, but pragmatists were more open to accepting foreign technology—as long as the terms could be made compatible with national goals. As Adler states, "although pragmatic dependentistas sometimes refer[red] to technological autonomy as their ultimate goal, their immediate goal [was] technological self-determination. The goal [was] instrumental; its basic purpose [was] the achievement of socioeconomic development."[88]

Despite the occasionally overblown NIEO rhetoric of autonomy or self-reliance, the goal reflected in the activist developing countries' legislation was technological self-determination. These countries sought to achieve the ability to adapt existing technologies and create new ones, as well as to ensure that the terms for foreign investment would emphasize national development goals. This strategy, adopted by the activist developing countries, gave the state a key role in setting the terms for foreign investment. In short, while structural and pragmatic antidependency schools of thought diverged on some important dimensions, both shared a critical perspective on foreign investment and advocated an increased role for the state in economic affairs. The NIEO rhetoric often smacked of structural antidependency, whereas the reality of the activist developing countries' (and NIEO champions') strategy was closer to the pragmatic antidependency school.

The Third World's critique of liberalism helped to forge Third World unity and provided coalitional glue. As Krasner suggests, "it provided a subjective identity that welded the Third World into an effective political bloc. This subjective self-identity was a critical complement to the objective international and domestic weaknesses that provided the basic motivation for Third World demands."[89] The developing countries' emergent dissatisfaction with the postwar economic order found its most forceful and coherent expression in their call for a NIEO and the Charter of Economic Rights and Duties of States, which the UN General Assembly adopted in 1974.

These declarations expressed the Third World's rejection of liberal, market principles in favor of a system based on the authoritative allocation of resources. The developing countries sought an international order that would be supportive of state-directed development. Seeking international agreements that mirrored assertive national and regional legislation, they wanted to rewrite the rules of international commerce to limit the power of private foreign capital in their countries. The NIEO covered a range of important international issues including: trade, shipping, commodities, the allocation of radio frequencies and geosynchronous orbits (which are the most desirable for communications satellites), managing the deep seabed and outer space, foreign aid, multinational corporations, and technology.

With respect to multinational corporations and the transfer of technology, the developing countries sought to internationalize the national and regional policies of the activist developing countries. The developing countries' demands across a wide range of substantive issues reflected a unified and coherent vision. According to Krasner, "all of these programs would either enhance the direct sovereign control of individual developing countries or establish international norms that would limit the ability of Northern actors to engage in exchange relationships."[90] These demands presented a fundamental challenge to the postwar economic order. While Prebisch and his followers were willing to work within the prevailing international economic system, the NIEO called for its complete overhaul. The system had to be reconstructed in order to redress past inequities and to tip the balance in favor of developing countries. Thus by the mid-1970s many of the developing countries, under the rubric of the NIEO, were united in their dissatisfaction with the postwar liberal order and their preference for a new system based on the authoritative allocation of resources in lieu of market principles.

Given the fact that the developing countries' NIEO program represented an attack on the postwar liberal economic order, which had been constructed by the developed countries, one may well wonder why the developed countries agreed to participate in these negotiations. Obviously the Organization for Economic Cooperation and Development (OECD) countries had a huge stake in preserving the postwar economic order from which they benefited. The main reason that they participated was their fear of commodity power. In 1973 OPEC was able to extract important political concessions by exploiting the vulnerability of oil-importing OECD countries. At the time this OPEC strategy exacerbated the OECD's prevalent economic uncertainty; OPEC also posed a credible threat and claimed it would raise prices even higher if the OECD countries did not engage in multilateral negotiations on development issues.

Furthermore, the example of OPEC helped to strengthen the identity and self-confidence of the Third World. OPEC's example held out the promise of more widespread commodity power. Producers of coffee, cocoa, bauxite, hemp, rubber, and other raw materials suddenly saw themselves as not merely, for example, "coffee growers" but rather as "commodity producers." Instead of remaining near the bottom of the international economic pecking order, the vision of future commodity power held out the promise of reversing one's fortunes and coming out on top for a change. While subsequent events proved that oil was the exception, in the early 1970s Northern policymakers feared that Third World commodity cartels would proliferate[91] and felt it necessary to placate the South by entering into negotiations.

However reluctant the OECD countries may have been, they entered into a series of UN-sponsored multilateral negotiations on a wide range of issues. Their primary aim in these negotiations was to minimize the damage that developing countries might try to inflict on a liberal economic order. The OECD countries were unconvinced of the substantive merits of the NIEO program and sought to prevent any weakening of the system based on market principles.

Substantively, with regard to international business activity and foreign investment, the Europeans and Americans had specific concerns that were reflected in the OECD deliberations on a code of conduct for MNCs. As might be expected, the OECD concerns were a far cry from those that animated the NIEO program. In the early 1970s the OECD countries began discussions on a code of conduct for MNCs. International investment relations were changing. "First, the OECD economies were entering a period of economic slowdown. Second, multinational enterprises were no longer an 'American' problem. European and Japanese firms were becoming significant actors."[92] In addition, European trade unions were becoming more powerful and were increasingly vocal about the negative effects of MNC activity on employment and collective bargaining. Among the toughest critics of MNCs were labor elites in the United Kingdom, France, and Canada.[93]

The United States, traditionally adopting a hands-off approach to activities of its MNCs abroad, became concerned about the misdeeds of its multinational corporations abroad in the wake of public scandals of bribery and illegal campaign contributions. Public pressure to regulate corporations was palpable. The United States overcame its initial resistance to a multilateral OECD code because "American business sought to deter congressional legislation and to internationalize any constraints placed on American firms through an international agreement."[94] American business managers feared the mood of self-righteous indignation that had swept the country after Watergate, and felt an international agreement would certainly be less stringent than what the U.S. Congress would put forth in such a highly charged atmosphere.

In the OECD deliberations, the member governments were far from unanimous about the best approach to adopt. Some favored binding regulations for multinational enterprises, while others argued for promoting further liberalization and stronger protection of foreign investment. The first approach focused on the behavior of foreign investors, whereas the second focused on their treatment by governments.[95] The OECD discussions included such issues as antitrust, the creation of standards for mergers, transfer pricing, the transfer of technology, and predatory pricing (or the subsidization of the subsidiary by the parent in order to keep prices artificially low). In addition, the OECD produced a report that "urged member states to use the information exchange and consultation procedures of the OECD to resolve disputes among themselves over matters involving MNEs [multinational enterprises]."[96] The Council of the OECD also issued a recommendation that urged member states to pay special attention to "known abuses arising from patent and licensing practices."[97]

In 1973 the OECD expanded a recommendation that parties notify each other in any antitrust enforcement actions and exchange information between interested parties. The 1973 amendment included a voluntary conciliation procedure within the OECD on disputes arising from enforcement of these laws.[98] Between these reports, recommendations, revisions, and discussions on a code of conduct, the OECD demonstrated a growing concern with the activities of MNCs. According to Levy, it came as no surprise that these governments arrived at additional rules of recommended behavior to avoid undue harm to other countries during a time of low investment, weak economic growth in the OECD, rising unemployment, and excess capacity in numerous sectors.[99] At the same time, these governments also felt that they should take steps to reassure foreign investors. "These concerns led to the establishment of the 1976 OECD Declaration on International Investment and Multinational Enterprises as well as to work undertaken in other forums, like the United Nations."[100] The OECD Declaration was strictly *voluntary* and emphasized the protection of foreign direct investment. In particular the guidelines established the principle of national treatment, under which foreigners are to be treated no differently than nationals, as proper conduct vis-à-vis foreign investors.

Thus it is clear that the OECD approach to the issue of foreign investment was diametrically opposed to the NIEO approach to this matter. However, the fact that the OECD adopted this set of guidelines shows that they were willing to go beyond previous national approaches to MNCs. This suggests that the OECD was not opposed to the notion of multilateral codes, per se, but a code devised by relatively likeminded parties who share substantive interests was a far simpler proposition than the North-South clash that was to follow in the UN context.

The OECD countries were initially interested in the international codes of conduct within the UN system because of the impact such codes might have on improving investment climates for multinational corporations. Home countries also welcomed the prospect of global codes as a possible means of "minimizing conflicts of international sovereignty by fostering the harmonization of competing legislation."[101]

Again, it is clear that the OECD's substantive interests in these deliberations were quite different than the interests of the developing countries. The OECD countries' interests were fully consistent with
preserving the postwar liberal economic order and at the very least
maintaining a holding action against the onslaught of the NIEO campaign. The developed countries participated because of OPEC's initial
success in extracting political concessions.

Summary

Technology transfer has become increasingly complex. As long as
economic liberalism prevailed, technology transfer was market led. It
was a simple transaction conducted between independent buyers and
sellers. Technology was relatively easy to acquire; there were very few
obstacles to diffusion. To the extent that governments were involved
in the process, such as in the cases of the Soviet Union and Japan,
their role was to promote the rapid acquisition of foreign technology.
Policymakers did not consider technology transfer a crucial international political issue.

  After World War II, the international economic order constructed
under the United States' auspices promoted global liberalism to an unprecedented degree. The postwar economic order's liberal trading and
payments system facilitated the rapid expansion of international commerce and the rise of the multinational corporation as the primary agent
of technology transfer. At the same time however, the creation of many
newly independent states as a result of decolonization helped to give
rise to a new source of tension. Long-independent and newly created
developing countries banded together under the mantle of compelling
new economic ideas that challenged the postwar economic order.

  The developing countries gradually challenged the prevailing
modes of foreign investment and technology transfer by asserting local
control over MNC activities in the 1950s and early 1960s. By the late
1960s and early 1970s they had passed novel national and regional
legislation that institutionalized their dissatisfaction with prevailing
modes of investment and technology transfer. Finally, armed with an
ideologically coherent critique of the postwar order and numerical
majorities in UN forums, they launched a full-scale attack on the

postwar economic order and called for a New International Economic Order on their own terms. They linked the global economic system to foreign investment, technology transfer, and economic development. They argued that their economic development required a new economic order and new international rules to govern patterns of foreign investment and, more specifically, the transfer of technology. The transfer of technology became far more complicated as both buyers and sellers took steps to control the process.

Developed countries, too, were rethinking previous approaches to these issues. Their central concern was to remain economically competitive during an era of low growth and economic slowdown. Furthermore, the spectacular postwar recovery of Western Europe and Japan began to change investment patterns as European and Japanese firms emerged as significant players. This led the OECD countries to adopt a code of conduct governing international business transactions, which promoted the principle of national treatment and maximized the value of efficiency.

Thus, by the mid-1970s, foreign investment and technology transfer became important international political issues. While the South was preoccupied with development, and the North was preoccupied with competition, they had both come to embrace supranational approaches to international technology transfer. Even though they had different ideas about the source and nature of the issues and problems, they came together to negotiate new international rules governing the transfer of technology.

The story of these multilateral negotiations is one of the clash of diametrically opposed views of the role of the state in multinational corporation activities in foreign investment and the transfer of technology. The Northern states advocated a minimal role for governments, while the Southern states advocated a maximal, distinctly interventionist role for governments. How and why did states representing such opposing views come together to negotiate new international rules governing the activities of multinational corporations and the transfer of technology? What happened as proponents of these opposing views directly confronted each other in multilateral negotiations? In the wake of the multilateral negotiations on codes of conduct governing technology transfer, intellectual property and antitrust, how have states redefined their interests? The next three chapters answer these questions.

3❖

NEGOTIATIONS ON AN INTERNATIONAL CODE OF CONDUCT FOR THE TRANSFER OF TECHNOLOGY

The demand for an international code of conduct for the transfer of technology came from the developing countries as part of the New International Economic Order. They wanted greater access to modern science and technology on more favorable terms and sought an international instrument to establish ground rules governing technological transactions. The purpose of the proposed code was to incorporate the specific concerns of developing countries into an international framework.

In important respects, the OPEC actions of 1973 created the opportunity for the developing countries' demands to be heard at the multilateral level. The industrialized countries were reluctant to negotiate over the NIEO but felt they had to because of the pressure of commodity power during a period of slow economic growth. At the time, no one fully understood how widespread the phenomenon of producers' cartels might become. However, the developed countries' approach to the negotiations was an exercise in damage control—to make sure that the South's call for increased state intervention in economic affairs would not become codified at the international level.

To understand the precise contours of this debate, which was central to the negotiations over a code of conduct for the transfer of technology, it is necessary to examine the origins of the developing countries' preferences in this issue area. In this chapter I will argue that while OPEC's actions made the negotiations possible, the true impetus for a code originated at the domestic (unit) level of key developing countries. The activist developing countries (Argentina, Brazil, Mexico, and the Andean Pact nations) had passed new legislation and had adopted key policies relating to foreign investment and the transfer of technology. The laws and policies codified these countries' redefinition of their interests in the TOT. Furthermore, these countries played a major role in forging a negotiating consensus within the Group of 77.

However, during the process of negotiation it became clear that the parties talked past each other. They clashed over the role of the state in economic affairs. The fact that the developed countries conceded nothing of substance to the developing countries in the negotiations supports the argument that the developed countries were engaged in a damage control exercise. The negotiations ended in a stalemate, without producing a code of conduct.

While bureaucratic factors (e.g., the role of UNCTAD) and the change in U.S. leadership from the Carter to Reagan administrations help to explain the fact that the last few UNCTAD sessions went nowhere, in the wake of these negotiations there has been a striking redefinition of interests on the part of the activist developing countries. The main factor that shattered the developing countries' former consensus was the global economic recession of the early 1980s. In response to severe economic pressure, many of the most vocal and strident NIEO champions have abandoned the core tenets that had animated the NIEO movement.

The first section of this chapter examines the evolution of the activist developing countries' interests in technology transfer and foreign investment, as expressed in novel legislation. The second section discusses the multilateral negotiations and the core issues in dispute. The third section analyzes the failure to reach agreement on a mutually acceptable international code of conduct. Finally, the fourth section discusses postconference developments, the redefinition of interests, and the dismantling of prenegotiation policies under economic duress.

Origins of the Demand for Cooperation

While the evolution of development strategies reflected developing countries' reevaluation of their relationship to foreign private enterprises, and the NIEO program packaged a variety of developing countries' demands, the more immediate impetus for a TOT code came from key developing countries' experiments in national and regional legislation in technology transfer. The leaders in the developing countries' push for a code were the Andean Pact countries (Chile, which withdrew from the Pact in 1976, Colombia, Bolivia, Ecuador, and Peru), Argentina, Brazil, and Mexico. These countries already had codified their dissatisfaction with the market principles governing technology transactions, and their desires were expressed in regional and national laws.

The major complaints of these activist developing countries were that technology was overpriced and that technology suppliers (mainly transnational companies [TNCs]) exploited developing country recipients. These developing countries felt that the terms of transfer set down by TNCs were unfair, and that the terms severely limited the recipients' control over the process. Acting on the basis of this assessment, Argentina, Brazil, Mexico, and the Andean Pact countries passed tougher laws that reflected their dissatisfaction with the earlier modes of technology transfer. The common element of these legislative measures was an increase in state intervention in the screening and control of technology transactions. The thrust of these efforts is summarized by Baranson:

> In the technology field, administered guidelines and regulations have sought to lead (or compel) enterprises into new channels of supply (from indigenous sources to replace foreign suppliers) or to screen technology imports to eliminate restrictive clauses in foreign licenses, to assure that the price paid is not excessive, and to influence decisions in the choice of technology "appropriate" to the national endowment and development goals.[1]

The countries of the Andean Pact, or Andean Common Market (ANCOM), adopted Decision 24 in 1970. Under this provision, contracts covering technology imports, patents, and trademarks had to be submitted to each member nation for examination and approval. This provision was designed to help increase technological capacity. Each member country's laws conformed to the Andean Decision's provisions. For example, Colombia's criteria for evaluating technology contracts were: "(a) effect on the balance of payments; (b) increase in employment; (c) productivity of foreign exchange spent in the project; and (d) use of internal resources."[2]

Articles 28, 30, 33, and 35 of the Andean Pact's Investment Code included mandatory fade-out requirements, whereby investors gradually had to relinquish majority ownership in joint ventures in manufacturing sectors within fifteen to twenty years. Through these Articles the ANCOM members tried to control the transfer of technology by limiting foreign ownership and control of domestic enterprises. The concern for reducing foreign economic dominance in local economies was further reflected in the Andean Pact's provision restricting foreign participation in select vital economic sectors, such as basic products sectors (oil, minerals, and other extractive industries). Foreign investment in these sectors was restricted to areas that did not compete with domestic investment.

Finally, the ANCOM Investment Code included provisions that prohibited the validation of contracts that contained restrictive clauses, such as limiting exports of goods made using the technology in the contract, or demanding that the technology recipient adhere to restrictive terms after expiration of the contract. In short, the purpose of the Andean Code was to engender technological self-reliance as a core objective in new technology and investment contracts. The new laws of Argentina, Brazil, and Mexico also reflected this objective.

Argentina's national measures for the transfer of technology sought to eliminate restrictive practices, improve terms for recipients, reduce costs of the technology transferred, and avoid the importation of technology if it was locally available. In 1971, Argentina established a Registro Nacional de Contratos de Licencia y Transferencia de Tecnologia. Under the 1971 law number 19,231, the Registro was given the authority to screen transfer of technology contracts. Law 19,231 regulated the technology market in order to protect local technological development and reduce the costs of technology transfer.[3]

In 1973 Argentine legislators devised stricter measures for foreign investors and technology suppliers and enacted Law number 20,794 to replace the 1971 law. This new law preserved both the spirit and essential features of the 1971 law but added new features, including the invalidation of clauses prohibiting the use of unpatented technology after the expiration of agreements, and new restrictions on parent-subsidiary payments.[4] The 1973 law was significantly stricter than its 1971 predecessor; for example, under the 1973 law all royalties paid by subsidiaries to parent companies were treated as profits and therefore substantially increased the tax burden on remittances.

Brazil's long-range national development objectives included the expansion of nationally owned enterprises and technological self-reliance. The central features of Brazil's efforts in asserting greater national control over the supply of technology and moving toward technological self-reliance were its National Institute for Industrial Property (INPI) and Ordinance 15 ("Normative Act") of September 1975. Brazil's Ordinance 15 was the most comprehensive and assertive effort by a developing country to achieve the goals of technological self-sufficiency and dependency reduction.

Established within the Ministry of Industry and Commerce's Industrial Technology Secretariat, the INPI played a crucial role in screening and regulating technology agreements in accordance with Brazil's Ordinance 15. As Baranson points out, the INPI's mandate was: "(a) to favor the importation of technology over the importation of capital goods; (b) to acquire technology instead of 'renting' it; (c) to eliminate contractual or implicit restrictions on local absorption and dissemination of technology; and (d) to discourage approval of patented contracts."[5]

Ordinance 15, a sweeping governmental act, set regulations for technology transfers to ensure that such transfers would promote Brazilian development. The ordinance covered five categories of technology transfer agreements: (1) patent license agreements; (2) trademark license agreements; (3) industrial technology license agreements; (4) technical and industrial cooperation agreements; and (5) technical service agreements. Agreements in each category had to be registered with INPI in accordance with a variety of specific regulations.[6]

In the case of patent license agreements, for example, "remuneration for a patent by the licensee to licensor [was] based on: (a) the degree of essentiality of the patent; (b) the start of the patent's effective use; (c) the sale of the product derived from the patent."[7] In other words, these regulations and their implementation through INPI were designed to ensure that the patent was necessary to Brazilian development plans and that remuneration was based upon the patent's use within Brazil. This allowed Brazil to combat patent abuses such as foreigners filing a patent in Brazil in order to capture a market, then not working it in order to keep competitors out.

The regulations on industry technology agreements covered contracts that provided the licensee with technology not protected by industrial property legislation (i.e., unpatented know-how) for manufacturing consumer goods. This know-how included:

> (a) the supply of all technical data of process or product engineering; (b) data required for upgrading product and/or process; and (c) transfer of technology compatible with current Brazilian policy of development of domestic technology which will contribute to improvement of the involved economic sector, leading to exportation of product. Licensed technology [was] also required to lead to replacement of imports involved product.[8]

Finally, the duration of terms of technology-licensing agreements was sharply limited "to the time period required for the licensee to assimilate the licensor's technology. INPI had power to rule upon effective and appropriate technology utilization."[9]

These provisions clearly reflected the Brazilian goal of technological self-sufficiency. They set firm time periods for such licenses that would be terminated when the Brazilian licensee was able to strike out on his own. They also stressed that the granting of these licenses was conditional upon demonstrating the licenses' clear benefit to Brazil's objectives of reducing dependency upon imports and achieving technological self-sufficiency.

Remuneration regulations for both the trademark license agreements and the technical and industrial cooperation agreements were similar to those governing patent license agreements. The regulations for technical service agreements reflected the same concerns as the other four types. Remuneration was sharply limited to a maximum of $20,000 for ad hoc technical services. This was "a fixed price based on costs incurred and the anticipated social benefit of the services. Non-residents shall not be remunerated as a percentage of gross earnings or production levels."[10] These provisions were designed to keep costs down. Furthermore, in technical service agreements the use of Brazilian engineering and consulting firms was encouraged.

Mexico's efforts to assert greater national control over technology transfer were equally bold and were especially important in the sense that Mexico's legislation predated both the Andean and Brazilian regulations. Since Mexico submitted the first draft proposal for a Code of Conduct for the Transfer of Technology on behalf of the Group of 77, its laws warrant close attention. Additionally, Mexico's Echeverria administration of the early 1970s sought a leadership role within the Group of 77. According to Baranson, "the Echeverria administration had strong underlying political motivations to take on a leadership role in the Third World, using the rhetoric of 'technological imperialism' and spearheading the drive toward technological self-reliance."[11]

Since 1970 Mexico had made the regulation of the transfer of technology a high priority. According to Baranson, "prior to that time, the technology factor in national development was not considered to warrant a policy of its own."[12] In December 1970, Mexico established the National Council of Scientific and Technological Research (CONACYT). This agency became the central coordinating and supervising agency for a National Plan for Science and Technology.

In 1972 Mexico passed the Law Governing the Registry for the Transfer of Technology and the Use and Exploitation of Patents and Trademarks. The spirit of this law and the purposes it was designed to serve anticipated the stated goals of the Group of 77 in the push for an international code of conduct. This 1972 law

> represented the first indication of unequivocal intent of the Mexican Government to intervene in negotiations between national firms and foreign technology suppliers. The regulations were drafted . . . : to regulate technology transfers so that their contractual conditions promote national development objectives; to strengthen and reinforce the bargaining leverage of the national enterprise; to impress upon the national entrepreneur the contribution technology can make to the country's development; and to establish an official register where the contractual conditions of technology transfer arrangements can be monitored and associated problems identified.[13]

The law was designed to boost Mexico's bargaining leverage, to save Mexico money by reducing royalty payments, and to eliminate

restrictive clauses in contracts. Under its provisions all patent, trademark, and technology agreements had to be registered with the National Registry of Transfer of Technology. The National Registry,
established within the Ministry of Commerce and Industry, had a
mandate to review technology transfer contracts and agreements. The
criteria used by the National Registry of Transfer of Technology to
judge the suitability of a proposed agreement were spelled out in the
1973 Contracts and Agreements Law and "require[d] comparison of
the investor's interests with the national interest and [were] used to
screen out dependency-creating investments."[14]

As of March 1976, one-half of all contracts submitted to the
National Registry were denied (seven thousand submitted, thirty-five
hundred approved). The main reasons for denial were: excessive duration of contract validity (42 percent were rejected on this basis);
limits on production levels or fixing of sales and resale prices (41
percent); unjustified or excessive payments (30 percent); and submis-
sion of arbitration to foreign courts.[15]

These activist developing countries—Mexico, Argentina, Brazil,
and the Andean Pact countries—set the agenda for the Group of 77's
demands. Their laws to control the transfer of technology all shared
basic features that provided the basis for the Group of 77's proposals.
All these laws included provisions for screening agreements and contracts with technology suppliers, prohibiting certain restrictive practices (e.g., grant-back provisions, restrictions on volume and structure
of production, tying clauses, restrictions on the use of personnel, price
fixing, and export restrictions), limiting foreign ownership and control
of domestic enterprises, and limiting payments to foreigners. The most
prominent underpinnings of these legislative measures were the themes
of technological self-reliance and dependency reduction. The laws were
particularly important to the case at hand because the United Nation's
Group of Experts used the Andean, Brazilian, and Mexican Investment
codes as models for the draft transfer of technology code.[16]

The Negotiations

At the September 1973 Pugwash[17] Conference in Finland the participants established a group of fifteen experts to draft a code of conduct

covering the international transfer of technology. Miguel Wionczek of Mexico chaired this group of experts and became the chief negotiator for the Group of 77 in the UNCTAD code deliberations. The Pugwash Group met in Geneva in April 1974 and drafted a code in the "deliberate attempt to strengthen the bargaining power of the LDCs."[18] The Pugwash Draft Code was important because it became the basis of the Group of 77's first proposal in the UNCTAD negotiations. The UNCTAD negotiations got underway in July 1974 when the secretary-general of UNCTAD convened a group of experts to prepare a draft outline of a code for international negotiation.

Prior to the conference sessions, each group (the Group of 77 was the developing countries; Group B was the industrialized countries) prepared and submitted draft codes for negotiating purposes. A brief overview of the content of the initial positions highlights how far apart the parties were at the outset of the full conference sessions. I will discuss the Group of 77's draft first, since Group B's draft was little more than a response to concerns raised in the Group of 77's more detailed proposal.

In May 1975 the Group of 77 held a week-long session to prepare for UNCTAD's first Group of Experts meeting on a code. Since Wionczek was chief negotiator for the Group of 77 in the UNCTAD deliberations, the Group of Experts heavily relied on the Pugwash Draft Code in preparing the first Group of 77 proposal. Most participants had been forerunners in LDC national and regional legislation. The Group of 77 consulted with UNCTAD's technology transfer section and the group's own experts before offering the modified Pugwash Code to the Intergovernmental Group of Experts as a whole.[19]

Mexico submitted this draft on behalf of the Group of 77. The Pugwash Draft Code was used as the basis for the Group of 77's first proposal, and like the Pugwash recommendations, the Group of 77 draft called for a legally binding instrument. Like the Pugwash draft, the Mexican draft proposed a code that embodied a very broad definition of technology, and that would apply to all types of technology transactions, "irrespective of whether the parties were private, public, regional or international parties, [and] the levels of development of the countries concerned."[20] The Mexican draft was essentially similar to the Pugwash Draft, except that it included a slightly more extensive list of prohibited restrictive practices; the

Mexican draft listed forty such restrictions while the Pugwash Draft included only thirty-four.

Debra Miller has traced the antecedents of the Group of 77's draft and identified the following elements and sources.[21] From the NIEO program, the Group of 77 draft included provisions that emphasized special measures for developing countries, that technology should be viewed as the common heritage of humankind, and that national regulation of technology transfer should be recognized as the fundamental right of each state. The Group of 77 draft's dispute settlement provisions (i.e., that disputes should be settled under the local law of the recipient country) were consistent with the Charter on Economic Rights and Duties of States. Finally, the Group of 77 draft included these elements from Latin American laws and practices: (1) technology should be transferred in an unpackaged manner designed to employ local materials and personnel; (2) the suppliers must guarantee the suitability and performance of the technology transferred; (3) forty restrictive business practices utilized by suppliers should be prohibited; and (4) the code should apply to relationships between enterprises' parents and subsidiaries.

The Group B countries were caught off guard by the detailed Group of 77 proposal. They prepared a hasty response that stressed the desirability of a *nonbinding,* voluntary code. Group B's document in response to the Mexican/Group of 77 draft set forth four principles as a basis for preparing a draft code. These four principles stipulated that: (1) the responsibilities of the various parties to a transfer of technology should be clearly distinguished; (2) the code should be a nonbinding international instrument; (3) the code's provisions should be general and voluntary; and (4) the parties to a contract should have recourse to international arbitration[22] (as opposed to an insistence on applying recipient countries' laws and jurisdiction).

While many international negotiations proceed on the basis of a common negotiating text, in this instance the groups' positions were too far apart. Therefore a working group was established to synthesize the positions on the basis of the regional draft proposals. Between 1975 and 1978 the regional groups (represented by one spokesman each in the working group) worked to synthesize their positions.

In these discussions, Group B presented a common front; as Thompson points out, they differed only "in the degree of liberalism they wished to show towards the developing countries."[23] The Netherlands, Denmark, and Scandanavian countries were the most generous, whereas the United States maintained a hard line. The OECD delegations included government officials, lawyers, and experts in industrial property.

The Group of 77 was the largest group, and since its expertise was not balanced (i.e., Mexico, Brazil, Argentina, India, and Egypt sent experts but most of the other member states could not), the group had trouble ensuring that specific interests of its subgroups (Latin America, Asia, and Africa) were represented. The UNCTAD Secretariat provided plenty of support for the Group of 77 by, among other things, preparing discussion papers and background on the various proposals. In interviews, the Group of 77 countries' delegates stressed that the UNCTAD studies were enormously influential in consolidating the Group of 77 negotiating position. The UNCTAD studies reflected the arguments advanced by prominent Latin American economists such as Prebisch and Vaitsos, and advocated measures similar to those adopted by the activist developing countries.[24]

After a rather cumbersome process of discussion and debate, the group made enough progress toward a single negotiating draft that the full conference was convened in 1978. Beginning in October 1978, negotiators met in six sessions, the last of which was held in Geneva in May 1985. The conference essentially was a series of concessions made by the Group of 77. There was considerable progress on several difficult issues during the first three sessions, but after 1981 the mood of the conference quickly became one of disillusionment and frustration. The last three sessions were characterized by heightened ideological rhetoric, a hardening of positions on both sides, and stonewalling tactics.

Among the most hotly contested issues were: (1) whether the character of the code should be binding or voluntary; (2) chapter 1 of the code (definition and scope of application); (3) chapter 4 of the code (restrictive business practices); and (4) chapter 9 of the code (applicable law and the settlement of disputes). At the outset of the conference these crucial issues remained unresolved and these tough issues haunted the conference. I will discuss each of these issues in turn.

The Character of the Code

The Group of 77 sought a code that would have teeth, and pressed for a legally binding code. Group B preferred a voluntary code. It quickly became clear that the United States would not continue to negotiate on the basis of a legally binding code. The Group of 77 eventually withdrew its insistence on a binding code once it realized that the main suppliers of the desired technology could not be compelled to abide by a provision that they so adamantly opposed. Without the support of technology suppliers, an international code would be meaningless. Thus the proposal for a legally binding code was an exercise in futility, despite last ditch efforts of some hardline Group of 77 states (e.g., Brazil) to resurrect this issue at the last session in 1985.

Chapter 1: Definition and Scope of Application

Paragraph 1.4 of the draft code stated that the code shall apply to the "international transfer of technology." However, the concept of "international transfer of technology" caused problems. Group 77 and Group D (socialist states) disagreed with Group B on what constituted an "international" transfer. The definition was important because it would determine what kinds of transactions would be subject to the code's provisions.

According to Group B, an international transfer was one in which technology was transferred across national boundaries. Group B wanted to limit the code's applicability to transactions across borders. In contrast, the Group of 77 and Group D favored a definition of international transfer of technology as "a transaction which is entered into between two or more parties who do not reside or are not established in the same country."[25] Furthermore, the text put forward by the Group of 77 and Group D specified that the definition also would apply to transactions between parties who are resident or established in the same country when at least one is a branch or subsidiary of a foreign entity, or when it is acting as an intermediary in the transfer of foreign-owned technology.[26]

These two views differed on the issue of parent-subsidiary relations. The Group of 77 and Group D saw subsidiaries as representatives of their parent companies. The Group of 77/Group D view considered a "transaction between a subsidiary and an enterprise owned and controlled by nationals of the acquiring countries"[27] to be an "international" transaction. For example, if a Brazilian-based subsidiary of an American parent company transferred technology to a Brazilian-held company, this transaction would be considered "international" and subject to the code's provisions, despite the fact that no national borders were crossed. This formula would encompass many more transactions than Group B's desired definition. In the hypothetical Brazilian example, Group B would consider the subsidiary as a principal in the transaction since no borders were crossed, the transaction would be exempt from the code's provisions. According to the Group B position, "it is immaterial whether the technology is already present in the country of the acquiring party or is brought into that country by the subsidiary of a foreign parent established there."[28] Since such a large volume of technology transactions involves subsidiaries of TNCs, the resolution of the parent-subsidiary question was important as well as problematic. This issue proved to be intractable in the full conference, and by the end of the sixth session it remained unresolved.

Chapter 4: Restrictive Business Practices

The issues contained in discussions on this chapter were perhaps the most crucial to the fate of the entire code. Failure to resolve these issues would place the entire code in jeopardy. The difficulties with this chapter reflected the almost diametrically opposed views on the purpose of a code of conduct, and the debates revealed hardcore ideological differences, especially between Group B and the Group of 77.

First of all, the preamble or "chapeau" introducing chapter 4 was supposed to set forth the purpose of including a restrictive business practice chapter. The central question was: What test shall be used in determining whether a given practice is restrictive and, therefore prohibited, in transfer of technology transactions? The Group B countries insisted upon a "competition" test, while the Group of 77 countries insisted upon a "development" test.

The Group B countries sought to restrict only those business practices that could be considered anticompetitive. In other words, they sought to prohibit only those practices that were forbidden under Group B countries' antitrust laws. These practices included abuse of a dominant market position and restrictive arrangements for licensing industrial property rights and know-how. Group B also insisted upon the principle of national treatment, whereby foreign investors in a developing country were granted the same treatment as that developing country's nationals. Group B wanted to ensure that developing countries could not discriminate against foreign investors.

By contrast, the Group of 77 countries were unconcerned with antitrust issues, which did not mean much to them, but saw restrictions as practices that were inherently unfair and represented the result of "undue influence by a strong supplying party over a weaker acquiring party."[29] The Group of 77 wanted to reserve the right to selectively discriminate against foreign investors, when necessary, to enhance bargaining power and to "catch up," and sought to control restrictive practices that could affect local acquiring firms' further development.[30] Specifically, Latin American laws on restrictive business practices reflected the presumption of starkly unequal bargaining power between suppliers and recipients. Lawmakers sought to prevent any practice that established a dependent relationship or unwarranted control over production, marketing, or technology. As Carlos Correa suggests, in these laws "the concept of restrictive practices [did] not exclude possible anti-competitive effects, but quite clearly [was] not limited to them."[31] Thus the essence of the "development" test was that any practice deemed to impede Group of 77 countries' development should be prohibited.

Another contentious issue surrounding chapter 4 concerned how the provisions should be formulated. Should they constitute blanket prohibitions, or more flexible guidelines? The Group B countries argued that it was rarely possible to "lay down legislation containing an absolute prohibition."[32] They maintained that some restrictive practices, while adversely affecting competition, may have other beneficial effects on the economy. Therefore, in an effort to introduce flexibility into the evaluation of restrictive practices, Group B argued that the code's chapter 4 provisions should be subject to the "rule of reason." In this view, provisions would be subject to a case-by-case analysis to determine whether, on balance, the practice in question would have beneficial or harmful effects. This argument was consistent with the United States' introduction of the "rule of reason" notion into the prohibition of anticompetitive practices under the Sherman Anti-Trust Act, and the European Economic Community's granting the Treaty of Rome Commission power to allow exceptions under Article 85(3). Group B wanted to add the qualification "unreasonably" to the restrictive practices listed in chapter 4.

The Group of 77, on the other hand, was suspicious of this argument and felt that adding the term "unreasonably" would facilitate arbitrary behavior by supplying parties.[33] The Group of 77 wanted the provisions to be subject to a "public interest" criterion, so that it could discriminate against potential suppliers if national authorities decided such measures were in the "public interest." Just as the Group of 77 feared that the "rule of reason" might lead to arbitrary behavior on the part of OECD-based suppliers, Group B feared that the "public interest" notion might lead to arbitrary discrimination on the part of Group of 77 recipient governments.

Early in the full negotiations, the Group of 77 made some concessions on chapter 4. During the first session, the Group of 77 agreed to pare down their original list of forty restrictive business practices to the following fourteen provisions to be prohibited under the code: (1) grant-back provisions; (2) challenges to validity; (3) exclusive dealing; (4) restrictions on research; (5) restrictions on the use of personnel; (6) price fixing; (7) restrictions on adaptations; (8) exclusive sales or representation agreements; (9) tying arrangements; (10) export restrictions; (11) patent-pool or cross-licensing agreements; (12) restrictions on publicity; (13) payments and other obligations after expiration of industrial property rights; and (14) restrictions after expirations of arrangements.[34] Not only was the list reduced to these fourteen practices, but it mirrored Group B's desired list because the provisions were consistent with industrialized states' antitrust, industrial property, and commercial laws. The Group of 77's concessions thus represented an important victory for Group B and a sharp disappointment for the activist Latin American countries' hopes to get their far more exhaustive conception of restrictive business practices incorporated into an international code.

Furthermore, Group B added a list of exceptions to exempt licensors from each of chapter 4's provisions. By including exceptions, Group B effectively called the legitimacy of developing countries' regulations into question. According to developing country legislation, licensors seeking exceptions had to bargain with the state; these countries feared that if a list of exceptions were internationally codified that their bargaining power would be undermined.[35]

In sum, progress in negotiating this chapter was the product of unilateral concessions on the part of the Group of 77. Despite the fact that these controversial issues were resolved, in a fashion—again by Group of 77 concessions in the RBP Code deliberations—by 1980 this resolution was met with deep suspicion by the Group of 77. Thus the fate of the RBP Code did not move the TOT discussions forward in any meaningful way.

Chapter 9: Applicable Law and Settlement of Disputes

This was the only other chapter that rivaled chapter 4 in its ideological component and in its importance for the code's successful completion. Chapter 9 covered the law to be applied in the case of a dispute between a supplier and a recipient, especially when one party (particularly the acquiring party) was the state itself.

The Group of 77 proposed that in such disputes, the national law of the technology-acquiring country should be applied, and its national courts should have jurisdiction to settle disputes. The Group of 77's concern for insistence upon its national laws and national courts stemmed from its contention that stronger supplying parties often imposed conditions for dispute settlement that required arbitration based on foreign laws or held in supplier countries' fora. The Group of 77 objected that such arbitration clauses removed disputed issues from their national courts and thereby abrogated their sovereignty.[36] The developing countries felt that international arbitration tended to favor developed countries, and therefore sought to tilt the balance in their favor by insisting on the application of acquiring countries' laws and jurisdictions. In particular, Saudi Arabia and other OPEC countries felt they had been unfairly treated in arbitral awards made in respect to petroleum concessions and took steps to ensure that only their national law would be applied in future cases.[37] The Andean Pact countries took similar steps.

Group B's position on these matters was to emphasize freedom for contracting parties to choose the applicable national law and national forum for the settlement of disputes. However, this freedom would be "subject to the condition of the existence of a substantial relationship between applicable law and the forum and the parties and the transaction, or another reasonable basis for the choices made."[38]

At the first session of the conference the Algerian delegate, Issad, insisted on the need to apply the acquiring country's laws in the case of disputes, as proposed in the Group of 77 draft. Group B preferred a more flexible formulation that would allow the contracting parties to choose the law and forum to be applied in case of disputes. As Issad argued:

> To accept the choice of the parties, i.e., the choice of the most powerful party, who always imposed the clauses that were most favorable to himself, would require the developing countries to endorse existing practice and thus give the suppliers of technology the whip hand. The arbitration being proposed to the developing countries for the settlement of disputes had often worked against them.[39]

During the first session, the conference chairman prepared compromise texts to try to bring the positions of the regional groups closer together. In particular, the Group of 77 made some important concessions on chapter 9 (on applicable law and disputes settlement) by accepting the chairman's compromise text.

Initially, the Group of 77 had opposed international arbitration as a means of settling disputes because it felt that arbitration usually favored technology suppliers. However, in a spirit of compromise, the group agreed to recognize arbitration as a means of settling disputes, "if the manners of selecting the arbitrators and the procedure adopted were calculated to ensure an impartial and equitable decision, and if the code and the national legislation provided for under the code were the same as the law applied by the arbitrators."[40]

During the third conference sessions the Group of 77 made a further substantial concession to Group B's position on the settlement of disputes in recognizing that "under certain conditions, the parties to a transaction involving the transfer of technology might choose the law applicable to questions of private interests in contracts and the jurisdiction that would decide on disputes."[41]

The Conference Sessions

Progress during the first three sessions of the conference largely resulted from unilateral Group of 77 concessions. Even as early as the end of the resumed first session in March 1979, changes in each group's attitude toward the code of conduct negotiations became apparent. At that time, the Group of 77 had made substantial concessions on chapter 4 and no longer argued that technology should be viewed as the "common heritage of mankind."

These concessions made by the Group of 77 led to a change in the groups' attitudes towards a code of conduct. Initially Group B had been unenthusiastic about a code, despite its active participation. The United States in particular had resisted on the basis of its opposition to the NIEO and its preference for a more laissez-faire approach to the transfer of technology. However, by 1979 official United States policy favored a code of conduct for technology transfer, and officials believed that such a code would pose no problems for the North or its enterprises.[42] By contrast, after the resumed first session members of the Group of 77 began to lose their conviction that the 1979 draft code would be a "panacea for their technology transfer troubles."[43]

The reason for this change of heart on both sides stemmed from the fact that the Group of 77 had made numerous substantive concessions that made the code far more benign, and even appealing, in Group B's view, and far less satisfactory from the Group of 77's standpoint. Through the process of negotiation, the code had increasingly come to resemble industrialized states' competition laws rather than developing countries' technology transfer legislation.

The third session, which ended in May 1980, was a major turning point in the negotiations. At the end of the third session the major issues left unresolved were: the legal character of the code and the mandate of the review conference; scope of application of the code (particularly the treatment of affiliated enterprises under the code's provisions); restrictive practices; international institutional machinery; and applicable law and the settlement of disputes.[44]

After the third session a mood of disillusionment and frustration set in. In retrospect, several key Group of 77 delegates felt that they should have agreed to the code as it stood in 1980, at the end of the third session and before the Reagan administration came to power in the United States.[45] Many Group of 77 delegates, as well as UNCTAD personnel, noted a dramatic change in the tenor of the negotiations beginning in 1981.

Specifically, the United States became more hardline and opposed to the code efforts. By 1981 other Group B countries followed suit. In the words of one Group of 77 delegate, many Group B countries "hid behind" the United States and let the United States take the heat. Often the position of the United States became the Group B position due to the United States' key role.

Particular features of the new U.S. administration that had a negative impact on progress toward a code after 1980 included its antiUNCTAD stance; its antiregulatory posture; and its penchant for bilateral as opposed to multilateral measures in dealing with Group of 77 member states. The new administration's anti-UNCTAD stance was clearly expressed by Gerald B. Helman in his address (on behalf of the U.S. delegation) to UNCTAD's Trade and Development Board in October 1981. Helman lamented the UNCTAD Secretariat's negative posture towards multinational firms and stated that "the continued attack by the Secretariat on these firms, which we see as an attack on the market economy itself, . . . is perhaps the single most important factor contributing to the failure of credibility in my government and elsewhere for the work of this Organization."[46] Roberts D. Hormats, U.S. assistant secretary for economic and business affairs, underscored the administration's antiregulatory posture in a 1981 speech. As he pointed out, "the Administration believes in the efficiency of the marketplace and has considerable skepticism about the effectiveness of government efforts to supplant it."[47] Finally, W. Allen Wallis, undersecretary for economic affairs, emphasized that the U.S. approach to stimulate growth in developing countries was to encourage the adoption of market-oriented policies through direct bilateral channels and international financial institutions.[48]

All these features led to U.S. resistance to the code negotiations, but since it was prominently involved under the Carter administration, it was committed to continue discussions. However, the character of the discussions changed. By the end of the third session, three-fourths of the code had been drafted on the basis of consensus. Movement on the remaining tough issues became impossible after the third session. The overall feeling in the negotiations was that if the United States didn't want a code, there would be none.[49]

At the end of the sixth and last session in 1985, the outstanding issues were the same as at the end of the third session: chapter 1, paragraph 1.4—criteria used for defining the international character of technology transfer; chapter 4—(a) characterization of practices to be avoided, (b) criteria for evaluation of practices in an individual case, (c) applicability of provisions to transactions between affiliated enterprises, (d) chapeau; chapter 9—applicable law and settlement of disputes; and chapter 8—the nature, timing, and mandate of the review conference, and the nature of the institutional machinery. In short, after the third session negotiators made no progress toward concluding a code.

The eventful failure of the conference to agree upon a satisfactory code was due to three factors: changes in U.S. leadership; bureaucratic factors (the group system in UNCTAD and a loss of faith in the organization); and changes in the world economic situation (a precipitous drop in foreign investment, the Third World debt crisis, and subsequent pressure to sacrifice ideological concerns for a more highly competitive environment, which led Third World policymakers to more aggressively seek foreign investment rather than strictly control it).

By the sixth session in May 1985, positions on both sides had been hardened to the point of no return. Not only was Group B thoroughly intransigent, but the Group of 77 consensus had vanished. The facade of Group of 77 unity persisted, fueled by the hardliners—Brazil, India, Egypt, and Yugoslavia. Just as Group B "hid behind" the United States, the Group of 77 formally backed the most hardline country—Brazil. Not only did Brazil resurrect the demand for a legally binding code, earlier Group of 77 concessions notwithstanding, but it found the entire code unacceptable.

Diplomatic Outcomes

At the sixth session, on paper at least, it seemed that if only the groups could resolve the parent-subsidiary issue, the definitional issue, and remaining parts of chapters 4 and 9, then the code would be acceptable. However this was not the case. Brazil found the code unacceptable and lost interest after the sixth session because it felt that the Group of 77 had made too many concessions. The code draft, as of June 1985, was considered to be unrecognizable compared to the first Group of 77 draft proposal and the objectives of the code.

While this position may seem puzzling coming from Brazil—the early champion of a code of conduct—in fact it should come as no surprise. One of Brazil's early objectives was to get an international code that resembled Brazil's national legislation. The code, in its 1985 form, was a much watered-down version of the first Group of 77 draft proposal and was far weaker than Brazil's laws (especially Ordinance 15). The same can be said for the other activist developing countries, but with a crucial difference. Countries such as Mexico and India, while their laws were tough on paper, applied their laws quite flexibly in practice and made numerous exceptions. Brazil, by virtue of its level of development and large market, was the only activist Group of 77 member state that consistently could afford to apply its tough legal standards for foreign technology suppliers.

The group system in UNCTAD, in which formal group unity was the order of the day, led to deep frustration on the part of more moderate Group of 77 countries. UNCTAD's group system became an arena in which the hardliners from every group held court. Ideological rhetoric predominated and substantive, technical discussions were virtually precluded by design.[50] With the United States and Brazil's hardline opposition to the code in its 1985 form, the possibilities for meaningful and constructive progress seemed hopeless. The Group of 77 members had the most to lose from this stalemate. In particular, African and other moderate countries without national legislation for technology transfers were the real losers in this situation. They were even eager for a relatively weaker code, as long as it contained principles and objectives to help developing countries.

UNCTAD felt pressed for results; the organization was eager for a success given its rather dismal track record in North-South negotiations. Some UNCTAD officials began encouraging the Group of 77 to be even more flexible (meaning, to make more concessions) than with the 1985 code draft. As a result, UNCTAD lost some credibility among many Group of 77 delegations. In the words of one Group of 77 delegate, UNCTAD "no longer inspires delegations."[51]

For its part, the United States clearly demonstrated its fundamental opposition to the code through its stonewalling tactics. After the sixth session, the general assembly passed a resolution to provide for consultations on the code of conduct to see if there was a basis for resuming the conference. According to the resolution, the consultations could include a restatement of positions, expressions of minor or major changes in positions, and statements reflecting general views on the outstanding issues. The United States supported the consultation process "fully" but insisted that no texts be produced in the process. The United States opposed the production of texts because discussion of actual texts would be tantamount to *negotiating* and would, in the United States' view, violate the mandate of the consultation process.[52]

The United States wanted a document prepared that would expose real positions but would include no texts. UNCTAD produced a document along the lines of the United States' wishes (e.g., outlining the "competition" and "development" tests for chapter 4's chapeau) but also included relevant texts from the sixth session. The United States was angry about this since the UN process was one of textual negotiations; therefore, adding texts would lead the consultation group into actual negotiations. The United States said it would walk out if this notion of consultation, as opposed to negotiation, were violated again.[53]

At this time, the United States expressed its dissatisfaction with chapters 4 and 9 (as expected) but added that it also found the previously agreed upon chapter 3 to be unacceptable. In particular the United States objected to provisions in chapter 3 allowing for the renegotiation of contracts, and it sought clarification of what was meant by "international law."[54]

When asked why the United States was interested in a code and what it would take for the United States to support a code, the United States delegate responded with three points. First, a code reflecting U.S. laws and practices would provide international legitimation for the United States procedures and make it easier to deal with countries that held a different philosophy. The United States could then point to the code as vindication of its practices.

Second, and related to the first point, the delegate emphasized the ideological dimension. The United States sought legitimation of its preference for limited state involvement, whereas the Group 77 sought a legitimation of greater state involvement. The key obstacle to reaching an understanding concerned the role of the state.

While the United States argued that in principle the main obstacle in the negotiations was the role of the state (prominent versus limited), UNCTAD personnel suspected that the United States really was just eager to get technology discussions out of UNCTAD and into a more hospitable forum, such as GATT. While there was no doubt that the United States publicly championed limited state involvement, the UNCTAD personnel's suspicions were justified. According to W. Allen Wallis, U.S. under secretary for economic affairs (speaking on behalf of the United States), the United States did not see UNCTAD as an appropriate negotiating forum and expressed its view that "negotiations of measures to ameliorate current economic difficulties or strengthen the existing trade or financial system are more properly handled within the specialized independent international agencies designed to address these issues—for example the IMF, the General Agreement on Tariffs and Trade (GATT), and the World Bank."[55]

Third, the United States favored a voluntary code because it could have moral force and long-term effects in the development of international law. It could serve as a building block in the evolution of technology transfer transactions.

The Group of 77, Group D, and UNCTAD saw the United States as stonewalling and interpreted the United States' behavior as evidence that the United States did not really want a code at all. The United States argued that it didn't want to "negotiate" in consultations because the experts who did the negotiating were in Washington, not Geneva. Thus the U.S. mission argued that its hands were tied.

In terms of the United States' mistrust of UNCTAD, the U.S. delegate pointed out that his country felt that the UNCTAD Secretariat was not appropriately fulfilling its role as an "international civil service" but rather was acting as a "Third World club."[56] The United States wanted to see UNCTAD become a technical body rather than a political forum, but that would have downgraded the status of UNCTAD in the eyes of the Group of 77. Even though the Group of 77 was disappointed by UNCTAD's performance in the code efforts, it was still the only forum of its kind for the Group of 77.

The story ended in disillusionment and disarray. Most Group of 77 delegations lost interest in the code. Besides the factors already mentioned (the group system in UNCTAD, a loss of faith in the organization, the change of leadership in the United States), the main reason for the failure of the conference lay far beyond the meeting rooms of Geneva. The world that existed in the early seventies, when the preparations for the conference were in full swing, changed dramatically by the early 1980s. The buoyant optimism of the Group of 77 of the early 1970s gave way to a mad scramble to stay competitive in a rapidly changing world economy.

Aftermath: Redefining Interests

As Harris points out: "sustained world growth from the late 1940s to the 1970s offered an external context highly favorable to growth in the newly industrializing countries."[57] However, the debt crisis and decline in world trade in the late seventies and early eighties ended that favorable environment. Faced with uncertain economic futures, in recent years many developing countries have reevaluated their national policies. There has been a marked retreat from the types of policies advocated by the dependentistas in the 1960s. According to Harris:

> Short-term financial exigencies combined with long-term changes
> in opinion . . . to produce a quite astonishing cult of "privatization,"

a catchword to summarize both denationalization of public companies and efforts to subject the public sector to competitive market measures. It went with a no less remarkable revision of attitudes towards foreign capital (governments now competed to attract it, rather than being preoccupied with minimizing or controlling it).[58]

For example, in 1985:

> The government of India had just announced a new policy to ban the takeover of "sick industries," to shut down twenty-six of the hundred textile mills held by the government and to sell others; private directors were to be put on public boards, and much more public-sector activity subcontracted to private companies. The Singapore government publicly limited its future intervention; it proposed that all state companies should be open to private share purchase on the stock exchange and that all minority shares should be sold.[59]

Furthermore, throughout Asia governments moved to denationalize sectors of activity, including telecommunications; airlines; shipping and shipbuilding; railways, buses, and highways; banks; oil and petrochemicals; general industry (textiles, chemicals, engineering); and hotels.[60]

Most significantly, the activist developing countries that helped galvanize developing country opinion to support a dependency-influenced code of conduct revised national policies along the lines mentioned by Harris. Mexico, Argentina, and the Andean Pact member states took steps to liberalize their policies vis-à-vis foreign technology suppliers in an effort to attract investment.

In 1978 Argentina amended its 1973 investment and technology transfer laws to make them less restrictive and more favorable for potential investors. In March 1981, Argentina enacted Law 22,426, abolishing the control of transfer of technology agreements between independent parties. The new law retained very limited supervision of technology prices in parent-subsidiary transactions for fiscal purposes only. The introduction to the 1981 law referred to the previous laws (19,231 of 1971 and 20,794 of 1973), acknowledging "the damages caused by restrictive policies and regulations,"[61] and reflected the view that "government cannot replace businessmen in making decisions."[62]

By 1986 the Argentine Congress was discussing further amendments to create a more open investment climate.

Due to the economic crisis of the early 1980s, the Mexican government was, as Harris points out, forced

> to commit itself to ending what was called an "indiscriminate import-substitution model." On a wide number of issues, the government relaxed regulations. The requirement on domestic ownership was quietly eased. A programme of denationalizing was begun (with over three hundred companies returned to private ownership in 1984).[63]

Finally, the Andean Pact countries' policymakers began to blame strict laws for the lack of, and decline in, foreign investment. These countries reevaluated their regulatory policies vis-à-vis foreign technology suppliers. The Andean Pact countries were eager to attract EEC investment, "which officials admit[ted would] be an uphill task, particularly against the stiff competition from other regions which are proving more attractive, like the Asian countries."[64]

In May 1987 the Andean Pact countries (Bolivia, Colombia, Ecuador, Peru, and Venezuela) took their first major step toward dismantling their restrictive policies vis-à-vis foreign investors. The pact members eliminated Decision 24, "which required majority national equity participation in new investment projects, demanded a gradual transfer of majority national ownership for old investments, and spelt out detailed restrictions on profit remittances, patents, and licensing contracts."[65] Ecuador first proposed the elimination of Decision 24; Peru was the only member state in opposition. Decision 24 was replaced by Decision 220, which allows each country to adopt whichever foreign investment regime it sees fit.

Since Decision 220 was enacted, Ecuador and Colombia liberalized their investment policies. In July 1987 Ecuador unveiled its new investment code allowing companies to transfer profits equal to 30 percent of their investment; up to 40 percent if they exported more than 40 percent of their production; those exporting over 80 percent and those working for tourism could transfer their profits freely.[66] Colombia also moved swiftly to change its policies. In July 1987 the Colombian government issued Decree 1265 and Resolution 44, which allowed investors to own up to 100 percent of a company, and retained "the obligation to turn into mixed corporations only if they wish[ed] to enjoy the benefits and privileges in the Andean regional markets."[67] Ceilings on profit remittance abroad were raised from 20 to 25 percent, and foreign investors suddenly were permitted to avail themselves of long-term internal loans from Colombian government channels with international lending institutions.[68]

Thus, changes in developing countries' policies, brought about by a world economic slump and heightened pressure to stay competitive, signified a drastic rethinking of policies adopted in the early 1970s. According to Harris, these changes reflected

> a shift from the belief that only the expansion of the domestic market could force growth . . . to a faith in the capacity to expand manufactured exports indefinitely; a movement away from hostility towards foreign capital to active pursuit of it; the liberalization of some imports; a shift of emphasis away from public-sector activity to the private market . . . ; and the privatization of public sector industries.[69]

The pressing economic problems faced by developing countries forced them to sacrifice many of the ideological premises that had fueled the effort to get an international code of conduct for the transfer of technology. The activist developing countries' legislation, which had inspired numerous provisions in the draft code, was called into question by the countries' own lawmakers and subsequently amended to reflect new economic realities. These trends, which became evident in the early eighties, led most developing countries to lose interest in the code effort. Apart from the fact that the latest draft version of the code was a far cry from what the Group of 77 had hoped for in the early 1970s, the whole enterprise seemed marginal at best. It seemed fruitless to pursue efforts to restrict and regulate the activities of foreign suppliers when foreign suppliers were so badly needed.

There was no enthusiasm for the code on either side by 1986. World economic trends heightened the United States' conviction that an international instrument codifying a stronger state role was a bad idea. The United States pointed to the success of the East Asian NICs as vindication of its neoclassical predilections. In a speech to the Foreign

Policy Association, U.S. Secretary of State George Shultz emphasized his view of the decisive elements in East Asia's success: "the developing countries that have grown fastest over the last decade have been those that opened themselves up to international investment. . . . It is no coincidence that systems which give the freest rein to economic activity are the most successful in liberating the talents, energies, and productivity of their people."[70]

The Group of 77 reevaluated its views as it faced a rapidly deteriorating economic situation. In fact, the solidarity of the group broke down. In preparation for UNCTAD VII sessions (held in July 1987) the African countries broke ranks with the Group of 77, and at the June 1987 meeting of the UNCTAD Trade and Development Board, the African block supported Group B's procedural proposals.[71] According to a Latin American trade expert, who refused to be identified, the African countries "want to see their immediate aid needs looked after as an absolute priority, and are quite prepared to block the financial reforms proposed by the Latin American debtor countries if that advances their cause."[72] He added that "the coming session will be a requiem for the original ideals of UNCTAD."[73]

Both sides shifted away from their old assumptions: the Group of 77 reevaluated its dependency reduction approach (and to some extent the theory of development upon which the approach is based), and Group B moved further in a neoclassical direction.

While the failure of the conference was due to changes in U.S. leadership and bureaucratic factors, this third factor—the economic slump of the late 1970s and early 1980s—was the most important. It was the strongest shock to the optimism of the Group of 77's member states. Not only did it take the wind out their sails, but it led them to abandon the whole ship.

4❖

INTERNATIONAL NEGOTIATIONS TO REVISE THE PARIS CONVENTION ON THE PROTECTION OF INTELLECTUAL PROPERTY

"Disaster" and "fiasco" are words often heard in reference to the Diplomatic Conference for the Protection of Industrial Property.[1] Developing countries tried to gain international support for a revision of the international system of patent protection embodied in the Paris Convention. The conference, held under the auspices of WIPO, began in 1980 and ended in March 1984. The differences between negotiating parties were fundamental from outset, and the depth and intractability of these differences only increased throughout the negotiating process. In June 1985, delegates consulted in Geneva to consider the wisdom of resuming negotiations, and the meeting ended in absolute deadlock.[2] The conference was never resumed. Since the last session in the mid-1980s the industrialized countries—especially the United States—substantially have redefined their interests.

In many respects the story of this conference mirrors the code of conduct negotiations discussed in the previous chapter. The impetus for the Paris Convention Revision came from the Group of 77. This was preceded by unit-level learning on the part of certain activist developing countries in Latin American and India, which had codified their dissatisfaction with the international system of patent protection by adopting new regional and national laws. As in the previous case, the industrialized countries held diametrically opposed views and were reluctant to negotiate; they entered the negotiations determined to prohibit any weakening of the system of patent protection. This status quo, antirevision stance meant that there would be no real dialogue in the full negotiations as ideological rigidity characterized both sides. Therefore it was not surprising that the conference ended in a deadlock.

However, as in the code of conduct case, after the negotiations there was a marked shift in positions. In particular, the United States redefined its interest from antirevision to actively seeking to strengthen the international system of patent protection. U.S. policymakers linked the issues of patent protection and international trade. The United States succeeded in getting intellectual property protection on the agenda for the Uruguay Round of GATT talks. The developing countries, as in the previous case, changed their policies under economic duress and U.S. pressure and, in large measure, abandoned the NIEO program in this issue area.

In 1883 eleven countries signed the Paris Convention for the Protection of Industrial Property. The convention was developed as a response to the increasingly international flow of technology and the increase in international trade. These developments created practical problems that could only be resolved through a greater harmonization of national laws. The convention established guidelines for industrial property law and also specified that contracting states constituted themselves into in *union* for the protection of industrial property.[3] As of January 1, 1986, ninety-seven states were parties to the convention. Sixty-four of these newest members of the Paris Union were developing countries. The provisions of the convention were formulated and revised by the adoption of new acts in 1925, 1934, 1958, and 1967, before developing countries belonged in large numbers. Over time the trend in the adoption of new acts has been in the direction of strengthening protection of the patent holder.

The Paris Convention serves two main functions. The first function is to protect inventors. The purpose of patent protection is to provide the stimulus for individuals to develop new technology and inventions and to share innovations with others. The second function is to establish guidelines for national patent legislation and practices to encourage and promote the development and diffusion of internationally new technology.

Patent protection and broad guidelines for national legislation reflect three principles of the convention: (1) nondiscrimination, (2) national treatment, and (3) the right of priority. Nondiscrimination means that there should be no barriers to the entry of foreign patentees in a member state's national market. National treatment means that once a foreign patentee has entered a member state's national market, that person should be treated no differently than nationals. Finally, the right of priority protects the patentee from unauthorized use of his or her invention for a designated time period; a patent provides the patentee a temporary monopoly. In effect, the Paris Convention sets the international standard for the minimum acceptable level of patent protection. Parties to the convention are free to pass national laws of their own design, provided that they maintain minimum standards of protection.

Nearly all technology supplier countries are parties to and supporters of the Paris Convention. If countries seek technology, they must play by the suppliers' rules. If protection of that technology is not guaranteed in recipient countries' national laws (adhering to minimum standards set forth in the Paris Convention), suppliers will be hesitant to transfer patented technology. Suppliers won't be willing to risk losing protection of and remuneration for the fruits of expensive research and development.

This chapter is divided into four sections. The first section examines the demand for revision of the convention and the interests of the various parties. The second section discusses the issues that were the subject of the negotiation and the fate of these issues through the conference. The third section addresses the aftermath of the negotiations and focuses on the redefinition of interests, particularly on the part of the United States. Finally, the fourth section presents conclusions about this case.

Origins of the Demand for Revision

The source of demand for a weakening of the international system of patent protection was unit-level learning on the part of certain activist developing countries, especially India and the Andean Pact countries. According to many developing countries, the standards embodied in the Paris Convention prevented them from adopting development provisions in their national laws pertaining to industrial property. After achieving independence, many developing countries adopted patent laws modelled after those of their colonial rulers. However, from the mid-1960s onward a good number of these countries revised their laws. "In modelling their national laws, quite naturally certain provisions have been carried forward from other existing systems and one of the most important sources which has influenced the formation of such national laws has been the Paris Convention."[4] According to an UNCTAD study, developing countries' adherence to the Paris Convention "circumscribe[d] their capacity to design their policies according to national needs and objectives."[5] Since most countries incorporated the Paris Convention's main provisions into their national patent laws and practices, UNCTAD concluded that developing countries' national laws "have legalized an anomalous situation 'which had come to act as a reverse system of preferences granted to foreign patent holders in the markets of developing countries.' . . . The developing countries, through their very laws and practices legitimized by the standards of the Paris Convention, have brought about this peculiar situation.[6]

Developing countries seized upon patent protection as a culprit behind import monopolies and patent abuse as a tool to prevent them from developing their own technology for the internal market and for export. As countries switched from an exclusive focus on import-substituting industrialization to export-led growth, they bristled at contractual provisions prohibiting them from exporting items produced with foreign-held patented technology. As Arcot Ramachandran, an Indian patent expert, points out: "a patent not only provides a right for a person to use this knowledge but also excludes others from using it. . . . This double-edged provision has caused patents to be put to several abuses."[7]

Perhaps no single writer has exposed these "abuses" more forcefully than Constantine Vaitsos. As head of the Andean Pact Secretariat's policies on foreign investment and technology, Vaitsos produced an influential and powerful analysis of the patent system. His study of the role of patents in developing countries led to a reappraisal of the merits of the patent system that influenced developing countries and UNCTAD.

Vaitsos argued that the patent system had a negative effect on developing countries. His main points, which were echoed by other voices throughout the Paris Convention Revision Conference, were: (1) patents granted by developing countries are overwhelmingly held by foreigners (usually foreign multinationals); (2) the main function of patents granted in developing countries is to assist profit maximization of large transnational corporations; (3) patents become a substitute for foreign investment and are a means to capture developing countries' markets; (4) patents are often the vehicle for the acquisition of local enterprises; (5) patents are a means for restricting the flow of technology from North to South; (6) patents can be a serious source of restrictive business practices.[8]

He emphasized the point that patents often amounted to monopoly privileges, and developing countries (through their patent laws) granted monopoly privileges while getting absolutely nothing in return except for stunted growth and balance of payments problems. According to Vaitsos, the monopoly privileges granted by patents are "exercised through the creation of secure import markets for the patented products in developing countries. International legal procedures have institutionalized the relationship between patent privileges and import markets."[9] These monopoly privileges, he argued, led to higher prices for imports and worse terms of trade for developing countries. This situation was further exacerbated by the practice of patent pooling or cross-licensing, which can create patent cartels.[10] Vaitsos argued that "international market control through patent cartels results in profit levels that would otherwise be unattainable for the corporations."[11]

Vaitsos' influential study underscored the view that developing countries could not afford to be neutral on the question of patents. He delved into a relatively neglected area of technology transfer policies, and his exposition helped to rouse developing countries from their previously unexamined complacency.

In 1974, India called for a revision of the Paris Convention. The Indian delegate formally requested a revision conference in a 1974 WIPO appropriations meeting. However, the real drive for revision began at least as far back as 1969.

In May 1969 the Treaty of Cartegena united Chile, Bolivia, Colombia, Ecuador, and Peru in a common front to minimize the negative effects of foreign investment and technology transfer. While their general approach to these issues is discussed in chapter 3, certain elements of their common policy pertained to industrial property in particular. The Andean Group's strategy was two-pronged; the five countries sought to (1) consolidate markets to attract foreign investment for building up industrial capacity and (2) regulate foreign investment to ensure that it met regional development priorities.

The main provisions aimed at regulating foreign investment are contained in Decision 24 on the "Common Treatment of Foreign Capital, Trademarks, Patents, Licensing Agreements and Royalties." This decision was adopted in a rather unusual way. It "was more or less conceived by a more or less closed group of reformist politicians, who were conscious of the need for reforms in order to alleviate the problems of underdevelopment. These politicians were aided by technocrats, who wanted to take part in the task of achieving higher economic growth rates."[12] Technocrats, such as Constantine Vaitsos, an architect of the Andean Group's policies, had a significant impact on the policies adopted.

Member states approved Decision 24 in December 1970. Decision 24 covered the treatment of foreign investments and established related measures for strict control in matters of patents and technology transfer.[13] Decision 24 firmly linked foreign investment and development goals. The decision also included "the establishment of a subregional office on industrial property for the coordination of national efforts on the transfer of technology."[14]

This regional coordination paved the way for the adoption of Resolution 85 of the Treaty Commission in 1974. Resolution 85 provided member countries with a common law covering patent, design, model, and trademark protection.[15] The thrust of Resolution 85 was to use the patent system to serve development goals. This created a tension between principles and priorities that was at the heart of the debate over patent policy. The purpose of Article 28 of Resolution 85 was to allow "the unhampered flow into the country of the results of patented technology which are available under more favorable conditions on the world market."[16] For example, Resolution 85, V. (28)

provided that a patent could not confer an exclusive right to import the patented product or a product manufactured by the patented process.[17] By contrast, the Paris Convention explicitly provided that a patent could confer an exclusive right of importation.[18] This discrepancy between the Paris Convention and the Andean Group's Resolution 85 pointed to a dissatisfaction with traditional patent protection on the part of some developing countries.[19]

Other key features of Resolution 85 that highlighted this dissatisfaction included: a provision to keep patent-free from the outset any technology that was important for a nation's development policy; a five-year limit on patent protection after which a patentee is limited to one renewal, and then only if he or she can show reasonable working of his or her invention; a provision that patents deemed important to the needs of national development could be subject to compulsory licenses at any time; and a provision that all licensing contracts had to be filed with the competent national authorities in order to ensure that such contracts conformed to public interest considerations.[20]

While the Andean Group's resolutions were particularly important in setting precedents and highlighting principles and priorities that competed with traditional notions of patent protection, the Andean countries were not alone in drafting new laws that presented a challenge to traditional precepts.

India's concern with regulating foreign investment dates back to 1948 when India established its general policy toward foreign private investment. India's "Industrial Policy Resolution" of April 1948 stipulated, among other things, that foreign private investment must be channeled into India's program of rapid industrialization.

India's patent system dates back to 1856. After attaining independence, the government undertook an extensive review of patent law in India. Two experts' inquiries determined that the Indian patent system failed "to stimulate inventions among Indians and to encourage the development and exploitation of new inventions for industrial purposes"[21] and for the public interest.

In 1970, India passed the Patents Act No. 39, which made certain contractual provisions illegal. Under the act, sellers of patented articles were not allowed to require the purchaser to acquire from the seller any article other than the patented article. Furthermore, sellers were not allowed to restrict purchasers from using an article or process that was not supplied by the vendor.[22] In short, the 1970 act asserted the rights of Indian recipients vis-à-vis foreign suppliers.

The Patent Act stated that patents "are not granted merely to enable patentees to enjoy a monopoly for the importation of the patented article."[23] India's Patent Act was based on the concern over getting patents worked in India, so that suppliers of patented technology would help establish production facilities on Indian soil. The act incorporated several provisions, taking into account the present state of development and its own and reported experience of patent acts in several other countries of the world. India was primarily interested in achieving rapid industrialization and increased technological capacity. According to Vedaraman:

> It was felt necessary to incorporate provisions for compulsory working of patented inventions in the country in the public interest, compulsory licenses and licenses of right to prevent abuse of patent rights by patentees who use the system as a means of securing an importation monopoly without commercially exploiting the patented invention within the country that granted the patent to promote its national industry and economy.[24]

Like the Andean Group's Resolution 85, the Indian Patents Act kept substances (not processes) intended for use as food, drugs, and medicines patent-free. The act also was designed to combat patent "abuses" such as import monopolies and nonworking.

India was not a party to the Paris Convention. India felt that state and public interests were not balanced with private interests in the convention. In 1974, India sought improvements in the existing convention before it would consider joining. India felt that developing countries lacked sufficient leverage in the Paris Convention and that developing countries needed special provisions to grant them effective bargaining power. The Indian delegation felt that the Paris Convention needed a stronger emphasis on states' rights vis-à-vis patentees. Vedaraman stated, "we look forward to the modification of the International Convention so that such measures which the developing countries may take are not rendered ineffective."[25]

While the Latin American and Indian developments comprised the broader context for the call for revision, in important respects the most immediate impetus for the Indian push in 1974 was the 1971 Revision of the Berne Convention for the Protection of Literary and Artistic Works. The 1971 Revision of the Berne Convention, administered by WIPO, granted special treatment for developing countries; it set a precedent at WIPO for preferential treatment and was fresh in the minds of the Indian delegation.[26]

Thus, certain key states were dissatisfied with past emphases in patent protection and perceived a need to alter the status quo. The sources of dissatisfaction were varied, but concerned states agreed that change at the international level was essential. They wanted the international system of patent protection to better reflect the burgeoning movement toward national legislation and regional agreements that incorporated notions of public interest to balance the private interests associated with patent protection.

The Andean Group countries were chiefly interested in enhancing their bargaining power vis-à-vis foreign investors (especially transnational corporations) and improving their balance of payments situation. India sought a more equitable balance between private and public interests, greater leverage for developing countries through preferential treatment, and a stronger emphasis on states' rights in patent protection.

Through the passage of national laws enhancing developing countries' bargaining power vis-à-vis foreign suppliers and patentees, these leading countries learned that they were not powerless to change their situations. These lessons were the product of experience: experience with balance of payments difficulties, entering into unfavorable contracts with transnational corporations, and implementing national legislation to correct perceived imbalances between public and private rights. However, these views were based on an analysis of the existing system of patent protection and industrial property rights that was consensual only *within* the Group of 77. These notions, for the most part, were not accepted by OECD countries.

The Paris Convention sets certain limits regarding national legislation. The earlier discussion of the Andean Group's Resolution 85 pointed out that its provisions did not fall within the range of acceptability according to the Paris Convention. Thus if a country sought to either join or remain a party to the Paris Convention, its laws could only go so far in asserting states' rights. The goal of the revision, then, was to change those limits in the interests of states' rights, even if it meant a diminution of the rights of the patent holder.

In 1974 the UNCTAD Secretariat, the UN ECOSOC, and the International Bureau of WIPO issued a joint report entitled "The Role of the Patent System in the Transfer of Technology to Developing Countries."[27] While the document was jointly authored, interviewees indicated that UNCTAD was the spearhead and major author of the report. It most closely reflected UNCTAD's position on these issues. At the time that WIPO agreed to be cited as coauthor, WIPO was trying to become a specialized agency of the United Nations. This helps to explain WIPO's cooperation with UNCTAD, even though the report contains many ideas and suggestions that run counter to WIPO's outlook, which conforms more closely to the OECD position. This study was a sweeping critique of the international system of patent protection and a call for changing the system in favor of developing countries. It challenged traditional principles of national treatment and nondiscrimination on the basis that they were merely legal niceties masking the true socioeconomic situation that kept developing countries at a disadvantage. In 1974 the journal *World Development* published a special issue on the international patent system. The contributing authors were all closely associated with UNCTAD.[28] The articles echoed the points made in the joint UNCTAD/ECOSOC/WIPO study of 1974.

In 1975, UNCTAD produced another report entitled "The International Patent System as an Instrument for National Development."[29] This report was exclusively devoted to the question of revising the Paris Convention, sharply criticized existing arrangements, and urged reforms to improve the situation of developing countries.

These studies did not present bold new arguments for those developing countries that had already passed laws incorporating the reevaluation of the existing system (such as the Andean Pact countries and India). However, the studies did open the eyes of those countries that did not have any patent legislation or had not considered the issue in any depth. The UNCTAD and *World Development* studies served an educational function within the Group of Developing Countries. The nonactivist developing countries learned from these studies, as well as from the examples of countries such as Brazil, India, and the Andean

Group, that their patent systems were disadvantageous, but that they could change them through a combination of national legislation and international negotiation. The combination of the studies, the examples of national and regional legislation in other developing countries, and firsthand experience with the disadvantages of the patent system all helped mobilize developing countries' opinions into a united front. The result was a powerful negotiating consensus on the merits of revising the Paris Convention to cater more effectively to the special needs of developing countries.

The OECD countries produced a mixed response to the developing countries' initial demands and the UNCTAD studies. However, the OECD countries were virtually unanimous in pointing out that the *positive* role of patent protection in industrial development had been overlooked by the forces for change.

Essentially the OECD countries reacted to the 1974 WIPO/ UNCTAD study. There was a marked lack of enthusiasm for the proposed revision (with some important exceptions: Canada, Spain, Portugal, New Zealand, Australia, and Turkey); the United States was particularly opposed to a Paris Convention revision. The U.S. delegation criticized the two previously mentioned UNCTAD studies on both methodological and intellectual grounds. The U.S. experts claimed that the critical assessment of the Paris Convention was based upon "selective use of experts' commentary and resort to hypothetical problems and abstract situations of unrealistic significance."[30] The United States argued that UNCTAD's and the Group of 77's assessment of the patent system was based on false assumptions, and that if the revision proceeded along UNCTAD's suggested lines, it would "have the effect of discouraging transfer of technology."[31]

Many of the OECD countries' responses to the UNCTAD studies reflected the view that the Group of 77 was looking at the international system of patent protection as a scapegoat for a myriad of ills, and that the revision would not be a panacea. Many OECD countries stressed the complex nature of the problems facing developing countries, including lack of training, lack of indigenous technology, lack of infrastructure to support industrial development, and the broader socioeconomic context. Both Britain and the United States emphasized the voluntary nature of technology transfer and warned that harsh measures against the owners of technology or patented inventions would not serve the goal of increasing that flow.

In short, the OECD countries argued that the developing countries' proposed policy instruments would not have the desired effect but would actually be detrimental to developing countries' objectives. Overall, what seemed to be a consensus on the Group of 77 side was flatly challenged by the OECD countries.

While consensus within one group led to the revision push, the fact that the more industrially and technologically powerful group rejected the Group of 77's challenge to the basis and the role of the patent system meant that the Diplomatic Conference on the Revision of the Paris Convention would proceed without a consensus on the merits of revision. There was an intragroup consensus on the side of the Group of 77, but since the basis of its consensual knowledge was rejected as such by the OECD countries, the prospects for a mutually acceptable agreement on a knowledge basis were dimmed.

The OECD countries had a different knowledge pool. A series of studies were conducted that explicitly or implicitly took issue with the UNCTAD analyses of the plight of developing countries in the patent area. For example, in 1975, Kunz-Hallstein pointed out that the tougher patent laws in India had led to a sharp decline in foreign patent filings in that country.[32] He argued that the new patent policies of developing countries were not leading to the desired goal of increasing the acquisition of foreign technical knowledge.

A study of the pharmaceutical industry in Latin America found that patent protection played both a smaller and more positive role than its critics suggested.[33] Another study, conducted in the course of the preparation of the National Paper of the Federal Republic of Germany for the UN Conference on the Application of Science and Technology for Development (Vienna, 1979), argued against the revision of the Paris Convention.[34] According to this study, adhering to the existing system would be more beneficial for developing countries than would the proposed reforms.[35] The author urged developed countries to reject all attempts to weaken traditional international rules and concluded that "it would be irresponsible, based on the current state of our knowledge, to suggest any weakening of the international patent system."[36]

Therefore, there was no knowledge consensus prior to the Diplomatic Conference. This lack of agreement on the basic notion of the purpose and function of international patent protection characterized the arguments made throughout the conference. Indeed, the gulf grew even wider since the last session of the Diplomatic Conference.

The Negotiations

The Diplomatic Conference for the Revision of the Paris Convention met in four sessions beginning in February 1980, in Geneva. After the fourth session in February and March 1984 a consultative meeting was convened in June 1985 in an unsuccessful attempt to break the negotiating impasse. Several salient issues were ardently debated, including the Group of 77's quest to obtain preferential treatment under the terms of the convention, and the Group of 77's proposed new policy instruments designed to encourage the working of foreign-held patents in developing countries' territory. This section discusses both the nature of the controversies over those issues as well as the fate of the Group of 77's quest during the negotiations.

While the issue of preferential treatment arose in a variety of proposed revisions for the Paris Convention, it was most extensively discussed in connection with Article 5quater (regarding importation and process patents). Article 5quater states that:

> When a product is imported into a country of the Union where there exists a patent protecting a process of manufacture of the said product, the patentee shall have all the rights, with regard to the imported products, that are accorded to him by the legislation of the country of importation, on the basis of the process patent, with respect to products manufactured in that country.[37]

Developing countries sought either to delete the article from the convention or at least be exempted from it.

Article 5quater "prohibits national law from distinguishing with regard to infringement between domestic and foreign products manufactured by the patented process."[38] The developing countries sought the ability to prevent importation of products manufactured under a process patent in cases such as those in which the product could be manufactured domestically. Developing countries felt that the system of patent protection was unbalanced; for them patent protection meant almost exclusively protection of foreign patents and that the international patent system operated only for the benefit of the economically and technologically stronger industrialized nations.[39]

The Group of 77 proposed that they be exempted from Article 5quater because they wanted the right to withhold protection from the owner of the process patent if that product was manufactured abroad. This was consistent with the group's quest to get patents worked in its countries to correct the perceived imbalance. It was also at odds with traditional principles of nondiscrimination and national treatment.

In addition to seeking a special exemption to Article 5quater, the Group of Developing Countries proposed two new articles under Article 5quater: Articles A and B. Article A would reduce fees for patentees from developing countries. Article B would lengthen the time period for the right of priority for patentees from developing countries. The purpose of these proposals for preferential treatment without reciprocity was to promote patent activity by developing country nationals. The idea behind it was that legal equality, as under the existing convention, was spurious in light of vast inequalities in industrial power and scientific and technological capacity. However Group B rejected these preferential measures under the convention's Article 5quater at the fourth session in Geneva in February and March 1984.

The Group of 77 argued that the biggest patent problem they faced was the nonworking or insufficient working of patents. "Working of an invention" means making the product or using the process that embodies the invention. The Group of 77 argued that importation of a product that embodied the invention did not constitute working. The obligation to work may be fulfilled by the patent owner himself or by somebody else under a license contract.[40] The patent holder would be obliged to work the invention, either himself or through a licensee, or else face the threat of a compulsory license to be granted at the request of a third party seeking to work the invention in the country.[41]

Developing countries claimed to suffer because so many foreigners filed and were granted patents in developing countries yet did not work the invention in the granting countries. While these figures have been widely disputed, UNCTAD estimated that 90 to 95 percent of patents granted in developing countries were not exploited, or properly worked.[42] Thus the Group of 77 argued that under the existing patent system, foreign filers did not contribute to Group of 77 development. The Group of 77's goal was to get the patents worked in their countries.

The policy instrument on which these countries desired to effect change was Article 5(A). Article 5(A) grants "member States the right to legislate against abuses which might result from the exercise of the exclusive right conferred by a patent."[43] The Group of 77 sought clarifications that (1) importation did *not* constitute "working" and (2) nonworking and insufficient working constituted abuses and should be subject to sanctions. The desired sanctions were *exclusive* compulsory licenses and forfeiture and revocation within shortened time periods.

Under the existing Stockholm text, the compulsory license for nonworking is nonexclusive. In other words, despite the granting of a compulsory license, the patent holder is still free to work his own invention or conclude license contracts with parties other than those that have been granted the compulsory license. Developing countries felt that this provision was too weak. Some suspected that patents often were filed by foreigners solely to block the use of the patented invention in the country or to promote importation of that article by the patent holder. In order to protect themselves from paying above-market rates for patented technology due to an import monopoly, developing countries preferred an *exclusive* license because it would be a much tougher sanction; exclusive licenses exclude the patent owner from using his or her patented invention.[44]

Nearly all developing countries felt that the Stockholm provision for nonexclusive compulsory licensing was ineffective and perhaps even detrimental to the development of indigenous enterprises. According to this view, if a nonexclusive license is granted to a small enterprise under the patent of a very strong competitor, the patent owner, who perhaps previously only imported into the country (if that), may see the licensee prospering in the local market and may "decide to start working himself in the country or to step up importation at prices undercutting the beneficiary's enterprise."[45]

The group of developing countries felt that the nonexclusive compulsory license was not an effective sanction in the case of nonworking or insufficient working. The possibility that the patent holder could jump into the market at any time, often with considerable advantages over the indigenous licensee, concerned developing countries. The often smaller and weaker indigenous enterprise could get squeezed out of the market very quickly.

Thus the developing countries felt that the grant of an exclusive compulsory license would be a necessary sanction against nonworking. No one argued that they actually intended to *use* the proposed exclusive compulsory license provision, but the Group of 77 thought that the presence of the threat would be sufficient to encourage working.

Compulsory licensing is one sanction designed to prevent patent abuses, but the harshest sanction is forfeiture of the patent. The Stockholm text of the Paris Convention provides that a patent may not be forfeited or revoked unless a compulsory license has already been granted. According to Article 5(A) 3:

> Forfeiture of the patent (i) shall not be provided for except in cases where the grant of compulsory licenses would not have been sufficient to prevent the said abuses (j). No proceedings for the forfeiture or revocation of a patent may be instituted before the expiration of two years from the grant of the first compulsory license.[46]

Brazil, in particular, was dissatisfied with this formulation. Brazil is a party to the Hague Act of 1925 and is not bound by the Stockholm Act on these matters. The Hague Act permits the forfeiture of a patent without first going through the compulsory licensing process. By contrast, the Stockholm Act sets down that a compulsory licensing procedure must be administered prior to any forfeiture. Brazil felt that the Stockholm text was not adequately explicit in identifying "nonworking" and "insufficient working" as abuses of the patent right warranting sanctions. Brazil felt that this last clarification would be important to encourage the working of patents in the granting country, The suggested remedy to this state of affairs was to adopt a proposed paragraph 8 under Article 5(A).

Paragraph 8 under Article 5(A) would give developing countries special treatment. The draft proposal would reserve the right to revoke patents in the case of insufficient working or nonworking for developing countries only. It would also relax the conditions for revocation, to make it easier for developing countries to use this sanction.[47] The purpose of the proposed special forfeiture provision and the exclusive compulsory license sanction was to extend the options available to developing countries to help them combat patent abuse. In the view of developing countries, these measures would increase their bargaining power and encourage working of patented inventions in the granting countries. Therefore the patent system could be used in a more positive way to help propel industrial development and facilitate technology transfer.

As it turned out, the measures that developing countries proposed to revise Article 5(A) in an effort to get patents worked in the granting countries became the main focus of the Diplomatic Conference. The first session in 1980 concentrated almost exclusively on procedural and administrative issues, but the remaining three sessions dealt with Article 5(A).

During the second session in Nairobi in September and October 1981, it appeared that the developing countries achieved some noteworthy victories. In particular it seemed as though they had prevailed on the issue of exclusive compulsory licenses. They were helped in their quest by a split among Group B. A group of six B countries (Canada, Australia, New Zealand, Portugal, Spain, and Turkey) played a key mediating role in trying to reconcile the divergent views on Article 5(A). The debates were quite heated, and participants became exasperated by the lack of progress.

In an effort to move the negotiations forward, the chairman of the committee charged with discussing Article 5(A) (Main Committee I), Argentine Ambassador Davila, convened a special group, "Friends of the Chairman."[48] The group consisted of three delegates from each of the three regional groups and met privately with Ambassador Davila. In consultation with the spokesmen from the regional groups, Davila then established a "Negotiating Group" for considering Article 5(A).

Six delegates from each of the regional groups negotiated for four days. Ambassador Davila presided over the deliberations, and the meetings were open to all participants and observers at the Diplomatic Conference. These sessions were well attended, and everyone in Main Committee I had firsthand knowledge of what transpired there.

The Negotiating Group resolved a number of issues, despite objections by the United States. When the Main Committee reconvened, the participants addressed the unfinished business of the Negotiating Group. The Group of Developing Countries reluctantly agreed to accept a Group B proposal for Article 5(A) (8) (a *bis*), which permitted the issuing of exclusive compulsory licenses. The Group of Developing Countries' profound reluctance about this provision was due to the highly diluted nature of the provision. The language of the paragraph (8) (a *bis*) emphasized that exclusive compulsory licenses could not be issued for *mere* nonworking or insufficient working (this was the developing countries' wish); rather before issuing such a license the national authority would have to determine that there are circumstances constituting *abuse* of the patent rights and that nonworking or insufficient working was *one* of the elements of the abuse. Therefore nonworking alone would not be an adequate justification for issuing an exclusive compulsory license.

Participants produced a compromise text, the so-called Nairobi text. There was a gentlemen's agreement to accept this compromise on Article 5(A), despite the objections of the United States and the dissatisfaction voiced by the group of six B countries that sought universal applicability of "special provisions" under 5(A) (8). However, the conference ran out of time and never formalized the acceptance of the Nairobi text. The crucial feature of the Nairobi text was that it allowed for exclusive compulsory licenses (albeit in watered-down form).

U.S. Ambassador Schuyler expressed his government's objection:

> A patent right is the right to exclude others from using an invention. A right to use one's own invention is an individual right. It is confiscation of private property, unrelated to the patent. The patent is the right to exclude others. The right to use one's invention is a separate property right and in reference with that right in the Paris Union, it is something that is out of place. . . . What abuse could possibly be so terrible that it warrants depriving an individual of his right to use his own property? . . . This Delegation repeats its objection; it will not be a party to any treaty which deprives an individual of his right to use his own invention.[49]

Switzerland also opposed the Nairobi text (especially Swiss industry—i.e., pharmaceutical concerns), but since the Swiss spokesman

Braendli was also the Group B spokesman, he did not want to come out too strongly in opposition to the majority group position.[50]

The proposed forfeiture provisions of the Nairobi text would allow patents to be forfeited or revoked without a prior compulsory licensing procedure for cases in which, "in the opinion of the national authorities competent for forfeiture or revocation, the grant of a non-voluntary license would not ensure sufficient working of the patented invention."[51] Ambassador Schuyler found this provision even more objectionable than the exclusive compulsory licenses. Schuyler argued that automatic forfeiture was more dangerous because a patent could be revoked based on an official's subjective and arbitrary judgement that

> a non-voluntary license would not ensure sufficient working, even though a license has not been granted. . . . Conceivably, a developing country may say that a high price for an imported product is an abuse, and grant an exclusive license unless the invention is worked in the country.[52]

Thus the United States raised the familiar fear of arbitrariness when the state is granted more power.

To summarize the discussion of the second session, the three main issues surrounding Article 5(A) were resolved (with the objections noted above) as follows: (1) The exclusive nonvoluntary licenses would be recognized in the convention. (2) The forfeiture or revocation measures without issuing a nonexclusive compulsory license first would be allowed in national laws via the convention, but with qualifications. (3) The special provisions in Article 5(A) would be restricted to developing countries. Although the Nairobi text restricts the use of special provisions (paragraphs 8, 8 (a), 8(a *bis*), and 8(b) to developing countries, the group of six B countries considered the matter unresolved and vowed to raise the issue at the third session. Ambassador Davila received unanimous praise for his role as chairman of Main Committee I; participants cited his fairness, objectivity, patience, and skill.

The third session represented an odd "about-face" from the last-minute conciliatory atmosphere of Nairobi. The Group of Developing Countries came to the third session in Geneva in 1982 fully expecting to move beyond Article 5(A), assuming it had already been resolved in Nairobi. The group was stunned to discover that between the second and third sessions the Group B countries had sharply reversed their position. The Group B countries came to the third session flatly rejecting the Nairobi text.

In between the second and third sessions, Group B countries' industries, deciding that they could not accept the Nairobi proposals, put pressure on the delegations to reject the Nairobi agreement.[53] Furthermore, "in the meantime some of the South American countries had been having second thoughts as well, probably because they were becoming worried about the conflict with the U.S. from where their new know-how came."[54] In particular, one official said that the United States put intense lobbying pressure on other Group B countries, as well as on Uruguay, Argentina, and Brazil. These Latin American countries were ruled by right-wing juntas at the time.

Acting in his capacity as chairman of Main Committee I's discussions of Article 5(A), Ambassador Davila began unofficial and informal consultations with various delegations from Group B and the Group of 77 to try to produce a consensus on Article 5(A) as it was conceived of at the end of the Nairobi session. Davila invited certain delegations to participate in this first round of consultations; after this round Davila prepared a text of Article 5(A) that he felt could be accepted by all parties. Davila circulated the text among various delegations and held a second round of consultations. The second round included representatives from each of the three regional groups, and the representatives were acting on mandates from their respective regional groups to represent the group's interests. This second round of informal talks failed to produce a consensus on the new text offered by Davila.

The Davila text's most significant departure from the Nairobi agreement was its omission of paragraph 8(a *bis*). The United States had always opposed 8(a *bis*) because it allowed for the granting of exclusive compulsory licenses. The Davila proposal eliminated the possibility of exclusive compulsory licensing and reverted to the pre-Nairobi situation. Group B and some developing countries initially accepted this formulation, but for the most part the Group of 77 was upset by and unhappy with the Davila provisions.[55]

The Group of Developing Countries rejected the Davila text because in its view even the Nairobi text was a compromise of significant proportions. The Davila text was contrary to their number one aim: to have an instrument available (exclusive compulsory licensing) to put pressure on patent holders to work patents in granting countries. As Fernandez Ballesteros, chief coordinator of the Group of 77 at the third session and delegate from Uruguay stated:

> The Group of 77 agreed to these [informal] negotiations primarily because the unofficial proposal mentioned in the report was presented by the person who holds the Chairmanship of Main Committee I, whose impartiality honesty are attested not only by the role that he plays in this Conference, but also by his well-known and universal admired line of conduct.[56]

While the Group of 77 admired the mediator, Davila, they could not accept the compromise.

Most of the developing countries were angry that the United States had orchestrated this new Davila compromise effort behind the scenes. Most of the Group of 77 hated the Davila text, and Cuba, Chile, Tanzania, and Tunisia were particularly opposed. In the end the Group of 77 displayed solidarity in rejecting the Davila text despite the embarrassment of having one of their "own's" name on it.

The Davila text waived Article 5quater for developing countries and allowed for forfeiture without prior compulsory licensing procedures. However, the conditions were unacceptable to developing countries. For example, Group B insisted that forfeiture be subject to judicial processes.[57] Why was this such a touchy issue? First, it lengthened the time period before forfeiture (courts are slower than administrative channels), and second, it displayed Group B's distrust of developing countries' governments. In this context Group B feared that developing countries' governments would be arbitrary and hostile, and thought that the courts would be a preferable safeguard from governmental fiat.

The Group B countries, by contrast, were virtually unanimous in praising the Davila proposal and were convinced that satisfactory solutions could be found on the basis of Davila's text. The only ripple in the smooth solidarity of Group B came from Richards of New Zealand, who once again reminded participants that not all "developed" countries were equally developed, and therefore the extension of special provisions to industrially weaker developed countries must be seriously considered. As Richards stated, "the final consensus on Article 5A will have to include an opportunity for access to special measures for certain technologically small countries such as my own. We are not seeking some soft option nor some free ride. All that we are seeking is fair and just recognition of our comparative level of development in patent matters."[58]

The third session ended in a deadlock; Group B maintained that the Davila text was as far as it was willing to go, and the developing countries argued that the Nairobi provisions were their absolute limit.

The fourth session was held in Geneva in February and March of 1984. Again the session focused on Article 5(A). The Group of 77 was united behind the Nairobi text and insisted upon exclusivity as an option for compulsory licensing. They did propose some new language for the Nairobi text, but the suggestions were too close to the spirit of Nairobi for Group B to accept them. The developing countries unanimously rejected the Davila compromise. The Group of 77 began to feel that no revision at all would be better than opting for the Davila text.[59] Group B restated its earlier position: "yes" to Davila, an emphatic "no" to Nairobi. Group B's intransigence "reinforced the conviction of the [Group of] 77 that exclusive compulsory licenses were the only threat which would force patentees who did not provide for manufacture to do so."[60] Positions hardened on both sides, creating a true impasse.

One notable change occurred at this session; the dissent of the group of six B countries vanished. All six quietly withdrew their earlier compromise proposals. These countries realized that they were not getting anywhere with those proposals, and there were also idiosyncratic reasons. In the case of Canada, the previous government had been replaced by a conservative Tory government. Spain and Portugal were busy trying to gain membership in the European Economic Community and felt that they had to "behave." Richards of New Zealand was no longer present at the conference, and with him left the impassioned pleas. In the case of Turkey the explanation is slightly less direct; Turkey's number one trading partner is Germany, and Germany began to follow the U.S. lead after the Nairobi session. Perhaps Australia withdrew its proposal because the old coalition fell apart. But the group of six ceased to be a factor in the deliberations.

While there was no forward movement at the fourth session, an interesting development occurred. Group B, and the United States in particular, expressed some dissatisfaction with the Stockholm Act of 1967. This was the first inkling in a multilateral setting that Group B might be seeking even stronger patent protection—beyond the status quo.

Steup, spokeswoman for Group B at that session, pointed out that her group sought clarification of the Stockholm provision regarding exclusive compulsory licensing. According to Bodenhausen's interpretation (one enthusiastically embraced by the Group of 77) the Stockholm text of Article 5(A) provides for *non*exclusive compulsory licenses only for failure to work. In other words, "the member states are . . . free to provide analogous or different measures, for example, compulsory licenses on conditions other than those indicated in paragraph (4), in other cases where the public interest is deemed to require such measures."[61] The Group of 77 welcomed this interpretation. According to one Group of 77 delegate, "developing countries now realize that they can use the Stockholm text to achieve as much as could be possible if the Nairobi text of Article 5A was accepted."[62]

Group B's spokeswoman objected to the so-called loophole interpretation whereby an exclusive compulsory license could be issued for reasons *other* than failure to work (i.e., "public interest"). Group B favored an interpretation in which "there are no exclusive licenses."[63] According to Steup, "the exclusive license is so troubling to us because it puts the patentee in a worse position than somebody who did not take out a patent. It creates a situation where the patent is not a benefit to him but some sort of punishment to him."[64]

Argentine delegate Mr. Pereira responded: "We have never thought that after four years of negotiations we would come to the point that Group B would state that the drafting of the Stockholm text . . . is not satisfactory, and that it is looking for a text that is more explicit."[65]

Steup qualified her group's position:

I did not say that my Group cannot on any account live with the Stockholm text; what I said is that we are looking for a balanced solution, and if one combines the Stockholm text with the provisions giving preferential treatment to developing countries, we consider such combination not to be the right balance.[66]

This exchange over the meaning of the Stockholm text was interesting because it foreshadowed later events, which will be discussed in the next section.

At the end of the fourth session, WIPO's International Bureau decided to postpone a fifth session until it felt reasonably sure that negotiating parties could find solutions and reach an agreement. In the meantime the bureau held consultative meetings to explore possible compromise solutions.

The first consultative meeting was held in Geneva in late June 1985. Article 5(A) was the only Article under discussion. More than two of the four days of the meeting were bogged down by procedural discussions. The delegates were frustrated, and the meeting ended in absolute deadlock.[67] A second consultative meeting was to be held in the summer of 1986, but it was never scheduled. Many delegations lost interest or gave up.

Aftermath: Redefining Interests

Not only did the Paris Convention Conference end in a deadlock, but the United States decided to raise the issue of intellectual property protection in GATT. The United States radically redefined its interests in intellectual property protection under industry-based pressure to stay economically competitive. This redefinition of interests culminated in a new trade-based approach to intellectual property protection. Institutionalized in its domestic laws, the new U.S. interests gained a multilateral dimension when the United States succeeded in getting intellectual property protection on the agenda for the Uruguay Round of GATT trade talks beginning in 1986. The international consequences of this redefinition have been dramatic; therefore it is useful to explore the evolution of the new U.S. thinking in greater detail.

This new interest, going well beyond the United States' initial status quo position in the Paris Convention context, grew out of domestic developments beginning in the early 1980s. In 1982 a chain of events was set into motion in the United States that led to a reinvigoration of patent protection. Two significant events occurred in 1982 and 1983 that ushered in what one commentator referred to as "the era of the patent."[68] The first event was the activation of the Circuit Court of Appeals for the Federal Circuit (CAFC) in October 1982 (under Public Law 97-164), and the second was a landmark Supreme Court decision regarding patent infringement in the *Devex* case. According to Robert Whipple, "no human mind apparently planned the almost simultaneous occurrence of the two episodes that taken together have created an environment for the onset of the new era in licensing which could be termed 'The Era of the Patent.' "[69] Whipple points out that during the era of the Black/Douglas Supreme Court (about 1946–1965), patents were not usually upheld and alleged infringers were rarely found guilty. When awarded, damages could be substantial but the amounts were rarely very large. Therefore, during this era businessmen did not need to be particularly worried about "trespassing on the claims of a patent."[70] This relatively lax attitude toward patent rights ended upon the establishment of the CAFC in 1982. Decisions of the court not only consolidated technical/legal criteria for determining patent infringement but have had the effect of raising substantially the level of damage/royalty compensation paid to successful patent-owner litigants.[71] Thus the activation of the CAFC signalled a more vigorous approach to the enforcement of patent holders' rights. The CAFC's decisions have reflected a more propatent approach and have supported higher damage awards than the decisions of previous Courts of Appeal.[72]

At about the same time, the U.S. Supreme Court handed down a landmark decision in *General Motor v. Devex*. Prior to the *Devex* decision, in infringement cases in which the patent owner prevailed, interest would be awarded from the date of infringement (as opposed to the date of judgement) *only* in exceptional cases. Under the old system successful litigants could not expect compensation based on damages from the date of actual infringement, but only from the much later date of the court's decision. *Devex* reversed this, and now prejudgement interest is common in infringement cases in which the patent owner prevails. Furthermore, since the *Devex* holding, numerous patent infringement awards have included "staggering" amounts of prejudgment interest.[73] In short, these two events ushered in a decidedly propatent trend and substantially raised the costs of patent infringement in the United States.

Several other U.S. developments in intellectual property protection were overt in their intended international dimension, and the trend beginning in the early 1980s gained momentum. The United States began to expand its newly invigorated propatent approach to encompass international trade. Alice Zalik, the former assistant general counsel of the Office of the U.S. Trade Representative (USTR), argued that inadequate intellectual property protection abroad caused "staggering" economic harm to American industries. She pointed out that American companies found themselves having to compete with mass-produced, unauthorized copies of their own patented, trademarked, and copyrighted goods both in source countries and third countries as well.[74] Industries felt the pain, and U.S. industry representatives initiated a series of measures to try to reverse this trend.

In the late 1970s agricultural chemicals producers—Monsanto Agricultural Company, FMC, and Stauffer—acting through the U.S. government, engaged in bilateral talks with the Hungarian government in a quest to end the piracy of agricultural chemicals and strengthen Hungarian law.[75] By 1982, responding to industry pressure, the U.S. government engaged in numerous bilateral consultations with Korea, Mexico, Singapore, and Taiwan on their patent, copyrights, and trademark laws.[76] As a result, Hungary, Taiwan, and Singapore took steps and enacted laws to ensure more vigorous protection.

These bilateral consultations were an important step in the evolution of the United States' new approach. Zalik pointed out that the participation of trade officials, rather than intellectual property administrators, in bilateral intellectual property negotiations helped increase the likelihood that targeted countries would change their laws because in developing countries trade policymakers have more clout than intellectual property officials.[77] Through these early successes, U.S industries realized that linking trade and intellectual property protection could be effective. According to James Enyart, the early U.S. bilateral negotiations with developing countries "began to make believers out of a large segment of high-technology and creative industries in America."[78] The agricultural chemicals producers joined forces with the U.S.-based International Anti-Counterfeiting Coalition (organized to protect trademarks in luxury and high fashion goods) and the Copyright Alliance to press for changes in U.S. trade policy.[79] As Chang Jae

Baik points out: "protection of U.S. intellectual property rights became a dominating issue only after a few firms and industry organizations initiated an intellectual property lobby. . . . Through astute marketing of their demands, the lobby gain[ed] broad support from the business community and elicit[ed] support even from liberal trade-oriented Congressmen."[80] These private sector actors represented vigorous export industries that enjoyed positive trade balances.

Most significantly, this spelled an end to the previous piecemeal treatment of intellectual property in the United States. Before the fall of 1984, the U.S. government had pursued an ad hoc approach to intellectual property problems, and U.S. embassies would assist individual companies when problems arose.[81] In 1984 the U.S. Congress, responding to increasingly effective industry lobbying, fashioned a more comprehensive approach to intellectual property. Two important trade initiatives were: (1) the 1984 and 1988 amendments of Section 301 of the Trade and Tariff Act of 1974 and (2) the revision of the terms for the extension of the Generalized System of Preferences for developing countries. I will discuss each of these initiatives in turn.

Section 301 of the Trade Act of 1974 gives the president of the power to take all appropriate and feasible action to enforce U.S. rights under trade agreements or to eliminate any act, policy, or practice that is unjustifiable, unreasonable, or discriminatory and burdens or restricts U.S. commerce. The act also permits U.S. industries, trade associations, and individual companies to petition the U.S. Trade Representative to investigate actions of foreign governments that they believe violate trade agreements or otherwise harm U.S. commerce.[82] If the USTR decides to investigate, he or she consults with foreign governments to try to resolve the problem. If these efforts fail, within a year (in all but subsidies cases that mandate a shorter time period) the Trade Representative recommends appropriate action to the president. "Appropriate action" often consists of retaliation via trade sanctions.

The 1984 amendment added two new features. First, the amendment permitted the USTR to initiate cases on his or her own motion; this change was designed to protect industries or companies that file 301 complaints from retaliation from foreign governments.[83] Second, for the first time the amended act explicitly included the failure to adequately protect intellectual property as actionable. The new language of the 1984 act identified as "unreasonable" those acts, practices, or policies that deny "fair and equitable provision of adequate and effective protection of intellectual property rights," and the criteria for finding an act "unjustifiable" was expanded to include any act, policy, or practice that denies protection of intellectual property rights.[84]

In 1988 the United States strengthened this trend with yet another amendment. Motivated by industry lobbying, in 1985 Congress pressed the administration to use Section 301 more vigorously. Congressmen bemoaned the fact that the executive branch shied way from trade retaliation because of its desire to use trade to barter for nontrade issues.[85] On August 23, 1988, Congress enacted H.R. 4848, the Omnibus Trade and Competitiveness Act of 1988, and adopted new amendments to Section 301. Since Section 301 is a core part of the main U.S. trade law designed to increase access to markets abroad for American exports and investments and, since 1984, to secure effective intellectual property protection abroad,[86] the 1988 amendments provided strong indications of how the United States sought to increase its ability to be economically competitive.

The 1988 amendments effectively transferred substantial authority from the president to the USTR. This change was intended to enhance USTR's position as the lead trade agency and reduce the possibility that trade retaliation would be waived for foreign policy or defense considerations.[87] In effect this change codified the elevated niche that trade has come to occupy in U.S. foreign policy—that trade interests should *not* be subordinated to issues traditionally conceived of as "high politics." The new act transfers to the USTR authority under Section 301 to determine whether foreign government practices are unfair and to take action.[88]

In addition, the 1988 Trade Act also strengthens the intellectual property components that were originally incorporated in 1984. Now the USTR must annually identify intellectual property priority countries—countries whose acts, policies, or practices deny effective and adequate intellectual property protection as well as those that deny fair and equitable market access to U.S. parties that rely on intellectual property protection. Within thirty days of identifying a country as a priority country, the USTR must self-initiate an investigation, determine whether the foreign activity is actionable and, if so, what action to take, within six months of the initiation. The USTR must implement Section 301 action within thirty days of an affirmative determination.[89] The 1988 amendments were important because they indicated that the United States would continue to pursue the carrot-and-stick approach in trade policy, and fortified the connection between intellectual property protection and international trade. Section 301 was strengthened and the message was clear—retaliation would be swift.

The second major initiative in U.S. policy in intellectual property protection was the revision of the conditions for granting developing countries Generalized System of Preferences (GSP) benefits. The U.S. Trade Act of 1974 gave the president authorization to waive tariffs on many imports from those developing countries designated as GSP beneficiaries. These nonreciprocal benefits help developing countries earn more foreign exchange. The GSP program was scheduled to expire on January 1, 1985. Industry associations that had participated in disappointing bilateral talks with Taiwan and Singapore over pharmaceutical, chemical, and copyright piracy in June 1984 indicated that they would press even harder for legislation that would make GSP benefits conditional upon adequate intellectual property protection.[90] The private sector began to see the GSP as an attractive trump card because these two countries were, at that time, GSP beneficiaries. The 1984 U.S. Trade and Tariff Act extended the GSP program until July 4, 1993, but, in response to industry pressure from the International Intellectual Property Alliance,[91] incorporated new conditions. Item 9 of the statement of purpose incorporates the effective protection of foreign nationals' intellectual property rights as an explicit condition for the granting of GSP benefits.[92] Furthermore the extension added patents, trademarks, and copyrights "to the definition of 'property' in the section that prevents the president from designating as a beneficiary a country that has expropriated the property of U.S. citizens."[93] The GSP extension provisions also require that the president "give 'great weight' to intellectual property protection" when making other decisions about developing countries' benefits under the program.[94]

The U.S. approach to intellectual property reflects the sentiments of U.S. businesses whose technology and intellectual property constitute invaluable assets. The chairman of Standard Oil remarked that the notion that intellectual property should be treated as the "common heritage of mankind" "assaults the basic morality of good business. What I have invented I own. I certainly don't mean this as a threat, but I am simply not going to license a process or build a plant in a country which turns around and steals my technology."[95]

From the foregoing it is clear that the United States has substantially redefined its interest in intellectual property protection. This interest in securing far more vigorous protection has evolved in a short time span and was codified in U.S. Trade Acts in 1984 and again in 1988.

Another domestic law pointed to the United States' concern with its industries' global competitiveness. In November of 1984, President Reagan signed into law the Semiconductor Chip Protection Act, Title III of H.R. 6163. This reflected the United States' response to competitive economic pressure in the computer industry. Notably, this was the first new form of federal patent protection in over one hundred years, providing protection both for "mask works," which are "fixed" in semiconductor chips, and the semiconductor chips themselves.[96] While this was a domestic law, the international ramifications were made quite clear from the outset. The United States broke new ground by extending protection to mask works, and the act incorporated extensive transition provisions to facilitate reciprocal protection by other countries. According to Mark Radcliffe, "Congress intended that the act would serve as an impetus to provide similar protection. The Act also has detailed provisions for coordinating protection with other countries who enact similar legislation."[97]

Under the provisions of the act, the U.S. Commissioner of Patents and Trademarks was authorized to extend interim protection to interested countries. Many OECD countries wasted no time in affirming their interest in this new approach. Japan immediately applied for interim protection (November 8, 1984) under the act and was quickly followed by Sweden, the United Kingdom, Canada, the Netherlands, Australia, and the European Economic Community.[98] The 1984 act illustrates the international intentions of the domestic legislation.

In the context of the Paris Convention revision efforts, in April 1986 the Office of the USTR went public with its dissatisfaction with current arrangements. The USTR was under increasing pressure from various industries (especially entertainment, computer, pharmaceutical, and chemical industries) to pursue a more vigorous program of protecting inventors. As revealed at the fourth session of the Paris Convention Revision Conference, U.S. industries felt that there were loopholes in the Stockholm Act. After April 1986 the United States criticized WIPO for the failed revision efforts. Prior to April the United States expressed no desire for Paris Convention revisions, but after April the United States raised the issue at GATT. The United States sought to link intellectual property issues to trade issues in the multilateral context. The United States felt it could be more effective in GATT where it felt it had more leverage than at WIPO. The United States preferred the GATT forum to WIPO for a number of reasons. The WIPO deliberations were open to the entire United Nations' membership (about 150 countries). GATT's membership was restricted to ninety countries, so the United States felt better able to use its clout at GATT. The United States sought to use market access and trade benefits as leverage; it felt it would be a direct, effective threat.[99]

The intense lobbying efforts of these industries led to the U.S. administration's policy change—from a status quo (antirevision) stance to a quest for much stronger patent protection. Industry representatives framed the problem and pushed hard for a multilateral approach. High-level executives from two activist companies, Pfizer and IBM, were members of the president's Advisory Committee for Trade Negotiations. They expressed their interest in getting intellectual property protection on the GATT agenda and got chief executive officers of twelve like-minded corporations to form the Intellectual Property Committee (IPC). The IPC represented computer, pharmaceutical, heavy and consumer manufacturing, electronics, creative arts, and chemicals industries. The IPC began by pitching its proposals to the U.S. government and then pressed its case abroad. It worked hard to convince the industrial associations of Europe and Japan that a code was possible, and then mobilized them to support its quest to include intellectual property protection in the Uruguay Round. The three groups then worked together to produce a consensual document, rooted in industrialized countries' laws, on fundamental principles for a multilateral approach to intellectual property protection. This industry coalition presented its document to the GATT Secretariat and Geneva-based representatives of numerous countries. This process, in which industry played such a central role, was unprecedented in GATT. Reflecting on the IPC's experience, James Enyart, of Monsanto, stated that "the industries and traders of world commerce have 'played simultaneously the role of patients, the diagnosticians and the prescribing physicians.' "[100]

The United States succeeded in getting most of what it wanted in the TRIPs (Trade-Related Aspects of Intellectual Property, Including Trade in Counterfeit Goods) agreement in the recently concluded GATT round. The industry representatives' demands are reflected clearly in the final agreement. For example, the TRIPs agreement affirms the principle of national treatment and mandates a twenty-year minimum period for exclusivity of patent rights from the date of filing the patent application.[101] Furthermore, the agreement restricts the issuance of compulsory licenses by forbidding exclusive licenses and sharply reducing the conditions for and scope of such licenses.[102] Chemical and pharmaceutical producers gained by the provision in the TRIPs agreement that reverses the former burden of proof in process patent infringement cases: before the burden of proof of infringement rested with the patent holder; now the alleged infringer must demonstrate that the process used is substantially different.[103]

However the TRIPs agreement includes some major concessions for developing countries. Articles 65 and 66 grant developing countries and least-developed countries five- and ten-year grace periods, respectively, before they are obligated by the terms of the agreement. Article 27(2) stipulates that

> members may exclude from patentability inventions, the prevention within their territory of the commercial exploitation of which is necessary to protect ordre public or morality, including to protect human, animal or plant life or health or to avoid serious prejudice to the environment, provided that such exclusion is not made merely because the exploitation is prohibited by domestic law.[104]

Article 27(3) exempts from patentability diagnostic, therapeutic, and surgical methods for the treatment of animals or humans; Article 27(4) exempts plants, animals, and their biological processes from patentability. These provisions will allow developing countries to continue to pursue conscious policies of drug patent exemption.[105] As Christopher Kent points out, these policies would reduce the profitability of multinational pharmaceutical corporations based in industrialized countries to the extent that they "are, and still would be, unable to capitalize on . . . [patent] protection in states opting to exempt pharmaceuticals from patentability."[106] Furthermore, agricultural chemicals may also fall under these exceptions, "provided the prevention of their commercial exploitation could be linked to a higher public order goal, such as the provision of an adequate food supply for the population."[107] The "ordre public" criterion is open to a variety of interpretations and enhances the role of state discretion in determining patentability.

Summary

In the Diplomatic Conference on the Revision of the Paris Convention, there was never any consensual knowledge. The Group of Developing Countries based its analysis and arguments on UNCTAD studies. The United States and most other OECD countries rejected the validity of the UNCTAD studies. The OECD positions were reflected in articles in the *International Review of Industrial Property and Copyright Law* (IIC). The two groups had conflicting knowledge claims and disagreed fundamentally about cause-and-effect relationships. While the Group of 77 believed that its revision proposals, if adopted, would improve the quality of technological transactions, the OECD countries argued that the proposals would have the opposite effect. The United States was intractable from the first session, and while its initial position was antirevision, by the end the United States desired revisions in the direction of increasing patent protection. The first traces of this shift within the conference itself were apparent in early 1984 at the fourth session but did not become full blown until April 1986 with the USTR statement and the U.S. efforts to get intellectual property on the agenda for the new round of GATT talks.

The conference debates became hardened as ideological arguments dominated discussions. The issue of patent protection became polarized between contractual freedom and states' rights. The debate got stuck on the issue of exclusive compulsory licensing, which reflected the broader ideological argument between liberal economic thought (or "managed liberalism") and dependency analyses. The liberal economic perspective favors market mechanisms for technology transfer, which depend on minimal state interference for smooth functioning. The dependency analysis favors strong state intervention to enhance developing countries' bargaining power and rectify past injustices. The participants were unable to build a bridge between these competing perspectives and lacked consensual knowledge to help find a mutually acceptable compromise. Consensus remained an *intra*group phenomenon. The groups flatly opposed each other's analyses and prescriptions.

In the case of the Paris Convention Revision Conference, consensual knowledge played no role in bridging the gap between competing values. However, the learning on the part of developing countries that took place prior to the negotiations was significant in shaping their multilateral demands. During the conference itself, many developing countries discovered what is permissible under the existing convention and found out that the Stockholm text was subject to an interpretation that favored developing countries' interests. However the significance of this discovery was somewhat diminished in the face of U.S. bilateral pressure, which has been effective in getting developing countries to redraft their intellectual property laws.

Learning and redefinition of interests took place prior to the negotiations—among the Group of 77—*and* later within the United States. The United States' redefinition of its interests in the intellectual property field arose not because of the Paris Convention negotiations but rather as a result of economic adjustment pressures in the early 1980s and the growing economic competition from countries such as Japan, South Korea, and Taiwan, which were catching up by using the strategy of the "fast second." U.S. industries felt that they could not be globally competitive if they were forced to compete with much cheaper knock-offs of their products. Industry representatives effectively pressured the U.S. government to undertake a series of measures to force other countries to respect the rights of intellectual property owners, culminating in the new GATT agreement on intellectual property. This case presents a vivid example of how states redefined their interests in response to economic pressure. The other OECD countries have jumped on the U.S. bandwagon to a large extent, and the effects of the United States' trade-based approach to intellectual property protection on developing countries will be examined in detail in chapter 6.

5❖

A CODE OF CONDUCT FOR THE CONTROL OF RESTRICTIVE BUSINESS PRACTICES

In December 1980 the United Nations General Assembly unanimously adopted the "Set of Multilaterally Agreed Equitable Principles and Rules for the Control of Restrictive Business Practices" (hereafter referred to as the RBP Set or the RBP Code). At the time, given the poor record of North-South negotiations, this was hailed as a great achievement. Since the South had expressed a desire to develop multilateral instruments to control restrictive business practices as a key component of the NIEO, the South saw the RBP Set as a victory of sorts. The North was more pleased with the RBP Set because the North (and particularly the United States) had eagerly embraced the idea of an RBP set, and its final provisions largely reflected the North's preferred position on RBPs.

The case of the RBP Set differs from the Paris Convention revision negotiations and technology transfer negotiations in several important respects. First of all, the negotiations were successful insofar as an international instrument was unanimously adopted. Second, in this case, unlike the Paris Convention and technology transfer negotiations, the North set the agenda. Furthermore, at least on the face of it, this case can be explained in the starkest of structural terms—the most powerful states got the instrument they wanted.

The story of the RBP Set is one of converging interests up until the time of its adoption, but one of diverging interests for nearly ten

141

years after the fact. Developments until 1989 suggest that in the years immediately following the RBP Set's adoption, the consensus evaporated. After 1980 the North began to distance itself from the agreement, and the South began to question the value of the RBP Set. The initial consensus disappeared when the ink was dry, and the agreement turned out to be less substantive than it had appeared. In short, the RBP Set was a success on paper, but at least until 1989 the achievements were questionable.

Restrictive business practices are business practices that are deemed to be detrimental to economic competition and international trade. In the words of a developed market-economy country expert on RBPs, the objectives of a multilateral instrument were "to ensure the benefits of competition in a free market; to secure the benefits of trade liberalization; and to protect sovereign prerogatives of national governments."[1] Examples of restrictive business practices include: abuses of dominant market power that pose severe danger to competitiveness; price fixing; tying clauses; restrictions on volume and structure of production; and export restrictions. The issue of RBPs arises in the context of international technology transfer because technology contracts have often included provisions—such as grant-back licensing provisions, restrictions on subsidiaries' bulk sales, and tied sales—that can be considered restrictive. Many of these RBPs were incorporated into technology transfer contracts concluded between Northern suppliers and Southern recipients. Therefore countries such as Brazil, India, Mexico, and the Andean Pact countries adopted prohibitions against restrictive business practices in their foreign investment and technology regulatory laws and policies.

The North and South displayed different approaches to the control of RBPs. In general terms the Northern approaches were designed to eliminate or curb RBPs that had an adverse effect on competition, whereas the South's application of RBP policies was designed to curb those practices that had an adverse effect on economic development.

This chapter is divided into four sections. The first section describes the interests of the parties in a multilateral RBP Code. The second section covers the issues raised in the negotiations and how they were finally resolved. The third section discusses developments after 1980. Finally, the fourth section presents conclusions about this case.

Origin of Demand: Converging Interests

The Northern countries were the main proponents of a multilateral RBP Code. The Northern interest in such a code dated back to as early as 1925, when the League of Nations considered proposals for an international antitrust code. The proposals were rejected at that time due to concerns over infringements upon state sovereignty and disparate national approaches to antitrust/restrictive business practices.[2] During the Great Depression business practices considered harmful to the free play of market forces—such as cartels and the rationalization of production and distribution—were actually encouraged in many countries (except the United States after the 1930s) as the key to global economic recovery. However, after World War II this permissive attitude toward international business activity and mercantilist policies was questioned. In particular, the United States felt that the considerable concentration of economic power in Germany and Japan contributed to responsibility for the war,[3] and was eager to reinvigorate international commerce. Therefore, the United States insisted that Germany and Japan adopt antitrust laws and helped to install similar laws in France and the Philippines.[4]

In 1948 the United States initially supported the Havana Charter, which would have established the International Trade Organization and a new international trading system. Chapter V of the charter focused exclusively on RBPs. The link between RBPs and trade was clear. While governments were negotiating the reduction of tariff and nontariff barriers to promote freer trade, those who drafted the charter sought to ensure that enterprise behavior would not maintain trade barriers through the use of restrictive business practices.[5] However the U.S. Congress ultimately rejected the Havana Charter; it was opposed by both the left and the right. In 1952 a UN Economic and Social Council committee endorsed a second draft of the charter's antitrust principles, but, at the behest of a conservative Congress, the United States withdrew its support based on the perception that such an agreement was premature because at that point too few states had adopted competition laws and policies. Policymakers feared that uniform implementation could not be guaranteed, and that international efforts should await further development at national and regional levels.[6] Two years later the Organization for European Economic Cooperation (OEEC) established a committee on RBP legislation; in 1961 this committee became a permanent part of OEEC's successor, the OECD.[7]

The grounds for the United States' rejection of the revised Havana Charter's antitrust provisions in 1952 no longer pertained by the mid-1970s. Twenty-two of the twenty-four OECD member nations and roughly a dozen developing countries had adopted competition laws and policies. Most of these laws, like U.S. law, covered issues such as undue restraints on competition and abuse of market power. However, no country adopted laws as stringent as those of the United States.

The movement to establish international antitrust rules first took concrete shape within the OECD. In 1967 the OECD passed a notification recommendation whereby all OECD nations with an antitrust enforcement program were asked to notify other member nations in advance of any investigation or prosecution that was likely to affect important interests of the other nations.[8] As discussed in chapter 1, the OECD further codified its concern over RBPs in 1976 by adopting the OECD Guidelines for Multinational Enterprises. The guidelines specify four competition principles for multinational corporations: no abuse of dominant positions of market power; no participation in international cartels that have not received government approval; granting of reasonable freedom for licensees and distributors to buy and resell; and providing requested information to antitrust officials.[9] Significantly, the adoption of the OECD Guidelines demonstrated the North's interest in a coordinated approach to these issues.

The guiding spirit behind the OECD's approach to RBPs was the belief in a relatively liberal international economic order. RBP rules are a core component of such an order. That order requires the lowering of tariffs, the elimination of nontariff barriers to trade and investment, the recognition of reciprocity in transactions, and the establishment of rules distinguishing between fair and unfair international competition.[10]

When UNCTAD was charged with the task of bringing experts together to negotiate a set of multilateral principles and rules for the control of RBPs in 1975, the United States was eager to participate since it had long been interested in an international approach to antitrust issues. The United States felt it had much to offer in deliberations on the topic; as the chief U.S. negotiator of the RPB Set, Joel Davidow, suggested, the United States believed that "it could offer more insight in the area of restrictive practices, at less ideological risk, than it could in any other area."[11] U.S. policymakers believed that their participation in drafting international RBP rules would lead to a more procompetitive and sophisticated document because the United States had much more experience with both antitrust and a free market economy than most of the other participants.[12] Thus the United States saw the negotiations as an opportunity to internationally codify its approach to RBPs and affirm the merits of a free market economy.

The North was not alone in its enthusiasm for an RBP code. While the developing countries had different reasons for supporting this multilateral effort, they too were eager for a code. The South's interest in an RBP code arose more recently and in a wholly different context than that of the North. Indeed the South's conception of the nature and purpose of RBP regulation was quite different than that of the North. The fundamental differences in approach to these issues became apparent in the negotiations.

The developing countries first raised their concern over RBPs within UNCTAD at its second session in New Delhi. There they adopted Resolution 25 (II), which called for a study of RBPs engaged in by industrialized countries' private enterprises, and the effects of those RBPs on the export interests of developing countries.[13] At UNCTAD's third session in Santiago in 1972, governments unanimously endorsed examining prospects for establishing international guidelines to protect developing countries from the adverse effects of RBPs.[14]

The UN General Assembly resolution on the Action Programme for the Establishment of a New International Economic Order incorporated RBPs and urged states to make efforts to formulate, adopt, and implement an international code of conduct for transnational corporations to eliminate RBPs.[15] At the seventh special session, the General Assembly stated that RBPs that hurt the trade interests of developing countries must be eliminated, and endorsed national and international efforts to negotiate a set of equitable RBP principles and rules.[16] Thus, an RBP code was identified as a crucial component of a New International Economic Order.

The developing countries' central concern over RBPs was economic *development* rather than competition per se. The South had three objectives in its interest in an international RBP code: (1) gaining greater access to Northern markets for their exports; (2) curbing restrictive practices of transnational enterprises generally and particularly in the context of technology transfer; and (3) curbing RBPs between parents and subsidiaries (intra-enterprise transactions).

In the eyes of the developing world, certain economic trends sharply revealed the need for international control of RBPs. As developing countries became more economically successful, their concern over RBPs grew. Brusick suggests that as developing countries had successfully exerted greater control over their natural resources and embarked on industrialization for exports, "the possible use of enterprise behaviour as a formidable obstacle to these aspirations of developing countries became increasingly evident."[17] Developing countries depend upon access to the markets of developed countries so that they can successfully export their commodities and manufactured goods. By the 1970s, their vulnerability was enhanced by the increased use of restrictive business practices as a means of entrenching developed country markets under new forms of protectionism. RBPs affecting developing countries' exports that reflected this new protectionism included: voluntary export restraints; agreements between enterprises in both importing and exporting countries to maintain set export levels and set prices; and the practice of parent companies instructing their subsidiaries to either limit or forego production for export.[18] The Group of 77 incorporated its quest for more open Northern markets in its proposal for the NIEO, "which called for a more equitable international trading and industrial structure and stressed the need to assist developing countries in these goals."[19]

The Group of 77 revealed its keen interest in establishing a more hospitable international trading environment in the group's statement of its objectives for an RBP Code, submitted by the expert from India on behalf of the group:

> (i) To increase the share of developing countries in international trade . . . (iii) To promote a more equitable balance in world industrialization and trade structure in the context of the establishment of the New International Economic Order; (iv) To maximize

> the benefits and to eliminate the disadvantages to trade and development deriving from the operations of transnational corporations so as to ensure that they make a positive contribution to the trade and development of developing countries; (v) To strengthen the participation of national enterprises of developing countries in activities undertaken by transnational corporations in their countries, particularly those relating to the import and export of manufactures and semi-manufactures. . . . (vii) To ensure not only that the activities of transnational corporations become a positive factor in export efforts and import substitution efforts of developing countries, but also to bring about greater control, by these countries, over the processing, marketing and distribution of their goods.[20]

Developing countries worried that without access to Northern markets, their export revenues would evaporate. Therefore, they sought a reduction of barriers to trade arising from RBPs and the creation of a more hospitable international economic environment.

The rapid and extensive expansion of transnational enterprises' activity in the developing world created controversies over the benefits to host countries. Many developing countries felt that these enterprises required careful monitoring lest they run roughshod over national development aspirations and goals. Policymakers in developing countries argued that when transnational enterprises engaged in abusive practices in host countries, developing countries had to (among other things) pay excessive prices for required imports and were denied the necessary inputs for successful industrialization and economic development. The developing countries sought the elimination of detrimental practices by TNEs in host countries. Developing countries desired "a reorientation in the activities of transnational corporations towards, *inter alia,* more complete manufacture in developing countries."[21] Furthermore, the Group of 77 saw the control of RBPs "as a step towards controlling the acquisition or abuse of market power by transnational corporations and in particular, the activities of such corporations in developing countries."[22]

While only about a dozen developing countries had enacted RBP legislation prior to the negotiations, those countries had substantially modeled their laws and policies after developed countries' laws. However, there were key differences between the application of these laws in the developing countries and those in developed countries. In addition, in both sets of countries there were differences in the role that RBP legislation played in controlling restraints on competition and abuses of dominant market power. As Eduardo White suggested in his comprehensive review of the control of RBPs in Latin America (Argentina, Brazil, Chile, Colombia, and Venezuela), RBP laws and policies in those countries were more a complementary instrument of control than a central one.[23] According to White:

> The industrial development characteristics of the region including the structure and size of markets, historical trends in state intervention, the presence and behaviour of a significant number of foreign firms (mostly subsidiaries of transnational enterprises) account for the fact that classical antimonopolistic legislation—introduced at least as a principle for action, developed from an operational standpoint in some of them—is often overtaken or replaced by different methods of State control of economic power in general. These include price control regimes, regulation of industrial development through, *inter alia,* the establishment of State-owned enterprises to provide countervailing market power, and controls of investment and technology transfers. These control methods still are, in most countries of the region, the main vehicle for the control of those restrictive practices of central concern to them.[24]

In contrast to the RBP laws and polices of most developed countries, the use of RBP legislation in developing countries played an indirect role in the control of market power. As White points out:

> an important function of such legislation seems to consist in increasing the visibility and accountability of the exercise of market power by dominant firms, in particular where it is not regulated or supervised under other instruments of government control. For example, foreign investment regulations tend to control *entry* to the market rather than the operations of foreign subsidiaries already established in that market.[25]

This reflected a "prior restraint" approach to regulation.

RBP control was incorporated into foreign investment policies and technology transfer regulations. For example, these regulations and policies in Brazil, Mexico, and the Andean Pact countries prohibited certain business practices such as grant-back provisions, restrictions on volume and structure of production, tying clauses, price fixing, export restrictions, and restrictions on the use of personnel. Reflecting this approach to RBPs, the Group of 77 proposed that an international RBP code cover "any international transaction involving the use of restrictive business practices oral or written and irrespective of its legal form, which refers to foreign investment . . . and to the procurement of technological know-how, equipment and processes, and including those on an intra-firm basis within transnational corporations."[26]

Developing countries were centrally concerned with RBPs engaged in by transnational enterprises in intra-enterprise transactions. According to Davidow, whereas the industrialized countries considered intracorporate transactions as a relatively minor technical issue of antitrust policy, developing countries considered these to be the most important group of restrictive practices that they wished to have eliminated.[27] This developing country perspective was shaped by a number of factors, including extensive experience with subsidiaries of multinational enterprises and developing countries' literal interpretation of the phrase "restraint of trade" (which traditionally had been interpreted as restraint of competition). As Davidow points out: "delegates from nations with a long antitrust tradition have tended to argue that the international goal should be to assure that traditional restrictive business practices do not hamper international trade or the trade and development of developing countries."[28] By contrast, developing countries argued that *any* business activity that has the effect of compromising their exporting ability or domestic purchasing power should be eliminated. The developing countries sought an RBP code that would regulate intra-enterprise transactions. They believed that the curbing of intra-enterprise RBPs would help to increase host country control over transnational enterprises' subsidiaries operating in their territory. Davidow suggested that the developing countries' emphasis was quite different from that of the developed countries, insofar as developing countries "generally want[ed] to complain about enterprise behavior rather than about antitrust prosecution."[29]

The Negotiations

Beginning in 1975, UNCTAD convened a group of experts to negotiate a multilateral RBP code. Many of the issues discussed in the RBP
negotiations paralleled those of the TOT negotiations. However, overall the RBP negotiations were far narrower and more technical in
scope. Among the core issues raised in the RBP deliberations were:
(1) Should the code be legally binding or voluntary? (2) Should there
be special exemptions for cartels originating in developing countries?
(3) Should the code incorporate the principle of national treatment, or
permit differential treatment for foreigners? (4) How should the issue
of parent-subsidiary relations (or intra-enterprise transactions) be dealt
with? (5) What philosophy of RBPs should the code embrace—one
emphasizing competition, or one emphasizing development? (6) What
kind of machinery should be established for the code's subsequent
implementation? I will discuss each of these issues in turn.

The North, as in the case of the TOT Code, sought a voluntary
code and rejected the idea of a legally binding code. The North's
preference for voluntary, nonbinding multilateral approaches in this
area was based on the view that "binding codes would be seen as
intolerable forms of control over private enterprise. . . . Binding codes
would inevitably regulate multinational enterprises to the detriment of
the enterprises themselves and of their home countries."[30] The Group
of 77 did not press as hard for a legally binding code on RBPs as it
had in other negotiations because in this instance the group was split.
Some group members favored a legally binding code to ensure widespread compliance, but the OPEC governments worried that a binding
antitrust code might jeopardize their commodity cartel. OPEC preferred a weak code and in this respect shared common ground with
Group B.[31] The negotiators agreed fairly quickly that the code under
negotiation would be strictly voluntary and nonbinding.

A related issue was whether the code would grant special exemptions for cartels originating in developing countries. In particular, OPEC
nations sought exemptions for their commodity cartel. Group B and
the Group of 77 were able to strike a deal on this issue in which Group
B agreed to exempt intergovernmental cartels in exchange for a nonbinding code and the inclusion of the consideration of other factors,

such as practices approved by national governments and restraints between affiliated firms.[32]

The exemptions for intergovernmental cartels were codified in the final document in two sections—B (ii) 9, and C (ii) 6. The first stated that "the Set of Principles and Rules shall not apply to intergovernmental agreements, nor to restrictive business practices directly caused by such agreements."[33] C (ii) 6 provided that "States . . . should take due account of the extent to which the conduct of enterprises, *whether or not created or controlled by States* [emphasis added], is accepted under applicable legislation or regulations."[34]

The North argued for national treatment in the application of restrictive business practices legislation and policies. It wanted that principle reflected in the RBP Code and proposed that "nations should formulate and implement their legislation to provide legal procedures ensuring fair and factual determination of the issues and *treat all enterprises justly without differentiation based on locus of origin or control* [emphasis added]."[35] The spokesman for Group B's experts argued in part that his group "did not believe that enterprises of developing countries should be able to compete under a different set of rules as this would be an entirely unworkable arrangement and one that would distort the market."[36]

By contrast the Group of 77's experts suggested that preferential treatment for developing countries' enterprises was necessary due to these countries' enterprises' generally weaker market positions. They felt special measures were called for to help create countervailing market power in developing countries to balance the powerful market position of transnational enterprises' subsidiaries. These experts suggested that "special or preferential treatment should be accorded at national and international levels to developing countries and national enterprises in respect of the multilaterally acceptable principles governing the control of restrictive business practices and concerning international collaboration."[37]

Again, the North prevailed on this point. The final language of the RBP Set was explicit in its insistence upon equitable treatment of enterprises. According to section E (3) of the RBP Set, "States, in their control of restrictive business practices, should ensure treatment of enterprises which is fair, equitable, on the same basis to all enterprises, and in accordance with established procedures of law."[38] Thus the RBP Set conformed to the Northern position that all enterprises should be treated the same; the RBP Set did not authorize developing countries to treat foreign enterprises any differently than domestic enterprises.

The issue of parent-subsidiary relation was hotly contested. Developing countries were particularly interested in this issue because one of their primary aims for an RBP code was to curb what they deemed to be restrictive practices engaged in by transnational enterprises—especially in intra-enterprise transactions. Part of the problem for developing countries, in their view, was that "the parent and subsidiaries of a transnational corporation are frequently treated under existing competition laws as a single economic entity and the restrictive business practices engaged in, in the context of intra-corporate relations affecting international trade, are by and large outside the scope of such laws, since they supposedly involve only one party."[39]

Developing countries had specifically targeted parent-subsidiary relations. The developing countries preferred an "arm's length" conception of parent-subsidiary relations to facilitate closer government scrutiny of business activity. They sought to treat subsidiaries as legally and economically independent from parent corporations in an effort to keep transnational enterprises' abuses to a minimum. Specifically the Group of 77's proposals for an RBP Code defined "enterprises" in such a way to imply that "branches were always a separate legal entity."[40] The Group of 77 also wished to treat "parent/subsidiary distribution of functions . . . as a restrictive business practice."[41] The spokesman for the Group of 77 stressed that, "branches needed to be covered by the definition of enterprises . . . [and] that the principles and rules needed to cover parent/subsidiary relations given the importance of such enterprises in the trade and development of developing countries."[42] The developing countries wanted to incorporate provisions regulating intracorporate transfer pricing and sought support for their position by reminding the other experts that transfer pricing had been explicitly considered a restrictive business practice by the OECD Guidelines.[43]

Group B rejected these proposals. As a Group B spokesman indicated:

the Group B experts adhered to the position that . . . internal decisions of enterprises were not deemed to be restrictive business practices. While accepting that a parent corporation could commit a restrictive practice by means of orders to its subsidiary, they considered that internal decisions generally raised questions not of restrictive practices but rather of investment, tax, or fiscal policies. As regards transfer pricing, Group B considered that this issue should be dealt with by the Commission on Transnational Corporations.[44]

Group B argued that transfer pricing was more of a financial or tax-revenue problem rather than a restrictive business practice. Furthermore Group B argued that if parent-subsidiary distribution of functions were to be treated as a restrictive business practice, "the effect would be detrimental to developing countries as it could well discourage foreign investment."[45]

So what was the outcome of the parent-subsidiary controversy? Negotiators resolved this issue in a manner that essentially reflected the Northern approach to intra-enterprise transactions. The developing countries' desired provisions regarding transfer pricing and intra-enterprise transactions did not survive the negotiations. The final document reflected the position of conservative economists who argued that vertical practices (e.g., between suppliers and customers, or licensors and licensees) should be presumed reasonable unless the parties seeking restraints possess dominant market power and "cannot justify the practice by its relation to quality, safety, service, or distributional efficiency."[46] The RBP Code focused on horizontal offenses such as price-fixing, market and customer allocation, and boycotts, but there were no strict rules governing intra-enterprise activity. Sections D(3) and D(4) of the code dealt with both vertical and horizontal abuses and "generally allowed normal intra-enterprise relations to be carried on without concern that such behavior might constitute restrictive business practices. Section D(3) excluded from its listing of harmful effects those which might arise when enterprises deal with each other 'in the context of an economic relationship wherein they are under common control.' "[47] The code further declared that allocations among firms were not to be treated as cartels. In addition, Section D(4) restricts the condemnation of vertical restraints to cases of dominant firms engaging in abusive practices.[48]

Finally, the North also prevailed on the issue of whether the code's provisions would constitute absolute prohibitions or would be subject to the "rule of reason" (or case-by-case) analysis. The section on intra-enterprise activity incorporated the "rule of reason" approach consistent with United States antitrust law. A footnote to section D(4), the "rule of reason" footnote, enumerated four factors that were to be examined on a case-by-case basis to determine whether or not acts or behavior are abusive. For example, factor (a) stipulates that certain acts generally are not abusive if they are "appropriate in the light of the organizational and legal relationship among the enterprises concerned, such as in the context of relations within an economic entity and not having restrictive effects outside the related enterprises."[49] "The purpose of the last clause is to provide the additional test of effect outside of the parent-subsidiary relationships; that is, if a practice limits access to markets or otherwise unduly restrains competition outside of the related enterprises, it may fall within those discouraged under Section D(4)."[50] Thus the RBP Code reflected the Northern position on the question of parent-subsidiary relations; the Group of 77 did not prevail in any aspect of this issue.

In the negotiations the parties clashed over a mutually acceptable definition of RBPs and an appropriate test for determining whether or not a given practice should be considered restrictive. This was hardly surprising given the gap between Northern and Southern perspectives on the philosophy and purpose of RBP legislation. According to the Northern experts, an RBP is a practice that harms competition. The appropriate test for considering a practice "restrictive" (and thereby prohibited) would be whether or not it restrained trade; if the practice restrained trade it could be considered restrictive. By contrast, the South advocated a definition of RBPs that was far more catholic; for the South an RBP included every abuse of a dominant position. The proposed test offered by the South was that a practice should be deemed objectionable when it harmed the development of an industrializing country.

The two groups finally reached a compromise, but one that substantially reflected the Northern conception. According to Miller and Davidow, Group B relied on the language of the Havana Charter to support its position.[51] For example, Group B resuscitated the Havana Charter's definition of RBPs as those "which restrain competition, limit access to markets, or foster monopolistic control."[52] The final language of the RBP Code condemned anticompetitive practices with adverse effects on trade and development, particularly those harming developing countries. Miller and Davidow emphasize that the code reflected a Northern position by establishing a two-part test including both competition and trade, yet also incorporated some development aspects.[53] Ultimately, in the balance between competition and development, the RBP Code favored competition as the main rationale behind the control of RBPs. Once again, the North prevailed in substantive terms and the code effectively reflected the more traditional conception of RBPs.

Section F of the RBP Set focused on measures to be taken at the international level to curb RBPs and implement the set. It included provisions for "facilitating and monitoring the development of national policies consistent with the code, and increased information, consultation, communication, and training programs on restrictive business practices."[54] Section G of the RBP Set established the international institutional machinery for the RBP Set's implementation.

The Group of 77 sought to give fairly broad powers to UNCTAD in implementing the RBP Set. The group proposed that the secretary-general of UNCTAD be empowered to convene consultations between countries when a developing country felt its trade and development interests were being adversely affected by RBPs engaged in by developed countries' enterprises. The group wanted the UNCTAD Secretariat to be authorized to assist developing countries in such consultations. Furthermore the Group of 77 proposed that if an RBP controversy, arising from the implementation of the RBP Set, could not be satisfactorily resolved, "the Secretary-General of UNCTAD will be requested to bring the matter to the attention of the Trade and Development Board for appropriate action. If considered necessary, the Economic and Social Council or a competent inter-governmental organization may also be consulted."[55] Group B opposed these suggestions, fearing that they would place too much pressure on the home governments of multinational corporations. Developing country negotiators agreed to give up those proposals in exchange for Group B giving up its insistence on notification of national proceedings.[56] Therefore, the North succeeded in keeping UNCTAD's role minor in comparison with the role that the developing countries had envisioned for UNCTAD in this issue area.

What about teeth: does the RBP Set have any? The answer is no. Davidow suggests that for the RBP Set to have teeth, it would have to establish a tribunal to pass judgement on the actions of states and enterprises. He argues that a rule prohibiting a firm's abuse of its dominant position of market power "by restricting exports when not justified by reasons of adequate distribution and service is so full of arguable and vague terms that a company would seldom acknowledge voluntarily that its conduct contravenes the rule."[57] However, as specified in Section G of the RBP Set, the only group charged with implementation and interpretation was an Intergovernmental Group of Experts. This group was charged with providing a forum for discussion, and undertaking and disseminating studies on RBPs. While the Intergovernmental Group could make recommendations to states, its mandate was strictly limited by Section G(4), which stated that:

> In the performance of its functions, neither the Intergovernmental Group nor its subsidiary organs shall act like a tribunal or otherwise pass judgement on the activities or conduct of individual Governments or of individual enterprises in connection with a specific business transaction. The Intergovernmental Group or its subsidiary organs should avoid becoming involved when enterprises to a specific business transaction are in dispute.[58]

In short the group, as established by the RBP Set, had no powers to pass judgement on states or enterprises; thus the RBP Set's implementation provisions were extremely weak. The industrialized countries preferred that the group of experts concentrate on discussions of national laws and enforcement experience, rather than treating the code as international law and UNCTAD as an enforcement agency.[59] The North preferred to keep UNCTAD's role as limited as possible due to the South's dominance in that forum.

Aftermath: Redefining Interests

The RBP Set, as unanimously adopted in April 1980 and unanimously endorsed in a General Assembly Resolution in December of that year, substantially embraced the Northern position on antitrust policy and the control of RBPs. The RBP Set's provisions were all consistent with Northern rules, and the RBP Set in no way endorsed the aims of the Group of 77's desired New International Economic Order. While, as in the Paris Convention and TOT cases, the Group of 77 pressed for a maximalist approach in the RBP negotiations insofar as the group sought the subordination of the market to the goals of states, the RBP Set provided the minimum rather than the maximum in terms of the scope and manner of control of RBPs.

The United States was pleased with the RBP Set at the time of its adoption. In a joint letter about the RBP Set dated November 9, 1981, the Departments of State and Justice announced to American businessmen that the U.S. government believed "that the recommendations it contains will contribute to a freer and fairer, more open and competitive international trading environment."[60] The letter further praised the RBP Set as being consistent with the United States' antitrust laws and policies, U.S. trade policy, and procompetitive, free market concepts, and characterized the RBP Set as a useful complement to the Tokyo Round under GATT, "which contributed toward minimizing government trade and tariff restrictions."[61]

This was clearly a case in which the most powerful states got the instrument they desired. Since the code was so unabashedly "Northern" in spirit and tenor, one may well be wondering why it received the unanimous endorsement of the Group of 77. Miller and Davidow offer several explanations for the Group of 77's acceptance of such a liberal code: (1) a code condemning at least *some* practices of multinational corporations was better than nothing; (2) agreement on a code was a welcome relief in light of the stalemates in other negotiations inspired by the NIEO; developing country policymakers could sell the code as a foreign policy success back home; and (3) for the least-developed and socialist countries, there was really very little at stake in the code, owing to the low levels of business activity there at the time.[62]

Initially the adoption of the RBP Code was hailed as a great success. The Group of 77 was hopeful that the code would be beneficial in curbing abusive practices of transnational enterprises. Members of the Group of 77 felt that they would benefit if industrialized countries and their enterprises took the code seriously, and if UNCTAD could use publicity and discussion generated by the code as an instrument for positive change.[63]

However, the initial exuberance over the code's adoption gave way to recriminations and an atmosphere of distrust and disappointment. In the years immediately following the code's adoption, both the United States and the European Community redefined their interests in antitrust and institutionalized these new interests in their domestic policies and practices.

In the United States, the ascendance of the Chicago school of economics fundamentally changed the implementation of antitrust policy and reflected the elevated role that economic analysis had come to play in antitrust. While the conventional wisdom credits (or blames) the Reagan administration for the new relaxation of antitrust policy, Marc Eisner has painstakingly documented the institutionalization of the Chicago school's approach throughout the late 1960s and 1970s.[64] The Chicago school challenged the conventional approach to antitrust by eschewing the former populist focus on market structure in favor of price theory. In this view, only business practices that reduce output and increase price are anticompetitive; business practices that expand output are procompetitive. According to this new interpretation, "high levels of market concentration and the exercise of market power may be indicative of efficiencies."[65] Therefore, in terms of antitrust enforcement the main objective is to prohibit horizontal cartel-like arrangements and price-fixing. As Eisner points out:

> the Chicago school reveals little if any concern over vertical restraints. They fulfill a positive function by allowing firms to minimize uncertainty; they can secure access to necessary resources and distribution sites. . . . The only type of vertical restraint which may be of justifiable concern is that which combines a dominant producer and a monopolist in control of some necessary primary resource.[66]

Eisner's analysis of the antitrust revolution emphasizes "the political force of economic ideas, their impact on administration, and ultimately the content of policy."[67]

The changes began at the staff level in both the Federal Trade Commission (FTC) and the Justice Department's Antitrust Division with the appointment of economists trained in the Chicago school. By the mid-1970s the Chicago school was playing an important role in structuring policy discourse on antitrust, and court decisions began to reflect this new thinking. The courts focused on price-fixing and deemphasized merger and monopolization cases.[68] Before the Reagan administration came to power, the Chicago school's approach was well entrenched in the institutions responsible for antitrust policy.

The Reagan administration publicly advocated the Chicago approach to antitrust, and the president appointed Chicago school lawyers and economists to lead the antitrust agencies. However, the "revolution" was already well underway within the bureaucracy. According to Eisner, "the Reagan antitrust philosophy did not encounter the bureaucratic resistance one might expect with dramatic shifts in policy. Indeed, the administration's proclamations were quickly translated into policy, as revealed by agency caseloads, which reflected distinct Chicago school priorities."[69] In this sense, "elite politics and organizational evolution were [mutually] reinforcing."[70]

The Reagan administration expressed concern about U.S. industries' ability to compete more effectively in world markets[71] and codified its more permissive approach to antitrust in the Antitrust Division's 1982 Merger Control Guidelines. In accordance with the Chicago school, the new guidelines stressed the beneficial role of mergers as efficiency promoting. The guidelines relaxed control over mergers and vertical restraints and were designed

> to reflect the current emphasis, both in the Antitrust Division and in the courts, on the need for economic evidence of harm or potential harm to competition before a merger will be challenged. . . . In general, the new guidelines allow some horizontal mergers (i.e., between competing enterprises) that the 1968 guidelines would have challenged and provided for the challenge of non-horizontal mergers only where there are indications that there would be some actual or potential horizontal effects.[72]

Furthermore, the new guidelines presented an expanded definition of relevant markets; this had permissive effects. Mergers could be exempted from challenge in light of assorted nonstructural factors, including foreign competition and possession of a new technology that was important to long-term competitiveness.[73] According to Paul Hoff, the Justice Department argued that "antitrust laws should not be applied in a way that hinders the renewed emphasis on increasing U.S. competitiveness."[74] The Reagan administration was very permissive in the area of corporate mergers, and between 1981 and 1984 the FTC approved the nine largest mergers in U.S. history; it also approved a joint venture between the first and third largest automakers in the world.[75]

Another indicator of this redefined interest was the 1982 passage of the Export Trading Company Act, which "provides immunity to export trading companies from prosecution under antitrust laws, where the particular behaviour engaged in has the approval by the Secretary of Commerce and the Justice Department."[76] This law addressed concerns that U.S. antitrust laws should not be a barrier to increased productivity and trade.

A central reason for this more relaxed approach to RBPs was the economic threat posed by Japan. Particularly regarding the intense competition in high-technology sectors, both the United States and the European Economic Community came to feel that the terms of trade in technology significantly favored Japan. Some U.S. analysts argued that through favorable licensing deals, the Japanese had gotten access to U.S. technology at prices far below the costs of developing that technology and therefore were free riding on U.S. research and development.[77] Others concluded that joint ventures between U.S. and Japanese firms imparted valuable knowledge about production processes that permitted the Japanese to become superior competitors.[78]

In seeking an explanation for this phenomenon, analysts pointed to Japan's relatively permissive approach to antitrust. Japan's policies allow for joint research and development in a wide range of high-technology industries such as computers, microelectronics, electronic instruments, optical communications, lasers, robotics, and aerospace engineering. For example, this permissive approach to antitrust in strategic economic sectors spawned Japanese research consortia such as the very large scale integration (VLSI) to facilitate the development of a new generation of microcomputers. As Barton, Dellenbach, and Kuruk suggested, the combination of a permissive approach toward corporate cooperation and extensive instances of vertical integration "may give

Japanese firms leverage in negotiations with foreign firms seeking cross-licenses."[79]

In response to this perceived advantage of antitrust policies, and the desire to become more effective economic competitors in high-technology sectors, both the United States and the European Economic Community took steps to duplicate this permissiveness. For example in 1984 the U.S. Congress passed the National Cooperative Research Act, providing new research and development consortia with an antitrust waiver.[80] Policymakers promoted this act to enhance the United States' competitiveness. According to Barton, Dellenbach, and Kuruk, "all sectors are intended to benefit from the certainty that research pooling will not bring antitrust actions. The Act recognizes that competition in many sectors is international; thereby domestic firms can cooperate to increase efficiency without decreasing competition."[81] Since this act was adopted, over 170 research consortia have been formed,[82] including Microlelectronics and Computer Technology Corporation (MCC, a consortium of ten of the United States' largest computer corporations) and SEMATECH (a group arrangement for U.S. semiconductor chip-manufacturers to conduct research on chip manufacturing processes). These research consortia are intended to promote export expansion and to counter foreign competition. For example, MCC arose out of consortium members' concern that IBM, AT&T, and Japanese corporations would soon completely dominate the global computer market.[83] However, the collaboration permitted under the 1984 act precludes joint manufacturing and production of innovative products and processes.[84] By contrast, "Japanese firms cooperating on innovation and commercialization of innovation have little to fear from Japanese antitrust law."[85]

The European Economic Community has not been immune to these economic pressures and in the early 1980s redefined its interests in response to the perceived failure of member governments' "national champions" strategies. In 1984 the European Commission relaxed its antitrust policies by adopting Regulation No. 418/85, which provided blanket provisions for horizontal R & D arrangements, including commercialization,[86] and also responded to trade imbalances and the loss of jobs due to U.S. and Japanese competition in high-technology industries by exempting joint ventures from antitrust enforcement under Article 85(1) of the Treaty of Rome.

Furthermore, between 1982 and 1985 three major collaborative R & D programs were established: ESPRIT, RACE, and EUREKA. ESPRIT and RACE addressed information technologies and telecommunications; EUREKA covered biotechnology, new materials, and the environment. As Wayne Sandholtz has demonstrated, ESPRIT and RACE originated from the process of cognitive change in which states discovered the limits of autonomy.[87] In addition, these two consortia were a product of policy entrepreneurship on the part of an international organization, the Commission of the European Communities (CEC) under the leadership of Etienne Davignon.

These revised U.S. and EEC approaches to antitrust were adopted in response to the facts that markets have become global rather than national, and technological competition has often emerged as important as price competition.[88] In any case, it is evident that the more permissive antitrust approaches of Japan, the European Economic Community, and the United States diverged rather sharply from the spirit of the 1980 RBP Code.

In 1983, the UNCTAD Secretariat produced its annual report on developments in restrictive business practices policies and legislation, as called for by the code. UNCTAD asserted that the international community's expressed commitment to curbing the use of restrictive business practices had waned. The first annual report expressed alarm at the "marked regression in the control of restrictive business practices."[89] The report stressed the link between RBPs and international trade by pointing out that the RBP Code was designed to complement GATT norms for business practices, and stated that "not to control restrictive business practices by enterprises is simply to provide a back-door for doing what governments are reluctant to do through the front-door, namely, to restrict trade, in particular through raising tariffs or imposing quotas."[90] In its survey the report pointed to a trend, cited as particularly ominous for developing countries, in which "the desire to strengthen the position of national enterprises in international markets, in times of reduced world demand, has resulted in action or legislation fostering the use of restrictive business practices."[91] While some experts argued that a relaxation of vertical restraints was irrelevant in the context of developing countries' concerns since such relaxation was confined to the domestic arena, the trend heightened developing countries' suspicions about the RBP Code.

The secretariat's report covering the period from early 1983 to January 1985 was similarly bleak in tone. In this period the report found that

> control of restrictive business practices with effects on the do-
> mestic market would in general seem to have been less rigorous,
> including with regard to practices involving a producer and his
> distributor, and to concentration of market power. With respect to
> restrictive business practices whose effects are outside the na-
> tional economy, there has been no attempt to bring such practices
> under control; rather, explicit encouragement is frequently given
> to their use, in particular as a means to strengthen the position of
> domestic enterprises in export transactions. Moreover, the ten-
> dency to encourage the use of restrictive business practices in a
> manner that will afford protection to domestic industries has
> continued to increase.[92]

Beyond these general trends, which deepened the Group of 77's dissatisfaction with the RBP Code, there were more specific features of the code's nonimplementation that caused controversy. In the wake of the code's adoption, the schism between the North and the Group of 77 became much wider and all too apparent. The main problems were a lack of implementation in three key respects: (1) the consultation pro-cedures established by the code had not been utilized; (2) there had been very little technical assistance; and (3) (as alluded to earlier) there had been very little compliance at the national level.[93] The latter two factors, in particular, revealed very different interpretations of what the set was meant to accomplish. Each of these factors will be discussed in turn.

In 1986, the RBP director of UNCTAD's Manufactures Division lamented the fact that since the code's adoption states had failed to take advantage of the consultation procedures. Under these provisions, if a country feels another country's enterprise is engaging in restrictive business practices, it can formally complain to UNCTAD. Then the accused country is to submit a report to UNCTAD about its enterprise's activities. However, these procedures have never been utilized. The fact that the developing countries did not use these consultation chan-nels suggests, as Davidow has argued, that they never really cared about RBP per se but rather were concerned with controlling the activities of foreign-based MNCs operating in their countries.

Two sections of the code dealt with technical assistance: F(6) and F(5). The Group of 77 attached particular importance to F(6) of the RBP Set, which called for "the implementation within or facilitation by UNCTAD, and other relevant organizations of the United Nations system in conjunction with UNCTAD, of technical assistance, advisory and training programmes on restrictive business practices, particularly for developing countries."[94] The Group of 77 looked forward to receiving special technical assistance in their efforts to curb RBPs. F(5) calls for work within UNCTAD on the elaboration of model laws, "to help countries in adopting, improving and effectively enforcing appropriate legislation."[95]

After the code's adoption, discussion of the implementation of these two technical assistance provisions revealed divergent views between the Group of 77 and Group B. The Group of 77 emphasized F(6), technical assistance programs for developing countries, whereas Group B emphasized F(5), model laws. At the Intergovernmental Group of Experts' second session (November 21–30, 1983), the spokesman for the Group of 77

> noted with great concern that no action had been taken with respect to technical assistance, advisory and training programmes on RBPs, particularly for developing countries, which were an integral part of the Set of Principles and Rules. . . . What was occurring in the area of technical assistance seemed unfortunately to be indicative of governments' attitudes to the Set as a whole.[96]

Furthermore, the Group of 77's spokesman stressed that

> his group attached considerable importance to the question of technical assistance in connection with RBPs and felt that all of the countries concerned should be given such assistance and should enjoy access to all the necessary information. . . . The Group of 77 was still concerned at the fact that it might be concluded from the data available that considerable efforts had been made to apply the agreed principles and rules. He did not believe that this reflected the actual situation.[97]

The spokesman for Group B indicated that his group was also supportive of technical assistance programmes for developing countries. However, due to lack of funds from UNDP to implement the provisions he

> emphasized that the extensive technical assistance that had been provided on a bilateral and multilateral basis outside the framework envisaged in section F(6) of the Set consisted of technical assistance that—at least in the present international institutional financial environment—was most effectively provided on that basis.[98]

The representative of the United States indicated that his government had dispatched high-level officials to Mexico, Ecuador, Panama, Costa Rica, the Dominican Republic, and Venezuela to consult with officials on RBPs and antitrust matters.[99]

The director of UNCTAD's Manufactures Division acknowledged that there had, indeed, been some bilateral activity in this area. Yet he expressed displeasure over Group B's statement that

> in the present institutional and financial environment it was unlikely that multilateral assistance would be forthcoming. That was not an encouraging element. . . . The Secretariat was . . . to some extent disappointed to be told that it should continue to try to ensure assistance or resources within the present resource availability.[100]

The spokesman for the Group of 77 expressed disappointment that funds had not been provided to implement F(6), while Group B pointed to its bilateral efforts as evidence of its compliance. Group B's response satisfied neither the Group of 77 nor the UNCTAD Secretariat.

A related issue was work on drafting a model law or laws on RBPs, as called for in F(5) of the RBP Set. The discussions over the intent and content of the model law or laws revealed further disappointment in the implementation of the code. Work on a model law was certainly less expensive than the extensive multilateral technical assistance programs cited in F(6), and Group B stressed that it attached great importance to the model law efforts. As the spokesman for Group B stated, his group

> had long considered the work on the model law or laws . . . to be essentially concerned with technical assistance. . . . Section F(5)

of the Set provided that this work should be "in order to assist
developing countries in devising appropriate legislation. . . . " He
trusted that the comments of Group B, based on the extensive
experience his Group had acquired in the control of restrictive
business practices, would be taken to heart by the Secretariat in
its next draft. By incorporating his Group's experience the model
law would surely provide an effective and substantial form of
technical assistance.[101]

He pointed out that "the model law document was based largely upon
laws in developed countries, and would, when completed, be in itself
an excellent form of technical assistance."[102]

In discussing a model law, Group B stressed that the core purpose of the law should be to promote *competition*. According to the
group's spokesman a model law should "start from the recognition
that RBPs might prevent the benefits of competition from being
achieved. Any other approach would require complete supervision of
business activity, thereby harming economic development, growth, and
efficiency."[103]

Controversy arose over the draft model law. The secretary-
general of UNCTAD submitted a revised draft of a model law to the
Intergovernmental Group at the second session. Between the first and
second sessions, the draft had been revised in a manner that incorporated provisions that Group B felt violated the spirit of the set and
downplayed the core aim of preserving competition in favor of development considerations.

Specifically Group B expressed dismay over the incorporation of
a development test "as a separate and independent justification for
taking actions against RBPs."[104] The language of the set defined RBPs
"as acts or behaviours which 'limit access to markets or otherwise
unduly restrain competition' *and* [emphasis added] had adverse effects
on international trade and economic development."[105] The revised draft
of the model law had changed the emphasized "and" to "and/or." The
Group B spokesman protested that "the Set did not say 'and/or' have
such effects. This was appropriate in a model law as well, because, a
model law should reflect the broadest agreed principles of maintaining
competition."[106] According to the spokesman, "the Set quite carefully
included the effect on development only a necessary consequence of

RBPs, not as a separate and independent basis for action."[107] He argued that the model law must be fully consistent with "the principles of furthering competition as embodied in the Set and should not go beyond the ideas in that document."[108]

In response, the spokesman for the Group of 77 reminded Group B that section E(2) of the RBP Set "called upon States to base their legislation primarily on the principle of eliminating or effectively dealing with RBPs as defined by the Set, having or being likely to have adverse effects on their trade and economic development."[109] He concluded that according to his Group's interpretation,

> the creation, encouragement and protection of competition was recognized by the Set to be one means to achieve greater efficiency in trade and economic development and not an end in itself. It was therefore important that the objective [of the model law] . . . should be in terms of controlling the adverse effects of restrictive business practices on the trade and development of the particular country in question.[110]

Thus during discussions on the model law it became clear that Group B emphasized *competition*, whereas the Group of 77 stressed *development* as the appropriate test for determining whether or not a business practice was restrictive. It seemed that both groups had very different ideas of what the RBP Code was for. The representative from Brazil aptly summarized the situation this way: "The emphasis placed by developing countries and other groups did not coincide. For the Group of 77 the major criterion for evaluation of restrictive business practices lay in the effects of these practices on international trade, and particularly the trade and development of developing countries. For Group B the predominant criteria were provided for in antitrust laws."[111]

Another aspect of the model laws that Group B objected to was a tougher approach to intra-enterprise transactions. Section 4 of article II of the revised model laws provided a "possible exception" to intra-enterprise transactions. Group B argued that this language went beyond the language of the Set's section D(3), which "made clear that the principles for enterprises . . . did not apply to enterprises when dealing with each other in the context of an economic entity where they were under common control, including through ownership, or

otherwise not able to act independently of each other."[112] In response
the spokesman for the Group of 77 defended the language of the
revised draft laws and argued that

> the authors of the revised draft had adequate reason to provide for
> a "possible" rather than an "across-the-board" exception of agree-
> ments or arrangements between parents and subsidiaries. . . . Many
> developed and developing countries did not have a specific ex-
> emption in their laws for parent/subsidiary agreements or
> arrangements. . . . It should be up to States to decide whether an
> exception should be provided or not in light of their national
> interest considerations and sovereignty.[113]

Finally, the two groups disagreed on the approach that the model
law should adopt on the "rule of reason." Group B objected to the
revised draft of the model law because it was based on the prohibition
principle (constituting blanket prohibitions as opposed to the rule of
reason); instead, Group B favored a rule-of-reason approach whereby
practices were evaluated on a case-by-case basis. The Group of 77 had
desired an absolute prohibition of certain practices enumerated in the
code. However, during negotiations on the RBP Set, Group B had
included a footnote to section D(4) that established a rule-of-reason
approach. The Group of 77's spokesman objected to the status of this
footnote, and he remarked that "it was important to note that the
footnote provision D(4) was not in itself a provision of the Set."[114]

The Group of 77 suspected that Group B was trying to elevate
the status of the rule-of-reason footnote to a part of the code's actual
text. The Group of 77 became upset by what it considered to be Group
B's reinterpretation of the RBP Set in the context of discussions of the
model law. To the Group of 77, Group B seemed to be suggesting that
development components of the Set were truly marginal and that the
only important elements were those relating to competition. As the
spokesman for the Group of 77 stated, "it was not appropriate for the
Intergovernmental Group to attempt, in the context of discussing the
model law, to renegotiate the Set of Principles and Rules. The only
body competent to renegotiate . . . [the Set] was the Conference on
Restrictive Business Practices."[115]

Beyond the moribund consultation procedures, and suspicion
surrounding the discussion of model laws, the UNCTAD Annual Re-

ports on RBPs pointed out that noncompliance at the national level had been the most distressing development in the wake of the RBP Set's adoption. Only Denmark, Norway, and Sweden (of the developed countries) had revised their laws in conformity with the code.[116] Since the RBP Set's adoption the use of RBPs had increased, and many countries—especially the United States and the European Economic Community—had relaxed their control of RBPs. The representative of Pakistan, speaking on behalf of the Group of 77, stated that

> a number of developed countries were not taking adequate steps
> to curtail or eliminate certain undesirable practices in the areas of
> exclusive dealings, resale price maintenance, tied purchasing, and
> other abuses by enterprises in dominant positions of market power.
> He felt that under the circumstances the statement . . . "it is one
> matter to have a Set . . . adopted but it is another to ensure that all
> countries implement their commitment to the Set" was well
> justified.[117]

The growing dissatisfaction, especially on the part of the Group of 77, came to a head at the 1985 Review Conference. The session was convened to review the implementation of the RBP Set five years after its adoption, as provided for in section G(3) of the RBP Set. The General Assembly, adopting the RBP Set in Resolution 35/63, decided to convene in 1985 an UNCTAD Conference to review all aspects of the RBP Set. The Intergovernmental Group of Experts met in 1985 to review the RBP Set.

As noted earlier, since 1980 the Group of 77 became increasingly alarmed by the nonimplementation of the RBP Code. The developing countries felt they had borne the brunt of the increasingly permissive environment for RBPs and, as Brusick argues, because the use of RBPs (including voluntary export restraints and orderly marketing arrangements—the so-called grey area of GATT)

> result[ed] in discrimination against the most competitive export-
> ers and frequently against those from developing countries; . . .
> tend[ed] to result in the maintenance of established trading pat-
> terns and thus prejudice[d] the position of new entrants to the
> international market, who are confined to small export shares;

[and] . . . transfer[red] the burden of adjustment to the exporting
countries.[118]

Therefore the Group of 77 came to the Review Conference animated
by their desire to put teeth into the RBP Code.

By all accounts, the Review Conference was a "disaster." Participants debated three major points, *none* of which was resolved. These
were: (1) the nature of the set; (2) the status of the Intergovernmental
Group of Experts; and (3) subsequent review conferences.

The Group of 77 and Group B disputed the nature of the set. The
Group of 77 proposed that the set become legally binding, in light of
the noncompliance at the national level. Group B responded to the
Group of 77's charge of noncompliance with countercharges that the
Group of 77 was not passing enough RBP legislation. Group B flatly
rejected the proposal to make the RBP Set legally binding and insisted
that the set remain entirely voluntary. Since this debate was not resolved at the Review Conference, the RBP Set remained strictly voluntary and nonbinding as desired by the North.

The discussions on the status of the Intergovernmental Group of
Experts were particularly volatile. The Group of 77, led by Brazil and
Egypt, sought to upgrade the IGE to "committee" status. The Group
of 77 bemoaned the fact that the RBP Code was entrusted to an IGE—
the lowest deliberative body on the United Nations totem pole. The
IGE was restricted to discussing technical questions. The Group of 77
sought to upgrade the IGE's status so that the "committee" would have
the power to monitor compliance. They sought to strengthen the consultation machinery and notification procedures and felt that gaining
acceptance of the elevation of the IGE to committee status would help
put teeth into the set. The Group of 77 members complained that
IGE's deliberations had become merely academic exercises at best.

Group B flatly rejected this effort, so the IGE remained a technical body. This was hardly surprising since Group B preferred to
confine the whole exercise to a technical level. Group B consistently
resisted efforts to strengthen the hand of UNCTAD, which was not
considered to be a friendly forum for the North. Thus the North was
unwilling to give the United Nations any real enforcement powers in
this issue.

Finally, the Group of 77 sought agreement to hold another Review Conference in 1990, but this too proved contentious so there was no agreement. In every respect the Group of 77's efforts to strengthen the RBP Code at the Review Conference met with failure.

Summary

Eight years after the adoption of the RBP Code, the disappointment of the Group of 77 was palpable. Whatever hopes the developing countries held in 1980 were dashed and dissolved into suspicion that they were somehow duped into endorsing the code. The Group of 77 became especially nervous about the reinterpretations of the code under the Reagan administration. Since the code's adoption, Group B increasingly downplayed the code's development components. As both Philippe Brusick, RBP director of UNCTAD's Manufactures Division, and Colin Greenhill (who later joined UNCTAD's Commodities Division but was instrumental in the formulation of the RBP Code in 1980) have argued, Group B had rejected the code's link to international trade, which was (in their view) tantamount to rejecting the entire code.[119] Group B countries emphasized that they could only control what went on "at home" and reinterpreted the code's provisions to refer only to *domestic* market competition. According to Brusick, Group B wanted to promote free market competitiveness *internally* in developing countries, because Group B's enterprises sought a more favorable market position as they were better able to compete.

Even though the case of the RBP Code, at first glance, appeared to be quite different than the failed efforts of the Group of 77 to revise the Paris Convention and establish a code of conduct for the transfer of technology, in the final analysis the results were very similar. In each case the most powerful states prevailed, and the Group of 77's attempts to establish a new scientific and technological order as a crucial step towards a NIEO were successfully resisted. While the North set the RBP agenda, the South had unsuccessfully tried to incorporate its development concerns into the multilateral code. From the standpoint of both the Group of 77 and UNCTAD, the RBP Code exercise had been a deeply disappointing one. However, Group B did not share this assessment since it succeeded—first, in getting the instrument it wanted in 1980, and second, in resisting efforts to strengthen the RBP Code since the Reagan administration came to power. The United States led Group B in 1980 and set the tone for subsequent deliberations on the code and its interpretation.

In retrospect it seems evident that in the case of the RBP Code there was never a true consensus—not even in 1980. The code was a document that papered over fundamental differences in outlook. Both Group B and the Group of 77 were interested in the code for diametrically opposed reasons, and the resulting text was vague enough to satisfy both the competition concerns of Group B and the development concerns of the Group of 77.

Group B's endorsement of the code, apart from the obvious fact that Group B prevailed on virtually every significant provision, was consistent with its more general perspective that excessive state intervention in economic affairs hampered economic development. Therefore its aim, as in the Paris Convention and Technology Transfer Code negotiations, was to reduce the role of the state in the economic affairs of developing countries. According to Group B's most vociferous spokesmen, the road to development should be paved by the free play of market forces and the unleashing of fair competition.

By contrast, the developing countries—initially embracing the NIEO conception that they must strengthen the role of the state vis-à-vis foreign TNEs—saw the code as a potentially effective means to that end. By establishing minimum international standards for business conduct in RBPs, they hoped to gain international legitimacy for an interventionist approach to development. By this standard, even a watered-down Code might serve their purposes.

Therefore the RBP Code was never a substantially consensual instrument. The illusory nature of the consensus quickly was exposed under severe economic pressure. The developed countries, under economic pressure from Japan, quickly reevaluated their faith in free domestic competition in certain critical sectors. The United States codified this reevaluation by passing new antitrust laws which substantially relaxed former stringent standards. The European Economic Community underwent a similar reevaluation, as it began to exempt certain strategic enterprises from its Treaty of Rome antitrust provisions.

The controversies over the RBP Code were further rendered obsolete as many developing countries, crippled by huge foreign debts and the nearly 25 percent drop in foreign direct investment in their countries between 1981 and 1986, reevaluated their previous approaches to development. In Latin America and Asia, states reduced their public sectors and increasingly exposed state enterprises to competitive market pressures. Laws regulating TNEs were revised to reduce restrictions on TNE investment, and existing tough laws became newly flexible in their application. As discussed in chapter 3, the Group of 77 became particularly vulnerable to the economic shocks of the 1980s and its initial NIEO consensus fell apart. The member states of the Group of 77 reevaluated their antidependency stance and increasingly sought to encourage foreign investment by creating more hospitable business climates for foreign investors. Countries such as Argentina, Mexico, and the Andean Pact member states became less concerned with controlling TNE activity and instead came to welcome it.

In some respects the story of the RBP Code looks like a simple structural tale—that is, the most powerful states got the instrument they wanted. The structural explanation certainly goes a long way toward explaining why the code was adopted. There was never a real agreement; there was no learning in the full negotiations. Yet in the wake of the code's adoption, it seems clear that ideational factors also were important. Both the United States and the European Economic Community undertook serious reevaluations of their prior approaches to antitrust and redefined their interests. When the new U.S. administration and the European Economic Community institutionalized their more permissive policies towards RBPs, these were clearly reflected in post-1980 deliberations on the code. The developed countries, especially the United States and the European Economic Community, continued to distance themselves from the "development" components of the code. The developing countries were powerless and not seamlessly enthusiastic in their efforts to resist this movement. They too have redefined their interests in this issue area; the next chapter explores this change in greater detail.

6❖

INTELLECTUAL PROPERTY PROTECTION AND ANTITRUST IN THE DEVELOPING WORLD: CRISIS, COERCION, AND CHOICE

In the past few years, the nations of the developing world have made a dramatic turn toward market-oriented policies. As recently as 1985, developing countries were still pressing for a NIEO based on economic nationalism and the rejection of global liberalism. Today, however, even the most ardent former champions of extensive state intervention in the economy and of discrimination against foreign investors have adopted policies that emphasize private sector initiative, nondiscrimination, and economic openness. What accounts for this change? Have these countries changed their minds, or just their policies? These are the questions addressed here, with specific reference to intellectual property protection and antitrust policy.

This analysis of intellectual property protection and antitrust in the developing world suggests the usefulness of decomposing the broad issue of economic liberalization to account for variation across issue areas. Despite the fact that developing countries increasingly are embracing a market orientation, the process of economic reform differs between intellectual property and antitrust policy. A nuanced analysis of the impact of both power and ideas is necessary to account for the differences.

Neorealism emphasizes the role of power and leads us to expect that weak states will comply with the preferences of powerful states. Neoliberal institutionalism examines how institutions can alter the incentives facing states and can play an important role in enhancing the credibility of commitments. By monitoring compliance, institutions also can reduce the incidence of cheating. In contrast, interpretivist neoliberalism examines the role of learning and norms as sources of change, and it focuses more squarely on the redefinition of national interests. For interpretivist neoliberals, institutions can play a more transformative role and can help states to redefine their interests by spreading new norms and value orientations. According to John Ikenberry and Charles Kupchan, norms are "general principles upon which a certain vision of international order is based. Value orientations are norm-based attitudes toward specific policy issues and types of behavior."[1] In both issue areas, the overriding interest is prosperity; the norm is liberalism. The value orientations in antitrust and intellectual property are competition and the protection of property rights, respectively.

At the outset I want to emphasize that the distinction between power and learning is hardly black and white. Both are present in these two issues. The line between learning and "being taught a lesson" can be very fine indeed.[2] External pressure can be used by elites in targeted states to realign coalitions or to push through painful reforms that the elites deem necessary. When elites redefine their interests (for example, to promote liberalization), external pressure often can provide a convenient boost for them to move against domestic opposition. However, with the sole exception of Mexico, there is as yet no strong domestic constituency for intellectual property protection in developing countries. Therefore I argue not that either perspective is right or wrong. Rather I indicate what aspects of each case the different perspectives help to explain. On balance, interpretivist neoliberalism provides a more thorough account of the changes in antitrust policy. In intellectual property protection, neorealism provides a compelling explanation for the adoption and substance of stronger policies for intellectual property protection, but interpretivist neoliberalism offers important insights to explain the discrepancy between policy adoption and implementation.

In the intellectual property case, learning on the part of U.S. policymakers was important in the adoption of a coercive strategy to force recalcitrant countries to pass laws strengthening the protection of intellectual property. From the point when the United States adopted a coercive strategy, this case is best explained by external coercion, as the United States has aggressively linked higher levels of protection to trade issues through Section 301 of the U.S. Trade Act. The United States has applied significant direct pressure on targeted states. These states are highly dependent on access to the U.S. market and are therefore vulnerable to U.S. threats of trade sanctions. Examining the effects of this coercive strategy suggests that explanations based on power can account for the substance, timing, and adoption of policies protecting intellectual property. However, this case also reveals the limits of a coercive strategy; weak states can resist external threats even at substantial costs to themselves. In nearly every instance, targeted states have chosen not to implement and enforce these new policies. In short, targeted countries have changed their policies, not their minds. If targeted countries do not accept the value orientation preferred by the powerful state, and no politically influential domestic constituency favors the new policies, one can expect nonimplementation and robust domestic resistance.

On the other hand, in the antitrust case no country has employed an overt coercive strategy. Pressure for change has come from within the developing countries themselves. General external pressure for market-oriented reform certainly is present in the form of the International Monetary Fund's conditionality policy and the World Bank's structural adjustment lending program. However, these two institutions have not pushed antitrust policies because their economists argue that import liberalization will achieve the efficiency goals of such policies.[3] While implementation has proceeded slowly, and though it is too early to make sweeping generalizations, evidence suggests that developing countries have changed their policies *and* their minds. Evidence that these states have accepted the value orientation of antitrust includes: the emergence of politically powerful domestic constituencies favoring the new policies; the sequence of policy change (norm change prior to policy adoption); and the voluntary and active quest for information and assistance in drafting laws and training officials to administer the new policies. The economic crisis of the early 1980s helped to resuscitate the moribund UNCTAD Restrictive Business Practices Code. In December 1980 the United Nations General Assembly unanimously adopted the Set of Multilaterally Agreed Equitable Principles and Rules for the Control of Restrictive Business Practices. Under its terms, an IGE is charged with implementing and interpreting provisions therein. Although the IGE has no enforcement powers, its mandate is to provide a forum for consultation and discussion of national and legislative experiences. This institutional mechanism has played an important role in expediting the adoption of antitrust policies in developing countries. Since 1989, developing countries have been flocking to UNCTAD to learn more about the operation of antitrust policies. The antitrust case reveals a process that has been more gradual, circuitous, and more dependent on domestic circumstances within developing countries. The interpretivist neoliberal emphasis on choice, learning, and the role of international institutions can account for the substance, adoption, and implementation of these policies. However, it cannot account for the timing of the change; in this regard, neorealism, with its emphasis on constraints facing weak states, offers the greatest insight.

These two cases highlight the usefulness of moving beyond the debate among neorealism, neoliberal institutionalism, and interpretivist neoliberalism. While it seems obvious that coercion is unnecessary if states have accepted the norms and value orientations at issue, the conditions under which coercion by the stronger party fails to yield the desired results are less clear. The United States has invested enormous amounts of time and energy in its coercive strategy and has thus far had little to show for it in intellectual property protection. I am not claiming that coercion never works; instead, I argue that it has largely failed in intellectual property protection. Furthermore, the prospects for the sustainability of the new policies seem to be much better in antitrust policy because the new policies are a product of these states' redefined interests.

Since the mid-1980s, developing countries have been adopting laws and policies for the protection of intellectual property based on a conception common to the industrialized world—namely, intellectual property as private property. Because the effective protection of private property rights is a cornerstone of a liberal economic order, these new policies reflect the developing countries' shift toward a market economy. Intellectual property protection is important for both international investment and trade. Investors are reluctant to build plants or issue licenses in countries where their technology and know-how are not protected. Exporters of products or processes based on intellectual property seek to recover costs of developing the property and to prevent counterfeiting and piracy. In the past, many developing countries refused to issue patents to foreign inventors because patent protection provides a temporary monopoly and raises the prices of protected property. Other developing countries did offer protection but on a relatively limited basis. Indeed, during the NIEO era, developing countries rejected the notion that intellectual property should be construed as private property. Instead, they argued that intellectual property should be transferred with no remittance because it was the "common heritage of mankind." Their new policies of protecting intellectual property as private and commercial reverse this conception.

Similarly, in the area of antitrust, developing countries are beginning to adopt laws and policies that resemble those of the industrialized world. As discussed in chapter five, in the past the few developing countries that had antitrust laws exclusively targeted local subsidiaries of foreign-based multinational corporations in the service of economic nationalism. Instead of using antitrust policies to promote domestic market competition, these countries had employed them to control foreign enterprises' activities. More recently, developing countries have come to perceive antitrust policies as relevant for their own domestic enterprises, and they are designing policies to break up domestic public monopolies left behind from previous eras of economic nationalism. The adoption of antitrust legislation and policies and the creation of domestic institutions to monitor and enforce such policies will become increasingly important as these countries continue opening their markets and stimulating private sector activity.

The two cases warrant comparison because the participants in the NIEO negotiations saw both issues as components of an integrated assault on economic liberalism. Developing countries sought changes in prevailing modes of both antitrust policy and intellectual property protection as part of their quest for a new international scientific and technological order. In the antitrust area, they sought to eliminate technology-transfer contract clauses that restricted their ability to use the technology to become more self-sufficient. In the area of intellectual property, they sought to weaken international standards of protection so as to gain access to technologies without paying royalty fees to the holders of intellectual property.

Indeed, the strategic incentives in each issue area are different. Free riding on others' intellectual property is an attractive option; the widespread piracy of patented goods underscores the point. In cases in which free riding is the most attractive option, those who seek to prevent free riding face the burden of changing the payoffs. Here neorealism and neoliberal institutionalism provide compelling insights; in particular, the incentives to forgo free riding must be supplied from the outside.[4] In contrast, antitrust policies reduce domestic monopoly power and can help stimulate both foreign investment and the importation of foreign goods. These policies reduce prices for consumers, whereas intellectual property protection tends to increase prices of desired goods. Once developing countries began moving toward market-oriented policies, they had economic incentives to adopt antitrust policies. The incentives are inherent in antitrust policies, since such policies can promote efficiency gains. These gains can accrue to the developing countries, rather than to the foreign holders of intellectual property rights.

The movement toward antitrust is being negotiated much more palpably in the domestic arena.[5] Previously privileged domestic groups, such as the *chaebol* (conglomerates) in South Korea, have marshalled their enormous powers to block antitrust legislation. The winners under the old policies stand to lose under the new policies; but their power is beginning to erode under pressures for social change and the leadership of bold reformers. Domestic constituencies for antitrust legislation are emerging in developing countries as a result of democratization and economic reform. Populist aspects of antitrust policy, such as protecting consumers, promoting small- and medium-sized enterprises, and recasting government-business relations are becoming important weapons in anticorruption battles and are changing the domestic balance of power within the state in favor of the urban middle class. Reformers have significant political incentives to promote antitrust policies. Under conditions in which incentives are built-in, such as in antitrust, neoliberalism provides a more compelling explanation. Finally, the fact that the NIEO negotiators themselves saw the issues as components of an integrated assault on economic liberalism suggests the usefulness of comparing the two cases and provides insights into the prospective fates of these policies in a markedly changed international economic environment.

This chapter proceeds in four sections. The first examines the role of the economic crisis of the 1980s. The next two sections analyze trends in intellectual property protection and antitrust policy, respectively. The fourth section presents conclusions about these cases and suggests further research based on this analysis.

Economic Crisis

The economic downturn that began in the late 1970s and progressively worsened in the 1980s heightened power differentials between the industrialized and developing countries. The euphoria of the NIEO gave way to a landscape of sharply reduced opportunities, and developing countries scrambled to adjust to this less hospitable economic environment. The consensus that had been crucial to the developing countries' multilateral NIEO agenda was shattered. Developing countries were far more vulnerable to these economic shocks than were the industrialized countries. For example, in 1982, Mexico announced that it was no longer able to service its debt.

These economic shocks prompted developing countries to adopt policies that promoted their integration into the global economy. Even a casual observer of current trends in developing countries must be struck by the extent to which their policies have come to reflect the wishes of the United States and other wealthy industrialized countries. Throughout the postwar era, the United States consistently argued that the road to development is paved by the free play of market forces, and it repeatedly urged the developing world to adopt liberal economic policies. Thus, to the extent that developing countries open their markets, liberalize trade and investment, offer greater protection for intellectual property rights, privatize public sector enterprises, and embrace market mechanisms, they "do the right thing" from the vantage point of the United States.

The economic crisis of the 1980s was an international constraint to which states had to respond. While constraints matter, responses to those constraints depend on choice. What were the more proximate causes for these policy changes? For example, why did developing countries wait nearly a decade to use the institutional machinery established for antitrust to facilitate the adoption of new policies? By what mechanisms did these changes come about? What were the sources of these new policies?

In short, the economic crisis of the early 1980s facilitated the policy change. However, it alone is insufficient for understanding the precise timing of the changes, the sources of the new policies, and the mechanisms through which these changes came about. We need to look elsewhere to understand why the effects of the economic crisis played out as they did.

Intellectual Property Protection: Coercion and Its Limits

The most important factor in the recent spread of intellectual property protection policies has been coercion. The United States has applied significant pressure on developing countries to offer stronger intellectual property protection. The ensuing analysis reveals, however, that this coercive strategy has produced quite limited results. The United States consistently sought to strengthen intellectual property protection abroad. Throughout the 1960s and 1970s, its exhortations at various multilateral forums, including the World Intellectual Property Organization and UNCTAD, produced paltry results. Beginning in the early 1980s, at the behest of various U.S. corporate interests, the United States achieved quick results through bilateral consultations with Hungary, South Korea, Singapore, and Taiwan.[6] From these early successes, the U.S. government learned that while exhortation alone was ineffective, linking trade and intellectual property protection could yield desired results. American policymakers learned through systematic bilateral consultations that a coercive strategy was more promising. The United States tightened this linkage between trade and intellectual property by amending the Trade and Tariff Act in 1984 and in 1988. It now can retaliate swiftly with trade sanctions in the event that targeted countries fail to adequately protect its intellectual property.

The U.S. ability to exploit the vulnerability of targeted states serves to link U.S. power and the move toward the market by developing countries. The United States possesses considerable market power, and access to the U.S. market is critical for many developing countries. In response to the economic crisis of the early 1980s, developing countries increasingly have tipped the balance away from import-substituting industrialization toward export-led strategies. The debt crisis, the perceived exhaustion of models of import-substituting industrialization, and the success of the East Asian countries all have contributed to this export-led shift. Access to northern markets therefore has become more important.

Tables 6.1 through 6.4 illustrate the extent of targeted developing countries' vulnerability to U.S. trade threats. Table 6.1 shows the value of selected developing countries' exports as a percentage of their gross domestic product (GDP) between 1982 and 1992. Table 6.2 shows the dollar value of these countries' exports to the United States. Table 6.3 indicates the percentage of selected developing countries' trade conducted with the United States. With the lone exception of China, the United States is the biggest importer of each of these countries' goods. In contrast, as illustrated in table 6.4, only two of the targeted states, Korea and Mexico, rank among the top ten trading partners for the United States (ranked sixth and third respectively). Therefore, these countries are far more dependent on trade with the United States than the United States is on them. By the mid-1980s, the U.S. market absorbed more than half of Latin American exports and a third of exports from East Asia. Thus the United States has significant potential leverage over these countries. As Alan Sykes points out: "If access to the U.S. market is restricted, the target nation cannot readily make up the losses by redirecting its exports."[7]

The United States has wielded its market power through Section 301 of the Trade Act of 1974, which allows it to threaten trade retaliation to induce policy changes in targeted states with inadequate intellectual property protection. Section 301 gives the president the power

Table 6.1 Exports of Goods and Nonfactor Services as Percent of Gross Domestic Product

Country	1982	1983	1984	1985	1986	1987	1988	1989	1990	1991	1992
Argentina	10.9	8.9	8.2	11.4	8.0	7.5	8.8	15.3	10.5	7.6	6.3
Brazil	7.9	12.0	14.5	12.4	9.0	9.5	10.9	8.4	7.2	8.5	—[a]
Chile	19.1	23.4	22.5	28.1	31.1	33.3	37.4	37.9	37.1	35.7	33.1
China (PRC)	10.5	9.7	11.0	11.8	13.0	15.6	14.5	13.7	19.0	21.9	—
India	6.5	6.4	6.6	6.1	5.8	5.9	6.1	7.2	—	—	—
Mexico	15.0	18.2	17.1	14.9	16.9	19.7	16.9	15.9	15.7	14.0	—
South Korea	37.0	36.1	36.4	34.5	38.5	41.8	39.6	33.7	30.4	28.8	29.6
Thailand	24.0	20.6	22.6	24.4	26.7	30.1	34.3	36.6	36.5	—	—

[a]Dash = data not available

Source: International Monetary Fund, *International Financial Statistics Yearbook*, Vol. 46 (Washington, DC: International Monetary Fund, 1993), pp. 136–137.

Table 6.2 Value of Exports to United States (in Thousands of U.S. Dollars)

Country	1987	1988	1989	1990	1991
Argentina	930,599	1,217,212	1,185,397	1,698,931	—[a]
Brazil	7,183,143	8,388,319	7,744,372	7,459,893	6,387,483
Chile	965,950	1,242,356	1,363,786	1,340,910	1,267,571
China (PRC)	3,020,413	3,357,938	4,404,887	5,175,334	6,147,516
India	2,252,391	2,556,216	—	2,643,570	—
Mexico	13,265,079	13,453,232	16,091,910	18,834,135	18,951,857
South Korea	18,362,736	21,477,257	20,694,317	19,419,654	18,607,413
Thailand	1,734,490	2,545,959	3,419,008	3,968,018	5,132,831

[a]Dash = data not available
Source: United Nations, *1991 International Trade Statistics Yearbook*, Vol. 1, *Trade By Country* (New York: United Nations, 1993), pp. 24, 102, 162, 170, 420, 498, 580, and 866.

Table 6.3 Percentage of Trade Conducted with the United States (Value as Percentage of World Total)

Country	1982	1983	1984	1985	1986	1987	1988	1989	1990	1991
Argentina (1)[a]	13.4	9.9	10.8	12.2	10.3	14.6	13.3	12.4	13.8	—[b]
Brazil (1)	20.5	23.1	28.6	27.2	25.8	27.4	24.8	22.5	23.7	20.2
Chile (1)	19.3	26.1	24.6	21.8	20.1	19.9	18.3	17.0	16.2	14.8
China (3)	8.0	7.8	9.3	8.6	8.5	7.7	7.1	8.4	8.3	8.6
India (1)	9.2	15.0	15.0	18.1	18.7	18.6	18.4	—	14.7	—
Mexico (1)	50.7	62.9	62.4	65.1	72.0	64.6	65.9	70.0	70.2	69.7
South Korea (1)	28.6	33.9	36.0	35.6	40.1	38.9	35.4	33.2	30.0	26.0
Thailand (1)	12.8	15.0	17.2	19.7	18.1	18.6	20.1	21.6	22.7	21.3

[a]Rank of the United States as a trading partner, based on 1991 figures, is shown in parentheses.

[b]— = data not available.

Source: United Nations, *1991 International Trade Statistics Yearbook*, Vol. 1, *Trade By Country* (New York: United Nations, 1993), pp. 24, 102, 162, 170, 420, 498, 580 and 866.

Table 6.4 Value of U.S. Exports in Selected Developing Countries (in Thousands of U.S. Dollars)

Country[a]	1987	1988	1989	1990	1991
Mexico (3)	14,572,859	20,621,656	24,843,516	28,245,178	33,143,982
Korea (6)	7,660,050	10,669,469	13,469,690	14,393,889	15,496,451
China	3,488,357	4,956,696	5,806,829	4,805,549	6,278,071
Brazil	3,998,894	4,247,215	4,798,002	5,061,527	6,147,835
Thailand	1,481,938	1,682,717	2,291,224	2,991,110	3,752,521
India	1,457,516	2,482,114	2,462,499	2,485,815	1,997,630
Chile	796,155	1,064,599	1,410,753	1,672,267	1,838,996
Argentina	1,088,909	1,054,663	1,036,744	1,179,126	2,044,691

[a]Rank of country as a U.S. trading partner (shown in parentheses) is included if country is among top ten partners.
Source: United Nations, *1991 International Trade Statistics Yearbook*, Vol. 1, *Trade By Country*, (New York: United Nations, 1993), p. 940.

to enforce U.S. rights under trade agreements and to eliminate policies and practices that discriminate or impose unjustifiable burdens on U.S. commerce. The section also permits industries, trade associations, and individual companies to petition the United States Trade Representative to investigate actions of foreign governments. If the USTR decides to investigate, it first consults with the foreign government to try to resolve the problem. If these efforts fail, within a year (in all but subsidies cases, for which a shorter time period is mandated) the USTR recommends appropriate action to the president. Such action often consists of the threat of retaliation via trade sanctions. After pressure from the private sector, the United States also linked the generalized system of preferences benefits, which grant preferential market access for developing countries, to the effective protection of intellectual property.[8]

Section 301 Cases

In a comprehensive analysis of the U.S. record in Section 301 actions, Sykes found that "Section 301 is fairly successful in inducing foreign governments to modify their practices when they are accused of violating U.S. legal rights; . . . success is more likely with a GSP beneficiary."[9] Table 6.5 provides a summary of the Section 301 cases in which intellectual property issues were at stake. In all eight cases, the targeted governments agreed to improve intellectual property protection along the lines desired by the United States. Furthermore, the timing of the changes demonstrates the strong link between this exercise of U.S. leverage and the reforms in targeted states. In short, both the substance and the timing of these policies can be explained as a product of coercion. The following detailed examination of several Section 301 cases against developing countries illustrates the relationship between the substance and timing of policy change in targeted states, on the one hand, and the exercise of U.S. coercion, on the other.

As the following cases demonstrate, there is a sharp disparity between the adoption of these policies and their implementation and enforcement. While developing countries have acquiesced in a formal sense by adopting new laws and policies, they have resisted imple-

189

Table 6.5   Intellectual Property Cases: U.S. Experience under Section 301

Case No.	Country	Area	Year Filed	Year Case Terminated or Suspended	GSP Beneficiary
301–49	Brazil	Infomatics	1985	1989	Yes
301–52	South Korea	Intellectual Property Rights	1985	Open	Yes
301–6	Brazil	Pharmaceutical Patents	1987	1989	Yes
301–68	Argentina	Pharmaceutical Patents	1988	1989	Yes
301–82	Thailand	Copyright Enforcement	1990	1991	Yes
301–84	Thailand	Patent Protection	1991	Open	Yes
301–85	India	Intellectual Property Rights	1991	Open	Yes
301–86	China	Intellectual Property Rights	1991	1992	No

Source: Adapted from Alan Sykes, "Constructive Unilateral Threats in International Commercial Relations: The Limited Case for Section 301," *Law and Policy in International Business*, Vol. 23, No. 2 (1992), pp. 263–330.

menting and enforcing these policies. This discrepancy between policy adoption and implementation underscores the fact that developing countries, though acting under duress, remain unconverted.

In the 1985 intellectual property rights case against South Korea, the South Korean government acquiesced in 1986 by enacting product patent protection for pharmaceuticals and improving enforcement procedures. According to the president of the U.S.-based Pharmaceuticals Manufacturing Association (PMA), Gerald Mossinghoff: "The Korean case was a major step forward and set an important example of what could be accomplished using trade instruments to achieve intellectual property objectives."[10] The South Korean case remains open because the private actors who have been monitoring South Korean compliance—the International Intellectual Property Alliance and the PMA— have been disappointed with South Korea's performance. The pharmaceutical manufacturer Bristol-Meyers Squibb Company charged South Korean companies with piracy and in 1989 filed new Section 301 complaints with USTR.[11] As a result, Korea has remained on the USTR's watchlists of intellectual property violators. The U.S. Business Software Alliance and the International Intellectual Property Alliance also have closely monitored South Korea's performance. In July 1992 the Business Software Alliance estimated that 86 percent of the personal computer software used in South Korea was pirated, accounting for more than $300 million in losses.[12] Despite the passage of the Computer Program Protection Act (CPPA) in July 1987, penalties for piracy in South Korea are still relatively low; the maximum fine for piracy is 3 million won (about $4,000).[13] The Business Software Alliance continues to press for amendments to the CPPA to raise penalties against piracy, and the International Intellectual Property Alliance has recommended that South Korea remain on the Section 301 watch list.

The 1987 PMA-initiated case against Brazil over its lack of patent protection for pharmaceutical products is noteworthy because it is the only case that resulted in trade retaliation by the United States under Section 301 provisions. After Brazil refused to alter its policy, the United States placed a 100 percent retaliatory tariff (totaling $39 million) on imports of Brazilian pharmaceuticals, paper products, and consumer eletronics.[14] Brazil filed a GATT complaint against U.S. trade retaliation, but it "withdrew its complaint when the sanctions were dropped [in summer 1990] in exchange for Brazil's patent commitments."[15] President Fernando Collor de Mello proposed patent legislation that would protect pharmaceutical products and process patents for the first time. The patent reform package presented to the Brazilian legislature in May 1991 "denies protection to drugs that are not made in Brazil, a provision intended to force patent holders to manufacture or license them locally."[16] These conditions do not satisfy the PMA, which will continue to monitor Brazil's approach. In the words of one TNC executive, "Brazil is looking for something to get it off the hook with the U.S. Trade Representative. But I'm not really optimistic."[17] The PMA recommended that Brazil remain on the USTR watch list in 1992. A 1993 USTR investigation was terminated in February 1994 after Brazil promised USTR Mickey Kantor that it would enact a new patent law. However, in the wake of the political scandals of the Collor administration, intellectual property protection has been put on hold by the Brazilian legislature. Brazilian and USTR negotiators met five times between May 1993 and February 1994 to discuss the possibility of trade sanctions for Brazil's failure to protect U.S. pharmaceutical patents. The 1991 patent bill still had not been passed, and Brazilian Senator Jose Richa indicated that he would not pressure the Senate to hurry passage of a new law.[18]

In 1988 the PMA filed a petition against Argentina. In consultations between the U.S. and Argentine governments, Argentina pledged to strengthen patent protection for pharmaceuticals by 1992. The PMA subsequently agreed to withdraw its Section 301 petition. The Argentine Congress considered various proposals for strengthened pharmaceutical protection that reflected the U.S. demands, yet quickly backpedaled on the issue of pharmaceutical patents. The Argentine government's agency in charge of intellectual property protection argued that a strong patent law would lead to higher drug prices and fewer jobs. The Argentine associations representing domestic pharmaceutical producers (primarily pirate labs) and distributors echoed these sentiments, citing the high cost of health care and specter of putting their employees out of work. An official from a wholesale pharmaceutical distributors' association, Reftels, told U.S. negotiators that "there were no saints in this issue—each side was simply protecting its own economic interests."[19] Argentina has remained on U.S. watch lists, and in early 1993 Argentina was ranked as the top Latin American violator of pharmaceutical patents "due to a powerful group of firms dedicated to copying patents and selling pirated drugs throughout Latin America."[20] The Argentine Congress is likely to water down reform proposals due to strong domestic opposition.

Similarly, Thailand agreed to improve its intellectual property protection in response to the 1990 Section 301 filing over its lax copyright enforcement. The United States is Thailand's largest export market, thereby providing the United States with significant leverage. The USTR has repeatedly cited Thailand on its priority watch list, and in the 1991 patent protection case Thailand indicated that it would consider compliance and "is looking to the results of the GATT negotiations for possible guidance."[21] Therefore the case is still open.

Intellectual property protection has placed Thai leaders in a difficult position. In 1987 Prime Minister Prem Tinsulanond's administration was ousted in a no-confidence motion after attempting to strengthen Thailand's copyright laws. Intellectual property protection is controversial in Thailand because piracy has become a lucrative business there. The government has a strong interest in protecting the piracy industry that provides jobs in manufacturing as well as in over 12,500 retail shops.[22] Because the domestic political stakes are high, "Bangkok's approach has been to compromise when necessary then fail to put the newly negotiated regulations in place."[23] Thai Commerce Minister Subin Pinkhayan rejected U.S. offers to help draft legislation, indicating that this would constitute a breach of sovereignty.[24] Thai officials repeatedly have complained about "the United States' tendency to use its 'economic muscle to throw its weight around and bully' its trading partners."[25] The United States has continued to pressure Thailand and has kept Thailand on its priority watch list as an intellectual property violator through 1994.

The 1991 Indian intellectual property case is still open. Due to progress in U.S.-Indian negotiations over patent protection, the United States decided to delay trade retaliation. Reporting in the *Far Eastern Economic Review*, Hamish McDonald pointed out that "India has taken steps to meet foreign concerns about enforcement of intellectual property rights under existing laws."[26] Beginning in 1991, Prime Minister

Narasimha Rao implemented a liberal economic reform package that substantially relaxed conditions for foreign investment. India softened its opposition to the inclusion of intellectual property rights in the GATT agenda. It has taken steps to strengthen protection for computer software, videos, and films, and it has improved its enforcement efforts. The Business Software Alliance has extended its activities to India and is keeping close watch on developments there, particularly regarding enforcement. Despite India's moves in the desired U.S. direction, it has remained on the USTR's watch list.

The last Section 301 case listed in Table 6.5 concerned intellectual property rights in the People's Republic of China. Initiated in 1991, this case has been the subject of intense negotiations. Trade linkage thus far has proven effective only on paper. China enacted its first patent legislation in 1984, but this legislation was deemed inadequate by interested parties in the United States. Section 301 consultations between the two countries in August 1991 proved frustrating, but China promised to resume discussions over copyright and patent protection in October of that same year. The value of China's exports to the United States was an estimated $18,969 million in 1991 and rose to $25,729 million in 1992, so the threat of trade sanctions was palpable.[27] After repeatedly threatening to impose sanctions, the USTR formally withdrew its Section 301 investigation in January 1992.

As a result of the negotiations, China agreed to enact new laws and regulations to expand the scope of protection and to join two international copyright conventions by the summer of 1993. As did governments in the other cases, the Chinese government superficially complied, but its piracy activities have continued unabated. In June 1994, the United States designated China a Section 301 priority country for copyright violations; deputy USTR Charlene Barshefsky noted that while China had "world class" laws to protect intellectual property rights, they were rarely enforced.[28] For example, the pirating of music recorded on compact discs and of computer software comprise two lucrative industries. An estimated 100 percent of the compact discs produced and 95 percent of the software used in China are pirated; indeed, the Chinese government helps the pirates by granting import concessions for machinery to produce CDs.[29] In the compact disc case, the Chinese set up factories as joint ventures with Korean

and Taiwanese investors who sought partners among relatives of the
Chinese Communist Party; according to industry officials, these connections "may explain why there has been so little copyright enforcement."[30] Furthermore, nearly all of the Chinese government ministries
use pirated computer software.

In late February 1995, Chinese and American negotiators narrowly averted a trade war by reaching a new agreement on intellectual
property. The Chinese government conducted several well-publicized
raids on pirate factories, this time with the participation of U.S. industry representatives, and pledged to implement tougher enforcement
and customs policies against pirated goods. However, distribution of
software and compact discs will continue to be done through Chinese
licensees. According to Eric H. Smith, president of the International
Intellectual Property Alliance, "Obviously we didn't get everything.
We would have liked a more open Chinese market."[31] While the agreement was not formally related to China's efforts to join the newly
created World Trade Organization, the Chinese clearly were motivated
by this.

As in previous U.S. efforts to secure stronger intellectual property protection in China, the bottom line will be whether or not the
Chinese implement and enforce these policies. As part of the February
1995 agreement, the Chinese had shut down a half dozen pirate factories, but they had all reopened within a few months. Various U.S.-
based industry associations reported huge increases in the Chinese
production of pirated goods for export. In February 1996 the USTR
again threatened to impose trade sanctions on China for its failure to
protect U.S.-held intellectual property. In a virtual replay of the 1995
brinkmanship over intellectual property, complete with U.S. threats
and Chinese counterthreats, in June 1996 the two sides reached another eleventh hour agreement. As in 1995, the Chinese mounted a
high-profile crackdown campaign, but made it clear that they would
not bow to foreign pressure. Rather than focusing on new agreements,
the 1996 talks concentrated on issues surrounding the enforcement of
the 1995 agreements. The Chinese agreed to close down pirate factories and to use police officers to carry out investigations of illegal
operations. However, they rejected the American demands for on-site
verification inspections by U.S. officials. No one involved in these

negotiations believes that the problem is solved once and for all, and the day after the agreement "nobody was dismissing the possibility that the two countries could confront each other over the same issues a year from now."[32] As Bian Zizhen, a China-based patent consultant points out: "China has a good structure as far as legislation goes. The main problem is education. People don't think of intellectual property like other property."[33] Representatives from the software, motion picture, and music industries will continue to monitor China's progress in enforcing intellectual property rights, but no one is expecting any miracles—nor should they.

The PMA also filed a Section 301 petition against Chile for failure to protect pharmaceutical patents, but withdrew it after consultations with the Chilean government, which promised to enact a pharmaceutical patent law by late 1989. Subsequently, several patent laws were proposed, but the PMA rejected them as inadequate. After continued bilateral discussions, Chile finally enacted an acceptable law, which went into effect in September 1991 and extended patent protection to pharmaceutical products for the first time. The law guarantees protection for fifteen years; the United States had requested a twenty- to twenty-five-year guarantee but agreed that Chile was moving in the right direction. In 1993 and 1994 the United States continued to pressure Chile to strengthen its copyright protection, due to rampant computer software, videotape, and audiotape piracy. The United States also is distressed that Chilean law provides neither semiconductor mask work (the individual design of the chip's layers) nor trade secret protection.[34]

Generalized System of Preferences Status

In its quest to secure more extensive guarantees of intellectual property protection, the United States also has threatened a target country's status as a GSP beneficiary. The 1974 Trade and Tariff Act included intellectual property protection as a new criterion for extending or maintaining GSP benefits. However, Washington did not pursue this avenue until the late 1980s, after consistent pressure from industry associations. In three instances involving India, Mexico, and Thailand,

GSP benefits were denied for failure to enact adequate patent protection. In 1987 Mexico continued its refusal to pass pharmaceutical product protection and thereby lost $500 million in GSP benefits.[35] The USTR cited Mexico again in 1989 under Section 301, but dropped Mexico from the list due to evidence that Mexico was considering major changes in intellectual property legislation in 1990.

In 1989, the PMA filed a complaint against Thailand, and when Thailand failed to acquiesce, it was denied its duty-free benefits under GSP in the amount of $165 million. In both cases, the targeted government faced strong domestic opposition to greater intellectual property protection from powerful local drug manufacturers and was concerned that extending pharmaceutical product protection would lead to higher consumer prices. Under continued pressure from the PMA via the USTR, in February 1992 the Thai government approved amendments to its Patents Act. The PMA still is dissatisfied because the new act does not offer pipeline protection (that is, for products invented but not yet marketed), nor does it eliminate compulsory licensing.[36] The Thai government cannot make further concessions without placing itself in a precarious position; the Government Pharmaceutical Organization dominates the local Thai drug industry and benefits from piracy, so pharmaceutical patents are a particularly sensitive issue. Finally, in 1992, India lost $80 million in GSP benefits over its weak protection of pharmaceuticals.

An especially sharp reversal from past policies of economic nationalism currently is underway in Mexico. Mexico's extreme trade dependence on it gives the United States extra leverage, but Mexico has successfully resisted U.S. pressure in the past. Many factors are at work, including: the Mexican decision to join the GATT in 1986; the change in leadership that brought President Carlos Salinas de Gortari to power by a narrow margin (50.7 percent of the vote) in December 1988; Mexico's placement on USTR's priority watch list; and Mexico's eagerness to participate in the North American Free Trade Agreement. The fact that the Salinas administration initiated the U.S.-Mexico NAFTA talks suggests that Mexico was motivated by the benefits that such an agreement might bring.

The Mexican government also announced a Program of Modernization of Industry and Foreign Trade for 1990 to 1994, which explicitly stated its commitment to stronger intellectual property protection. The connection between the Section 301 pressure and the Mexican response was clear, as the United States immediately took Mexico off the priority watch list. On June 28, 1991, Mexico enacted a new industrial property law that represented a marked reversal of past policies. The new Mexican law extended patent protection to chemical, pharmaceutical, agrichemical, and biotechnology products for the first time. The law also included provisions for the protection of trade secrets (which had never been protected by Mexican law), stipulated that the importation of patented goods would constitute "working" the invention, and virtually eliminated the grounds for granting compulsory licenses.[37] According to Mike Privatera, the public affairs director for the U.S.-based pharmaceutical Pfizer Inc., "the Mexicans gave us everything we wanted."[38]

However, despite these changes and the apparently considerable incentives for Mexico to comply with demands for stricter intellectual property enforcement, Mexican enforcement efforts are still notoriously weak. Industry leaders have complained that Mexico has violated the intellectual property provisions of the NAFTA agreement and that enforcement is virtually nonexistent. As recently as April 1996, the International Intellectual Property Alliance noted that "Mexico has become one of the biggest pirate markets in the world."[39] The Business Software Alliance estimated that four-fifths of all business software programs used in Mexico are unlicensed copies. Music, video, and software pirates, when caught, are usually released on bail as low as a few dollars and fined $150 or less. While hundreds of cases have been brought before Mexico's antipiracy prosecutor's office since 1994, only six pirates have been convicted and none have served substantial jail terms.[40] The prosecutor's office is grossly understaffed, with only fifteen agents serving the entire country. Thus, despite powerful incentives to comply with demands for greater protection, even Mexico is falling far short of the mark.

These Section 301 and GSP cases demonstrate that the U.S. strategy has been largely successful in securing compliance on paper. The timing of the new policies can be explained by a neorealist approach that emphasizes coercion. Indeed, even though most analysts argue that neoliberal explanations are superior in accounting for the *substance* or *content* of policies, in this case the neorealist analysis appears to be sufficient. The policies have been the result of direct pressure from industry representatives (via the USTR), who have been instrumental in shaping the substance of the new policies through consultations with targeted governments. However, in nearly every instance the targeted countries have engaged in foot dragging and have chosen not to implement and enforce the new policies. The continued monitoring and repeated threats of renewed Section 301 action in the absence of satisfactory enforcement of the new policies suggest that the trend toward greater protection of intellectual property is not being embraced as ardently as the United States would wish. The targeted states acquiesce on paper and do just enough to free themselves of U.S. pressure—but no more. While these countries have changed their policies, they have not changed their minds about the merits of intellectual property protection. Even when the United States has carried out its threats, as it has with Brazil, India, Mexico, and Thailand, the targeted governments did not comply. Gains from free riding on others' intellectual property and the profits from piracy still outweigh the liberal norm of respect for these property rights. At this stage in their development, they do not yet see intellectual property protection as being in their interests. While some evidence suggests that this is beginning to change, the widespread acceptance of the norm of intellectual property protection is still a long way off.

Antitrust Policy as a Choice: Changing Their Minds?

In contrast to the intellectual property protection case, the adoption of antitrust policies in developing countries has been based on choice within constraints rather than coercion. These policies have been adopted voluntarily, and the international institutional machinery established in 1980 under the RBP Set has played an increasingly important role since the late 1980s. As with intellectual property rights, the economic crisis of the early 1980s promoted the policy shift in developing countries. However, the effects of the crisis were different in this case; in the antitrust context, industrialized countries have refrained completely from direct hegemonic coercion and threats.

On one level, the antitrust case is consistent with the neorealist expectation that the weak conform to the preferences of the strong. However, this case also is consistent with an interpretivist conceptualization of international relations that focuses on the diffusion of ideas—here, neoliberal economic ideology. In the intellectual property case, learning on the part of U.S. policymakers led to the adoption of a coercive strategy; external coercion led developing countries to change their policies. The sequencing of policy change in the antitrust case is different, and norm change may have preceded policy change. While the underlying cause for norm change in this case was the economic crisis of the 1980s, the more proximate causes are to be found in the realm of ideas.

As Thomas Biersteker points out, "in most instances, the 'demand' for policy reversal came from technocratic groups . . . within the state. Although their factions were present . . . before the early 1980s, the magnitude of the economic crisis, along with the failure of past policies, provided them with an opportunity to articulate an alternative set of ideas."[41] These ideas were borrowed from the international pool—the Reagan and Thatcher economic revolutions and the academic economists (i.e., the Chicago school)—and were given further credence by the demonstration effect of the East Asian success stories.[42]

The switch toward export-led industrialization and attendant economic liberalization has raised a host of economic issues that did not seem salient to developing countries during the NIEO era. Undeniably, certain coercive elements have been at work, for economic policy changes have been driven in part by structural adjustment programs through the IMF and the World Bank.[43] Economic liberalization is a core component of IMF conditions for loans to developing countries. Furthermore, a spillover effect from coercive economic policies could account for the timing of the changes in antitrust policy and could help explain the ten-year lag between the establishment of institutional mechanisms to expedite the passage of antitrust laws and the developing countries' use of those mechanisms.[44]

Deregulation, privatization, and the liberalization of trade and investment climates pose new challenges for developing countries. For example, when deregulating economic sectors, states need to ensure that the former regulations are not replaced by private sector anticompetitive behavior, such as market allocation or price fixing. As states privatize formerly state-owned enterprises, they need to ensure that private sector owners do not abuse their positions and replicate the inefficiencies of the former state sector. When breaking up former state monopolies, states must ensure that the new entities do not engage in restrictive business practices. In addition, by liberalizing trade and investment climates, developing countries are abandoning their former stance of discrimination against foreign-based multinational corporations.

In this way, an economic logic is at work, insofar as a country eventually gains an interest in promoting competition in its domestic market as a consequence of liberalization. Even so, what distinguishes this case from intellectual property protection is that an international institution, established in 1980 through the adoption of the RBP Set, has played a significant role in spreading the industrialized countries' conceptions of antitrust and competition policy. The institutional mechanisms established under the terms of the RBP Set provide a forum for education, drafting legislation, and training officials in implementation and enforcement of antitrust laws and policies. Policymakers in developing countries are recognizing the connection between liberalization and antitrust policies. Instead of having the United States dictate the substance of the policies under the threat of trade sanctions, these countries are taking the initiative and are actively requesting the help and advice of the IGE established by the RBP Set. In other words, the more proximate explanation suggests a significant role for international institutions and choice. The voluntarism in this case contrasts with the transparent coercive hegemony of the intellectual property case.

A decade after the adoption of the RBP Set, the president of the Second Conference to Review the Set opened the conference by noting:

> The world was now quite different from what it had been 10 years ago when the Set of Principles and Rules had been adopted, or even 5 years ago when the first Review Conference had been held. The past year, in particular, had seen very rapid changes in the international economy and there was now a greater and more widespread appreciation of the benefits of the free market and competition.[45]

Indeed, the UNCTAD Secretariat has received requests for technical assistance under the terms of the RBP Set from fifty-nine developing and Central European countries since 1989. The countries have requested many different types of assistance, including organizing regional and national seminars or workshops, drafting legislation, and training RBP officials. Table 6.6 lists the countries that have requested assistance and the nature of the requested assistance. UNCTAD initially provided assistance in the form of regional workshops to introduce interested countries to the operation of antitrust policies and the control of restrictive business practices. Due to the huge demand in this area, it has expanded its activities to include national seminars, advisory missions, training workshops, and on-the-job training internships.[46]

As Table 6.6 shows, fifty-two countries have participated in UNCTAD's regional workshops, and an additional five countries have requested UNCTAD assistance in conducting regional seminars. Twelve countries have participated in national seminars on restrictive business practices, two countries plan to participate, and an additional twenty-one countries have requested help from UNCTAD for their national seminars. Currently, fourteen countries have RBP laws on the books, four currently are drafting legislation, two plan to draft such legislation, and four have requested UNCTAD assistance in preparing laws. Finally, the training missions sponsored by UNCTAD address issues of implementation. Three countries thus far have participated in training missions, four plan to participate, and four more countries have requested UNCTAD assistance in training antitrust officials.

The first country to adopt RBP laws after the UNCTAD negotiations was South Korea. According to a spokesman for the South Korean government, his country "responded immediately after the adoption of the RBP Set by introducing the Act for Monopoly Regulation and Fair Trade and had started a systematic control of anti-competitive and unfair business conduct."[47] The South Korean government modeled its law after those of Japan and Germany, but added uniquely South Korean elements. For example, violators of the law have been required to issue public apologies. The staff of the Fair Trade Office judges this remedy to be "perhaps even more powerful than monetary remedies."[48]

Another key difference between South Korea's antitrust policies and intellectual property protection is that South Korea is implement-

**Table 6.6 Status of Restrictive Business Practices Technical
Assistance Programs, by Country**[a]

Requesting Country	Regional Seminar	National Seminar	Drafting Legislation	Training RBP Officials
Albania	Request	Request	—	—
Argentina	Action	Action	Law	Plan
Bangladesh	Action	—	—	—
Botswana	Action	—	—	—
Bolivia	Action	—	—	—
Brazil	Action	NA	Law	Request
Brunei	Action	Request	—	—
Bulgaria	Request	Request	—	—
Cameroon	Action	Request	Request	—
Chile	Action	Action	Law	Action
China	Action	Action	Request	Request
Colombia	Action	Request	Draft	—
Costa Rica	Action	Request	—	—
Cuba	Action	Action	—	—
Dubai	Request	Request	—	—
Ecuador	Action	Request	—	—
Egypt	Action	Request	—	—
Ethiopia	Action	—	—	—
El Salvador	Action	—	—	—
Fiji	Action	—	—	—
Gambia	Action	—	—	—
Ghana	Action	Action	Draft	Plan
Guatemala	Action	—	—	—
Guinea	Action	Action	Request	—
Honduras	Action	—	—	—
Indonesia	Action	Action	Request	Request
India	Action	—	Law	—
Iran	Action	—	—	—
Kenya	Action	Action	Law	Action
Korea, Democratic People's Rep. of	Action	Request	—	—
Lesotho	Action	—	—	—
Liberia	Action	—	—	—
Madagascar	NA	Request	—	—
Mexico	Action	Request	—	—

Table 6.6 Continued

Requesting Country	Regional Seminar	National Seminar	Drafting Legislation	Training RBP Officials
Mongolia	Action	Request	—	—
Morocco	Action	Request	—	—
Myanmar	Action	Request	—	—
Nepal	Action	—	—	—
Nicaragua	Action	—	—	—
Nigeria	Action	Plan	Plan	Plan
Oman	—	Request	—	—
Pakistan	Action	—	Law	—
Peru	Action	Action	Law	Request
Poland	Request	Request	Law	—
Philippines	Action	Action	Draft	—
Romania	Request	Request	—	—
Russian Federation	Action	Request	Law	—
Somalia	Action	—	—	—
South Korea	Action	—	Law	—
Sri Lanka	Action	Request	Law	Action
Swaziland	Action	—	—	—
Thailand	Action	Action	Law	—
Trinidad and Tobago	Action	Request	—	—
Tunisia	Action	—	Law	Request
Uruguay	Action	—	—	—
Vietnam	Action	Plan	—	—
Venezuela	Action	—	Law	—
Zambia	Action	Action	Plan	Plan
Zimbabwe	Action	—	Draft	—

Note: Request = action has been requested; Dash = no action currently planned; Action = action has taken place; Law = a law has been enacted; Plan = action is planned; NA = not applicable; Draft = drafting of legislation is in progress.
Source: Adapted from UNCTAD, "Activities Relating to Specific Provisions of the Set: Technical Assistance, Advisory and Training Programs on Restrictive Business Practices," TD/B/RBP/83 (6 August 1991), p. 5, par. 20, and TD/B/RBP/90 (28 July 1992), pp. 11–12.

ing and enforcing antitrust policies. South Korea has targeted the *chaebol*, or domestic industrial conglomerates; in 1981 the thirty South Korean *chaebol* comprised less than 1 percent of corporations, yet accounted for 39.7 percent of sales in mining and manufacturing.[49] Between 1981 and 1985, "in every case involving a major chaebol, violations of the statute were found, and the subsequent corrective orders indicate that the chaebol were treated no less harshly than other defendants."[50] In this case, there is no discrepancy between the adoption of the policies and their implementation; South Korea's National Assembly both supports and approves of the activities of the Fair Trade Office.[51]

The domestic consumer demand to restrain the power of the *chaebol* has increased over time. Once viewed as engines of development, in the popular mind they now are perceived as corrupt and inefficient. Between 1986 and 1992, however, not much forward movement on antitrust policy occurred; the *chaebol* actively resisted government policies and became adept at dodging them. With the recent democratization of South Korea, public pressure against the *chaebol* has increased. South Korea amended its Fair Trade Act in November 1992 "to strengthen restrictions on cross-ownership and capital investment limits for large business groupings."[52] This was the strongest legislative measure yet to curb *chaebol* power. Elected in December 1992, President Kim Young Sam launched an aggressive anticorruption campaign that has focused on the *chaebol* and their use of financial power to buy elections. In November 1993, Chung Ju Yung, founder of Hyundai (one of the largest *chaebol*) and a presidential candidate in the 1992 election, was sentenced to three years in prison for violating election laws by diverting $62.8 million from the Hyundai Group to finance his campaign.[53] According to Koo Suk-moo, vice president of the Korea Economic Research Institute, "The general public has linked business activities with personal wealth accumulation. . . . They now look at them [the *chaebol*] as entities of destructive power and influence."[54] In response to this negative assessment, John Burton reported that in April 1993 the chairman of the Fair Trade Commission, Han Lee-hun, announced that the new government of President Kim "will use anti-trust laws as its main weapon to curb the economic power of the chaebol. . . . Han explained that . . . their dominance of the domestic economy prevented the growth of small and medium businesses."[55] In the summer of 1993, Han unveiled a new line of attack by initiating FTC investigations into the *chaebol*'s internal trading practices. According to Burton, the *chaebol*'s extensive internal trading "reduces the ability of small businesses to sell products and services to the conglomerates."[56]

President Kim rode into office on a populist wave; thus far he has exhibited bold leadership and has been unafraid to confront the *chaebol* directly. He has made it clear that antitrust instruments will become increasingly important in the battle, and he has added campaign finance and tax reform to his arsenal. According to an UNCTAD report, looking back on South Korea's decade-long experience in the RBP field, the South Korean spokesman noted that "technical cooperation from international organizations such as UNCTAD and from developed countries had been very useful. During the past 10 years, the various international meetings on antitrust or RBP control, including the IGE meetings and seminars held by UNCTAD, had provided his country with good advice which had been instrumental in the efficient enforcement and improvement of fair trade policy in Korea."[57] Thus, in contrast to South Korean efforts to strengthen intellectual property protection, the South Korean implementation of antitrust policy has been undertaken for domestic reasons, has been influenced by UNCTAD activities, and is supported by the populace.

While South Korea was in a sense the post–RBP Set pioneer, several other developing countries also have adopted antitrust legislation and policies to control RBPs. Venezuela hosted an UNCTAD regional seminar in September 1990. Its new antimonopoly law established the Anti-Monopoly Superintendency to implement its policies. A 1992 test case suggested that the superintendency would apply the new law stringently. In this case, the Venezuelan Sugar Distributor Company contracted with domestic sugar mills to be the exclusive distributor of sugar to the mills, and it asserted its right to set prices. *Business Latin America* reported that Superintendent Ana Julia Jatar challenged these contracts and "says the firm must negotiate contracts without exclusive clauses in order to open the way for competition. Observers say Jatar could be testing the water with 'small fry' before confronting the powerful cartels that have traditionally dominated

Venezuela's distribution system."[58] During 1992 and 1993, the superintendancy expanded its activities by initiating its own investigations and rendering numerous opinions and consultations, "the most important of which related to proposed mergers and acquisitions in electric power, airline, vegetable oil, beverage, paint, ceramic, automobile, and insurance sectors. Decisions to date reflect the practical approach of the agency in addressing problems of economic efficiency and consumer welfare."[59] Importantly, the Venezuelan law targets domestic monopolies; this is a clear departure from the Andean countries' earlier antitrust approach of targeting only transnational enterprises.

The Venezuelan Anti-Dumping and Subsidies Commission of the Ministry of Industry (Fomento) published a block exemption to the Anti-Monopoly Law in July 1993, defining "certain activities which because of their relatively minor impact on the total market would not be considered an abuse of dominant market position (designed primarily to help small businesses)."[60] The Venezuelan government passed a new antimonopoly law in August 1993 and a new privatization law that provided that "the privatization process shall be null and void if the results violate the Venezuelan anti-monopoly legislation."[61] This underscores policymakers' concerns that the privatization process should promote domestic competition rather than merely transfer economic concentration to private hands. At least through the end of 1993, Venezuela was implementing this law; for example, in November of that year the antimonopoly authorities barred the local airline Avensa from bidding for the privatization of Venezuela's other local airline, Aeropostal, so as to avoid the creation of a dominant market position for Avensa within the country.[62]

Chile began liberalizing its economy most recently in 1985.[63] After returning to democracy in March 1990, the Chilean government strengthened the institutions responsible for promoting and implementing liberalization and free competition. In 1990, Chile revised its former antimonopoly law (Decree 211 of 1973) to expand the responsibilities of the National Economic Tribunal (Fiscalia Nacional), which has extensive investigative powers, to include the control of price distortions with respect to imports (Law 18.525).[64] Chile also participated in UNCTAD's regional RBP seminar in Caracas in September 1990 and discussed its experience in the control of RBPs. Furthermore, Chile participated in the UNCTAD-sponsored RBP officials–training program. The Chilean delegate to the second RBP review conference stated that "his country was keen on constantly improving its legislation with the objective of promoting free competition. All these developments were fully in line with the Set of Principles and Rules. Moreover, Chile was willing to share its experience with other countries wishing to adopt and implement competition legislation."[65] By organizing and conducting the seminars and meetings, UNCTAD has created a forum where developing countries can compare notes as they begin adopting and implementing these new policies.

In light of its intellectual property stance regarding pharmaceuticals, Brazil launched an interesting investigation into Brazilian pharmaceutical companies under its antitrust laws. Although Brazil lifted price controls on Brazilian pharmaceuticals, the Ministry of the Economy has continued to monitor prices in an effort to protect consumers and prevent unfair business practices.[66] Brazil's Administrative Council for Economic Defense (CADE) is charged with investigating and punishing unfair business practices (i.e., monopoly and cartel formation). In 1992, CADE fined several Brazilian pharmaceutical companies for the abusive practice of trying to raise prices by withholding consumer goods.

In early 1994, the Brazilian Ministries of Finance and Justice began drafting a new antitrust law.[67] The president of CADE, Ruy Coutinho, indicated that the new law will substantially speed the processing of antitrust cases from nearly two years to forty-five days. The bill also will define the term "abusive prices," an important step because government officials previously have interpreted this term in politically convenient ways that often bore no relationship to anticompetitive practices. Strengthening these policies is an important step; in the past, these policies have not been frequently enforced, and Brazilian courts have overturned most CADE administrative decisions when appealed by businesses.

Mexico passed a new antitrust law in December 1992 that came into effect in June 1993. As Natalia Delgado and Steven Martin suggest, "essentially, the Act is the Mexican government's attempt to implement United States antitrust policy in Mexico."[68] As in the intellectual property case, Mexico is strongly motivated by NAFTA. Chapter

15 of the NAFTA agreement covers competition policy and, according to Jeffrey Lang and Laura Brank, requires that "each Party adopt measures preventing monopolies and state enterprises from unfairly discriminating against, or engaging in, anti-competitive practices with respect to investments of other NAFTA parties."[69] Mexico has moved swiftly to implement the law and establish an intensive training program to develop the necessary expertise for staffing the Federal Competition Commission (FCC).[70]

India has fundamentally changed its treatment of foreign investors and, since 1989, has relaxed barriers to entry. The Monopolies and Restrictive Trade Practices Act (MRTP) of 1969 had been used to limit the entry of foreign multinationals into the Indian market. However, as *Business Asia* reported, a senior executive of a large Indian enterprise (the Tata Group) pointed out that "the way the law is being applied now 'has the effect of keeping the legislation intact while dismantling, in practice, the entire edifice of regulatory controls built up in the 1970s.' "[71]

Relaxing the former stringent criteria for industrial licenses, in late 1988 the Indian government approved a major collaboration between Tata Iron and Steel Co. Ltd. (TISCO) and U.S.-based Timken Co. to produce bearings. As characterized by *Business Asia*, "The controversial project won government permits despite vocal opposition from existing manufacturers—on the very grounds that likely would have led to its rejection a few years ago."[72] Other Indian bearing manufacturers argued that the Tata-Timken venture would flood the market and hurt local producers. The government's Monopolies Commission rejected their arguments and defended the venture on the grounds that: (1) it would result in product upgrading due to access to superior technology and (2) the venture would not seize the dominant market share but instead would create a countervailing force and thus stimulate domestic competition.[73] Thus India has eased its discrimination against foreign multinationals and has gone so far as to defend the merits of foreign multinational investment against local opposition. The Indian government also has approved numerous joint ventures between Indian firms and transnational enterprises such as Minnesota Mining and Manufacturing Company (3M) and Honeywell Company; while it is entirely possible that some joint ventures may have anticompetitive effects, the Tata-Timken ruling suggests that India's Monopolies Commission is concerned with stimulating domestic competition.

In another strong reversal of past discriminatory policies, in 1993 the Indian cabinet approved Coca-Cola's plans to set up a wholly owned venture to produce its soft drinks in India.[74] In the words of *The Economist*, "Keeping soft drinks makers out of India has been a fetish with Indian socialists ever since a previous government chucked out Coca-Cola in 1977."[75] India's leading soft drinks company, Parle, had been protected from foreign competition due to the stringent limits on shareholdings in local affiliates. Under the 1973 Foreign Exchange Regulation Act, foreign ownership was limited to 40 percent of equity.[76] The Indian government lifted this restriction in August of 1991, and in 1993 alone over one hundred companies won approval to increase their equity in Indian affiliates.[77] Welcoming Coca-Cola back on such generous terms demonstrates the complete reversal of policy.[78]

While the following cases do not reveal extensive implementation, these countries voluntarily have sought UNCTAD counsel and availed themselves of UNCTAD's training programs. In Latin America, the Andean Pact countries participated in UNCTAD regional seminars and each requested national level workshops. As the Colombian spokesman said, "as economies were liberalized the Set of Principles and Rules had shown its usefulness. . . . The dismantling of quantitative restrictions in Colombia had led to the adoption of antidumping and countervailing duty statutes, and the beginning of revision of antimonopoly legislation."[79]

Peru also adopted antitrust policies. It participated in regional and national seminars conducted by UNCTAD, and it has requested further UNCTAD assistance in training antitrust officials to implement and enforce these policies. In November 1991 the legislature passed more than 126 laws, many of them designed to stimulate private sector activity, and it radically reoriented the country's formerly statist economic policies. As part of this sweeping change, Peru eliminated state monopolies in telecommunications, postal and railway services, and utilities.[80]

In 1987, Sri Lanka adopted antitrust legislation and created the Fair Trading Commission of Sri Lanka, which applied the principles laid down in the RBP Set.[81] Sri Lanka also received assistance from

UNCTAD in the forms of a regional seminar and a program to train RBP officials.

The Philippine government introduced Bill No. 996 in 1989 to address antitrust and RBP issues. This bill proposed to establish an independent antitrust commission and was inspired by the RBP Code, U.S. laws and court decisions, and European models and experience. Speaking on behalf of the Group of 77, the Philippine delegate emphasized that "in the 10 years since the adoption of the Set, the functions of the Intergovernmental Group of Experts had assumed greater importance as Governments made competition policy a priority."[82] In November 1992 at the IGE meeting, the spokesman for the Philippine government indicated that UNCTAD had provided generous technical support for the development and institutionalization of Philippine competition policies.[83]

Many African countries, such as Ghana, Kenya, Nigeria, and Zambia, also have actively sought UNCTAD assistance in designing policies to control RBPs. For example, Ghana availed itself of UNCTAD's services by participating in a national seminar in February 1991; hosting an UNCTAD consultant and UNCTAD RBP staff member for a working visit for advice in drafting legislation; meeting with UNCTAD RBP experts in London in May 1992 and visiting London's Office of Fair Trading; and returning to Geneva to discuss Ghana's RBP program with the RBP Unit of UNCTAD.[84]

The institutional mechanisms established in 1980 have come to serve a number of important functions. Multilateral assistance in the form of UNCTAD's regional seminars has introduced large groups of government officials to basic RBP control principles. The IGE has become a forum for informal consultations; as summarized by UNCTAD, it "served in the past to identify problems that developing countries . . . faced in RBP control, had provided a forum for discussions of possible solutions to such problems and had served to establish important contacts between experts of developed and developing countries."[85] UNCTAD also has compiled and distributed a list of RBP control authorities in numerous countries, complete with phone numbers, addresses, and fax numbers, and a standardized checklist for information requests and of steps that countries must take in preparing a case and requesting consultation.[86] In this sense UNCTAD is reducing transaction costs for interested states and thereby is providing important benefits to participants.

Beyond reducing transaction costs, the IGE has become a source of detailed, substantive information about the rationale for and operation of the control of RBPs. During each session of the IGE, states are encouraged to engage in multilateral and bilateral consultations on RBPs, address specific problems, and establish contacts with experts. Participants have praised these consultations as helpful and informative, and in response to the IGE's request, the UNCTAD Secretariat has pledged to continue to provide facilities for these consultations. UNCTAD has encouraged states to present seminars at these meetings on specific substantive topics, including deregulation and the treatment of natural monopolies.

In contrast to the acrimonious first conference to review the RBP Set in 1985, the second conference in 1990 was characterized by a high degree of consensus on the merits of both the RBP Set and the activities of UNCTAD in this area. At UNCTAD VIII in Cartagena in February 1992, member states agreed that "UNCTAD should pursue, through the Intergovernmental Group of Experts on Restrictive Business Practices, its work with regard to policies and rules for the control of restrictive business practices to encourage competition, to promote the proper functioning of markets and efficient resource allocation, and to bring about further liberalization of international trade."[87] The NIEO focus on economic exploitation is absent from this formulation. As the spokesman for the industrialized countries noted, "an increasing number of developing and eastern European countries were following the Set's principles in developing their own RBP legislation. . . . The Set . . . had stood the test of time better than could have been imagined in 1980."[88]

Clearly, the institutional mechanisms for RBP control established in 1980 have played an important role in providing information, facilitating transnational learning, and getting others to join the growing number of countries accepting the principle of RBP control. In Ikenberry and Kupchan's terms, this is a case of "normative persuasion," in which the participating countries have learned more about and accepted the idea of RBP control prior to adopting policies.[89] By actively approaching UNCTAD for help in the design of these policies and for consultations to improve their functioning, developing countries have been volunteers rather than coerced targets of manipulation by the powerful states. Developing countries have redefined their interests, and the institutional mechanisms provided by UNCTAD have expedited the adoption of new antitrust policies. Furthermore, UNCTAD has provided an arena in which developing countries can choose from an array of approaches to RBPs, design and adopt RBP control policies for their own reasons, learn from each other as well as from industrialized countries' experts, and do so in such a way that does not compromise domestic legitimacy.

Conclusion

The intellectual property protection case is an example of what Ikenberry and Kupchan refer to as socialization through external inducement, or "acts before beliefs." They describe the causal chain of behavior change as externally induced policy change (i.e., "cooperation through coercion") leading to norm change (i.e., "cooperation through legitimate domination").[90] The process of normative change is still underway and is, therefore, still reversible. The distance between adopting policies on paper and believing in their intrinsic merits is significant. The fact that developing countries have not vigorously enforced these new policies suggests that domestic opposition is still robust. Interested private parties in the United States, such as the Business Software Alliance, the International Alliance for Intellectual Property, the PMA, and the Semiconductor Industry Association, know that the distance between formal policies and actual commitment to the value of heightened standards of protection and enforcement is great. Thus, they are continuing to monitor the implementation of these policies and to threaten Section 301–based action.

Business associations also are pursuing alternative channels to both secure compliance and convince developing countries of the merits of protection. For example, the PMA has funded research demonstrating the negative effects of lax protection on developing countries' economies. Ad hoc groups, led by representatives of U.S. licensing interests, have lobbied actively in Brazil and Mexico for increased patent protection. These groups engage in educational activities and meet with local business leaders. According to Robert Sherwood, who has represented the Brazil Ad Hoc Group, nearly every Brazilian business leader that he met with "has suffered losses when key technical employees have been hired away from competitors, taking proprietary technology with them."[91]

The depth and sustainability of these recent policy reforms in intellectual property protection will depend on the emergence of politically influential indigenous interests committed to this direction. Domestic resistance is still strong, but evidence exists that this may be changing. Pockets of nascent indigenous interests in stronger intellectual property protection are beginning to emerge. For example, Sherwood documents a case in which a Brazilian company owner sought to acquire a metal-etching technology from abroad, "but if he reached an agreement with a foreign source, he stood the risk of losing that technology through employee departure to a competitor while still being obligated to pay for the acquired technology. He dropped his plans."[92] Robert Merges cites a link between stronger intellectual property protection and the new dynamism of indigenous industries: "a recording industry flourished in Hong Kong for the first time after the passage of a copyright act protecting sound recordings; the Indian software industry saw a growth surge after a copyright was extended to software."[93]

As more developing countries' domestic industries suffer from a lack of adequate intellectual property protection, and as their high value-added export products that incorporate intellectual property begin to be pirated, these industries will support stronger enforcement. Video and record producers in Brazil, Korea, Mexico, the Philippines, and Singapore, computer associations in Thailand and Malaysia, and some drug manufacturers in India all have demonstrated an interest in stronger standards of intellectual property protection. In the late 1980s the associated chambers of commerce urged the Indian Government to join the Paris Convention,[94] and in 1991 Indian computer software exporters formed the Indian Federation Against Software Theft (INFAST).[95]

Additionally, as Pacific Rim countries continue to promote joint ventures with transnational enterprises, a greater stake in intellectual property protection will be necessary if they expect to acquire leading-edge technology. Without such protection, prospective partners will not be willing to share their most valuable technology. In fact, private investors have been able to secure commitments from joint venture partners that the U.S. government, Section 301 notwithstanding, has been unable to secure. For example, in order to curb piracy Texas Instruments, IBM, and Microsoft all have become partners with local industries in Taiwan through licensing agreements for computer hardware, software, and chip production.[96] This suggests that corporations may be better able to create situations of mutual benefit by extracting guarantees of intellectual property protection from parties that have been recalcitrant in the Section 301 process in exchange for sharing know-how and technology in joint ventures.

Developing countries have begun to encounter new problems as their enterprises have expanded to manufacture technologically sophisticated goods for export. In fact, computers exported from Taiwan have been copied by companies in England, China, and Southeast Asia, thus turning the tables on an old pattern: "before they copied others, now others copy them."[97] In response to domestic demand from large, well-established export-oriented enterprises in Taiwan, three industrial organizations (the National Anti-Counterfeiting Committee of the National Federation of Industries R.O.C., the Association for Computer Industry, and the Taiwan Toy Manufacturers Association [TTMA]) have lobbied for policy changes to curb piracy and counterfeiting of Taiwanese goods.[98] Taiwanese toy manufacturers may now register their intellectual property based on guidelines developed by its industry association (TTMA). Nonetheless, these indigenous efforts have yet to succeed in changing government policy to the extent that the United States desires. Continuing Section 301 and U.S. private-sector pressure bears this out. These policies will be implemented effectively only when these countries embrace them for their own domestic reasons.

The prognosis for the control of RBPs appears to be more positive. Developing countries are moving in the same market-led direction by adopting antitrust policies. They are proceeding more slowly than is the case with intellectual property protection, but with the help of UNCTAD, they are tailoring these policies to fit their particular situations. They also are voluntarily making use of the resources provided by the RBP IGE. These policies will be more politically palatable and will be perceived as more legitimate because they cannot be construed as the result of "buckling" under crude foreign pressure.

Developing countries face a delicate challenge ahead, and the commitment to liberalism hardly is carved in stone. The U.S. Section 301 strategy in intellectual property has helped to mobilize developing countries' domestic opposition, particularly among local pharmaceutical manufacturers and others who profit from piracy.[99] It also has put elites in developing countries in a difficult position. If they succumb to U.S. pressure, they are subject to criticisms of selling out their sovereignty to foreign interests. The sentiments that animated the NIEO are still present in the developing world, especially in Latin America. For example, despite the fact that the Partido Revolucionario Institucional (PRI) won the 1994 Mexican election, questions of social justice dominated the populist campaign of Cuauhtemoc Cardenas Solorzano (Partido de la Revolucion Democratica, or PRD). While he received only 17 percent of the vote, his focus on the roots of the political violence that erupted in Chiapas in early 1994 highlighted distributive issues that the PRI will have to face in order to keep political peace. In the wake of the Brazilian financial scandals and resignation of President Collor, the populist candidate Luis Inacio Lula de Silva began reviving interest in economic nationalism. In December 1993, disillusioned Venezuelan voters elected former President Rafael Caldera with just over 30 percent of the vote. Caldera's campaign rhetoric appealed to nationalist sentiment with his harsh attacks on the IMF and World Bank; he also pledged to reverse many of the market-opening "fatal economic policies" of his predecessor Carlos Andres Perez.[100]

This chapter suggests that neorealist analysis provides powerful insights into factors such as asymmetrical power relations and international constraints. However, these factors do not capture some important aspects of the story. The spread of hegemonic norms is hardly automatic. Interpretivist analyses that focus on learning, choice, international institutions, and nonstate actors, such as industry associations and transnational enterprises, provide compelling insights into variation across issues.

While an in-depth treatment of the domestic politics of all the countries discussed herein is beyond the scope of this chapter, it would be fruitful to examine the domestic politics of both the powerful states and the states that are the targets of powerful states' efforts to alter their policies. A more precise understanding of the conditions under which targeted states find external pressure beneficial for domestic reasons, and those under which they will resist such pressure, would provide insights into the process of hegemonic socialization. Furthermore, the role of nonstate actors, such as industry associations and transnational enterprises, in the domestic politics of both the initiating and targeted states should be highlighted. Both the mechanisms for and the impacts of transnational links between these parties merit further investigation.

The spread of hegemonic norms alters domestic political incentives. The sustainability of the new direction in developing countries will depend on both the emergence of politically powerful domestic constituencies committed to the new direction, and the ability of interested private parties to mobilize these constituencies to uphold and enforce these policies. Forging transnational links between private parties will become increasingly important to marshal lasting support for an open international economic order.

Conclusion

The North-South politics and diplomacy of intellectual property and antitrust underscore significant changes from the NIEO debates to the impact of the new emphasis on deregulation, privatization, and globalization in the 1980s and 1990s. Developing countries still have deep reservations about intellectual property protection but not about antitrust. In the 1970s, emboldened by OPEC's commodity power, activist developing countries set the multilateral agenda for North-South conference diplomacy. The negotiations revealed fundamental differences between the North and South that could not be bridged. While negotiators unanimously approved the Restrictive Business Practices Code, this sole multilateral agreement reflected the North's preferred conception and in no way endorsed the goals of the NIEO. The economic crisis of the 1980s forced developing countries to rethink national development policies and embrace elements of a market model.

As power shifted against the South during the debt crisis, the United States pursued an agenda to strengthen intellectual property protection in response to its new realization of the importance of intellectual property for international competitiveness. The United States' agenda emerged out of domestic developments, including the gradual

strengthening of patent holders' rights in U.S. domestic law and practices and the concerted lobbying efforts of industry associations representing powerful export industries with a high intellectual property
content. The United States exercised coercive diplomacy via Section
301 of the U.S. Trade and Tariff Act in an effort to force developing
countries to strengthen intellectual property protection. Finally, the
United States succeeded in codifying its trade-based approach to intellectual property in the both the NAFTA agreement and the TRIPs
accord in GATT.

This reappraisal and examination of the North-South politics and
diplomacy of intellectual property protection and antitrust reveals the
limits of standard structural, power-based analyses of North-South
relations. Certainly power matters, but an exclusive focus on power
obscures as much as it reveals. Yes, the strong made the rules, but
power-based analyses cannot tell us why the weak are not obeying
them. Ideas matter too. Intersubjective aspects of politics are as important as power. An interpretivist analysis does more than merely flesh
out the descriptive scenario. It also accounts for an important anomaly.
Developing countries' skepticism about the merits of intellectual property protection has remained intact, despite the death of the NIEO.
Even though the power disparities are glaring, there is still no shared
understanding between the North and South about the operation and
benefits of intellectual property rights. Furthermore, an exclusive focus on power would obscure the fact that developing countries voluntarily accepted the norm of competition, as evident in their increasing
implementation and enforcement of antitrust policies. Power considerations had little to do with this change. Finally, to the extent that
structural analyses marginalize domestic politics, they provide little
insight into the increasingly blurred boundaries between domestic
regulatory policies and international commerce. As Mowrey and
Rosenberg point out:

> in many cases, long-standing domestic policies that were devel-
> oped with little or no attention to their effects on international
> trade are now the subject of negotiations among trade policy-
> makers. Negotiations over these policies involve a far larger com-
> munity of policymakers and domestic interests than talks over
> border measures, which greatly increases their complexity.[1]

Over the past thirty years we have seen multilateralism in the 1970s, bilateralism in the 1980s, and a return to multilateralism in the 1990s with NAFTA and the TRIPs accord. While competition policy was incorporated into NAFTA, we may yet see an extension of multilateralism in competition policy in the next GATT round.[2] In all these periods the demand for multilateral approaches grew out out redefined interests, institutionalized in domestic policies, that the agenda setters sought to globalize. In the 1970s, the activist developing countries sought a global extension of their domestic legislation that emphasized technology suppliers' *obligations*. In the 1990s, the OECD countries, led by the United States, sought a global extension of their domestic laws that emphasize technology suppliers' *rights*.

In the late 1960s and early 1970s the activist developing countries redefined their interests in technology transfer. In the beginning of these cases the developing countries had redefined their interests and linked issues in more comprehensive way. While industrial development had always been the ultimate goal for these countries, the developing countries adopted a new intermediate goal—technological self-reliance. In addition, they fashioned new means to achieve that goal. They linked issues, which had been previously approached in an ad hoc manner, under the umbrella concept of technology transfer. The activist developing countries institutionalized these new interests in their domestic laws and policies. These formed the basis of a developing country negotiating consensus and of their multilateral demands. No longer passively accepting the market-led transfer process, they adopted an assertive stance vis-à-vis foreign investors in an effort to further their development goals. Their domestic regulatory environments posed new challenges for foreign firms seeking to do business there, and confronted the OECD's market-led approaches.

The success of the OPEC cartel provided opportunities for these new interests to be heard at the multilateral level. The activist countries sold their Group of 77 counterparts on their agenda and, with the exception of the East Asian countries that did not participate, presented a united negotiating front. However, their new consensus was flatly rejected by the industrialized countries. As the Paris Convention and Transfer of Technology negotiations wore on, the specter of commodity power disappeared. OPEC fell apart, and the widespread Northern fears of broad Southern commodity power evaporated. The developing countries' new ideas were not accepted by the more powerful actors and thus did not shape diplomatic outcomes.

In the 1980s, the exogenous shock of economic crisis had profound domestic effects in both developing and developed countries. By the early 1980s there was growing evidence that both developing and developed countries were redefining their interests in technology transfer. The economic shocks of the early 1980s prompted this new thinking. The apparent solidarity of the South fell apart as these countries scrambled to adjust to a less favorable international economic environment. The economic recession also heightened competitive economic pressures among the developed countries and led to the adoption of new policies. For the developed countries the ultimate goal remained the same: to be economically competitive. But many developed countries altered the means thought to lead to that end.

Overall, developing countries have been exposed as far more vulnerable than the OECD countries to the economic shocks of the 1980s. They have revised their earlier restrictive approaches and blamed those previous practices as the source of their economic woes. They have also succumbed to increasing pressure from developed countries to open their markets for Northern goods and investments by entering into bilateral investment treaties that guarantee foreigners a more liberal economic environment. They have revised their NIEO approaches and have opted for more liberal rules.

By adopting more liberal economic policies and enforcing antitrust policies, developing countries have embraced the norm of competition. The switch from exclusively targeting subsidiaries of transnational corporations to promoting competition among domestic enterprises reveals the depth of this change. The institutional mechanisms established by the RBP Code in 1980 have come to play an important role in expediting this change. Furthermore, the sequencing of policy change in this area suggests that developing countries have adopted the norm *prior* to adopting the policies.

In intellectual property protection, the collapse of the Paris Convention negotiations coincided with a newly invigorated United States effort to globalize its emerging trade-based conception of intellectual property rights. The United States, faced with competition from Japan and a hemorrhaging trade deficit, realized the significance of intellectual property rights for global competitiveness. The United States' new interests were, in large part, a product of the concerted effort of industry associations. These private sector actors were well positioned to capture the government's attention, in light of the fact that their industries enjoyed positive trade balances and for whom intellectual property constituted valuable competitive assets.

These domestic developments led to amendments to U.S. trade laws to incorporate intellectual property. Later, this trade-based conception of intellectual property rights was incorporated into both NAFTA and the TRIPs accord. The purpose of these efforts was to get other countries to adopt legislation mirroring that of the United States. Developing countries became the objects of coercive bilateral diplomacy, via Section 301, and began to comply with U.S. wishes *on paper*. However, even when faced with credible threats of trade sanctions, developing countries have resisted implementing and enforcing intellectual property protection. Developing countries have yet to be convinced of the benefits of protecting these rights.

In intellectual property protection, cause-and-effect relations are still contested. While the North claims that stronger intellectual property protection will benefit developing countries, this relationship has yet to be demonstrated in either economic theory or empirical proof.[3] Referring to a user-oriented strategy for technological innovation, van Wijk and Junne suggest that, "as international competitiveness is not so much determined by the *production* of new technologies but rather by the *application*, technology policy actually puts increasing emphasis on the *diffusion* of new technologies to their users."[4] This raises questions about the social value of providing inventors with a twenty-year monopoly right, as established in the TRIPs accord. In an era of rapid technological change, unimpeded diffusion has much to recommend it; otherwise, "strong protection of a key innovation may preclude competitors from making socially beneficial innovations."[5] Furthermore, safeguarding these monopoly privileges provokes justifiable fears among technological latecomers seeking to emulate the Japanese strategy of the "fast second" by reverse engineering and rapidly commercializing foreign technologies. The past president of the Licensing Executives Society (LES) Britain and Ireland, Donal

O'Connor pointed out in his candid assessment of the TRIPs accord that the hypothesis linking increased intellectual property protection to technology transfer and investment flows for developing countries "has not by any means been proven. It is one that we in LES wish to accept because it is one that we consider attractive."[6]

Nonetheless, this hypothesis shaped the TRIPs accord. The U.S. TRIPs proposals were based on analyses and estimated loss reports provided by transnational corporate exporters and their industry associations. One developing country critic of the TRIPs agreement suggested that "the governments have simply reproduced these reports without the slightest verification. . . . We now see a new paradigm: the losses of private companies are losses of the developed countries. And the losses of the developed countries are losses for all countries, for all peoples of the world."[7] Despite this skepticism of the basis for the TRIPs accord, developing countries finally assented to its inclusion. Developing countries have limited leverage in the GATT forum, which is precisely why the United States found this venue more attractive than WIPO. Their shift to export-led industrialization makes access to Northern markets essential, and their participation in the WTO will provide benefits, such as Most-Favored Nation status. Yet as indicated in chapter 6, their adherence to these new standards remains an open question and undoubtedly will be a continuing source of tension in the foreseeable future. Developed countries accepted some concessions for developing countries—for instance the opportunity to delay implementation for periods ranging from five to eleven years.

The Dispute Settlement Understanding (DSU) is elaborated in Article 64 of the TRIPs agreement, and instruments range from consultation and voluntary mediation to the suspension of trade concessions. The TRIPs agreement notwithstanding, the United States expects to preserve its right to pursue both Section 301 and GSP action against countries that fail to protect intellectual property. The Industry Functional Advisory Committee on Intellectual Property Rights for Trade Policy Matters takes the position that the United States can continue to pursue these actions, but acknowledges that the extent to which the sanctions of domestic law can be invoked are more limited with the acceptance of the GATT 1994 agreements.[8] Under TRIPs, the United States is supposed to submit complaints to the Dispute Settlement

Body of WTO and abide by the WTO ruling. In its legislation on TRIPs, the U.S. House of Representatives stated that "nothing in this Act shall be construed . . . to limit any authority conferred under any law of the United States, including Section 301 of the Trade Act of 1974, unless specifically provided for in this Act."[9] However, as Shrader suggests, "once the Dispute Settlement Understanding becomes fully effective in the year 2000, the extent to which unilateral action can be taken to remedy a trade practice may become a contentious issue for the United States."[10]

This is important because many of the U.S. industry representatives still are not fully satisfied with either the TRIPs or the NAFTA. Given the fact that they have been the most active in pressing for Section 301 action and GSP suspensions, one should expect this activism to continue. For example, even though industry associations praised NAFTA as the most comprehensive intellectual property agreement ever negotiated, the Business Software Alliance has complained that, "despite the NAFTA, Mexico has neither taken effective action against infringement of intellectual property rights, not has it provided 'expeditious remedies' as effective deterrents to intellectual property violators."[11] Another commentator recently warned high-technology businesses that NAFTA offered little protection. He stated that Mexico's intellectual property enforcement efforts are "an inheritance of past policies and a lack of understanding of the parameters of 'adequate' enforcement. The Mexican administration is making real efforts to educate itself and adapt its system to properly enforce the protection of its grants. . . . Such efforts take far more time than simply changing the wording of laws."[12]

Industry representatives are even more dissatisfied with the TRIPs agreement, which is substantially weaker and less comprehensive than NAFTA. Industry associations have expressed dismay over the transitional period for developing countries, the lack of an obligation to protect against parallel imports (lawfully made goods that are not authorized for distribution in the country where importation is sought, also known as gray-market goods), the "public order" loophole, and weaker border enforcement of infringing articles than they desired.[13] Therefore, industry pressure to pursue Section 301 and GSP actions against infringing countries is unlikely to vanish.

In the area of RBPs, at a time when more developing countries are revising their approaches to conform to more procompetitive antitrust policies of the United States and the European Economic Community, the United States and the European Economic Community are rethinking their former stringent policies. As discussed in chapter 5, both the United States and the European Economic Community have responded to new competitive challenges posed by Japan in high-technology sectors by waiving domestic antitrust provisions for economically strategic industries. In the United States, the economic staffs of the antitrust enforcement agencies adopted the new Chicago school of economics as enforcement criteria.[14] This shift in economic thinking was well-entrenched before Reagan's 1980 election. Therefore, when the Reagan administration sought to weaken antitrust enforcement, implementation proceeded swiftly. The United States redefined its approach to antitrust; it relaxed standards domestically and permitted corporate mergers on an unprecedented scale in an effort to help U.S. industries become more competitive globally. The Justice Department issued new Merger Control Guidelines in 1982 that reflected a more lenient approach to antitrust. The Federal Trade Commission approved the nine largest mergers in U.S. history between 1980 and 1984, and the United States passed the 1982 Export Trading Company Act, granting immunity to export trading companies from antitrust prosecution if approved by Commerce and the Justice Department. The 1984 National Cooperative Research Act spawned over 170 research consortia, including MCC and SEMATECH.

Europeans also redefined their interests in this area and abandoned their "national champions" strategies in favor of technological collaboration. High-technology joint ventures became exempt from the Treaty of Rome's antitrust provisions, and horizontal R & D was encouraged under the European Commission's 1984 Regulation No. 418/85. The European Economic Community also formed several important research consortia. Additionally, "joint production ventures are eligible for automatic exemptions from antitrust laws if the participating firms control less than twenty percent of the market. Ventures that cannot obtain this automatic exemption are eligible for individual exemptions."[15]

As in the case of intellectual property protection, there is currently little consensus on the merits of antitrust policies in the context of competitiveness. For example, David Teece and Thomas Jorde have joined the chorus against strict domestic enforcement on the premise that it is a hindrance to innovation.[16] As discussed in chapter 5, some commentators have indicated that Japan's more lax laws in this area have provided the Japanese with unfair advantages. Deborah Wince-Smith, speaking on behalf of the U.S. Department of Commerce in 1993, said that "friction is on the rise because there are very real disparities among various nations' policies governing competition, trade, investment and, of course, intellectual property rights. Too often these disparities have created an uneven playing field."[17] Yet in the domestic context, a number of observers have concluded that "the time has come for the pendulum to swing back towards stricter enforcement."[18] For example, Anne Bingaman, the assistant attorney general in charge of the Justice Department's Antitrust Division, has become an outspoken critic of lax domestic enforcement. Taking issue with the arguments that foreign firms are succeeding because of permissible cartel and collaborative activity denied to U.S. firms, she indicated her belief that cartel activity did not promote innovation and that "firms that prosper are more likely to be those that face fierce rivalry in their home markets rather than the sheltered monopolists."[19] While expressing a commitment to tightening domestic standards, the Justice Department has pursued an aggressive enforcement policy against anticompetitive practices abroad.

The United States has pressured Japan to adopt tougher laws in the Structural Impediments Initiatives agreements. The United States has also continued to consult with the European Economic Community and concluded an antitrust cooperation agreement in 1991 that expands information sharing obligations on both sides. In April 1992 the Justice Department restored its pre-1988 position of enforcing anticompetitive conduct abroad that harms U.S. export commerce; according to Rill, this is "consistent with and more accurately illustrates the increasingly global nature of markets and the increasingly significant role of import and export commerce on the U.S. economy."[20] However, a June 1993 U.S. Supreme Court decision, *Hartford Fire Insurance Co. v. California*, provided insight into the debate over antitrust policy. The majority held, in a 5-to-4 decision, that U.S. antitrust laws apply to conduct by non-U.S. citizens occurring outside the United States, even if that conduct was legal where it occurred. The dissenting opinion maintained that "the majority had stated a 'breathtakingly broad proposition . . . that will bring the Sherman Act and other laws into sharp and unnecessary conflict with the legitimate interests of other countries—particularly our closest trading partners.' "[21]

While the dissenting opinion revealed concerns over potential conflicts engendered by an aggressive enforcement policy abroad, the United States has continued to pursue this policy. In May 1994 the Justice Department filed a complaint against the British company Pilkington PLC and a U.S. subsidiary. Pilkington was charged with abusing its patent and trade secret rights by incorporating territorial and use restrictions deemed to reduce licensees' incentives to innovate.[22] Pilkington settled the case in order to avoid expensive litigation, and Bingaman remarked that "the *Pilkington* case is a paradigm for how U.S. antitrust enforcement can foster innovation and open export markets previously closed for anticompetitive practices."[23] Market access considerations were central to a June 1994 complaint, *U.S. v. MCI Communications Corp.*, over a proposed vertically integrated joint venture between MCI and British Telecommunications PLC. The consent decree issued by the Justice Department incorporated provisions to prevent discrimination against U.S. carriers seeking the opportunity to interconnect with British Telecomm's U.K. network. Bingaman praised the decree as contributing to nondiscriminatory access to the U.K. market for U.S. firms, and pointed to the decree as an example of using U.S. antitrust laws to "protect U.S. competition from mergers that threaten the misuse of foreign monopoly power."[24]

Governments' concerns over market access are shared by firms, and the transfer of technology has become increasing complex. As Cowhey and Aronson point out, "one of the most dramatic changes of the past three decades is the growth of political and economic activity outside the traditional jurisdiction and organizing principles of states."[25] Overall, developed countries' policymakers and industries all realize that this new era is qualitatively different than that which preceded it. Brian N. Smith, chairman and chief executive of Metal Box PLC, expressed this awareness: "we live in world markets and can no longer shelter within our own country, secure in the knowledge of our local competitors and the loyalty of our customers. Changes in markets, technology, interest rates, currencies, government controls, suppliers' costs and competitors' thrusts are all happening all the time."[26] Whatever consensus existed in simpler times has been thrown into doubt. The experts do not agree, nor do policymakers. Peter Waite, chief executive officer of a large chemical and petroleum concern based in London, pointed out that changed economic conditions and lack of consensus among the experts have been coupled with the economic challenge posed by Japan and the East Asian NICs.[27]

Both the private sector and developed countries' governments have responded quickly to these new challenges in an effort to remain economically competitive. In TOT investment patterns, RBPs, and intellectual property, significant changes have taken place. Firms face new challenges. According to Mowrey and Rosenberg, "rising development costs place severe strains on the ability of firms to sustain ambitious R & D programs and increase the importance of penetration of foreign markets to ensure commercial success."[28] Faced with uncertain economic futures, technology suppliers and investors have felt increasing pressure to reduce economic risk; this pressure has important consequences for the international transfer of technology. For example, in sectors particularly reliant on patent protection, such as chemicals and pharmaceuticals, firms are most concerned with maintaining control over their valuable technology. Referring in particular to the chemical and pharmaceutical majors, a technology contractor pointed out that in an effort to control their destiny, producers have begun "to maximize their profit from each technology by extending their involvement and control from feedstock to final packaged product. . . . Risk has been subordinated to control—the control of the market—and as a consequence of that control dependence, the hurdle rate for new technology has been raised."[29] This preoccupation with control of market volume is manifest in specialization in fewer product areas and reduced product diversification. Waite suggests that this trend has had negative effects on licensing new technology because it has become less available. As a contractor he has seen his technology portfolio decline.[30]

Sectors such as microelectronics, commercial aircraft, and telecommunications equipment are less reliant on patent protection. Yet they too face rapidly increasing product costs and a variety of nontariff trade barriers, such as government procurement policies. Furthermore, technological capabilities, in part increased as a result of "fast second" strategies and changes in the economics of innovation, have become more global. These industries increasingly have pursued technological collaboration through strategic corporate alliances with foreign firms in order to spread the economic risks, gain access to foreign capital and technology, and, most significantly, gain market access. As Mowrey and Rosenberg point out, "the asset provided in exchange for market access is technology."[31] Cowhey and Aronson suggest that these emerging international corporate alliances are "part of the problem for policymakers but part of the solution for private firms."[32] They challenge policymakers by blurring regulatory boundaries, but they help corporations address pressures of escalating costs and the quest for market access. These alliances have accelerated the diffusion of internationally new technology.

It is clear that international technology transfer has become far more complex than it was just a few decades ago. Developing countries have abandoned restrictive policies and have begun to play by the developed countries' rules in an effort to attract foreign investment and technology. However, due to competitive economic pressure among developed countries—particularly the United States, Europe, and Japan—new tensions between technological diffusion and domestic regulatory policies have come to the fore and served to create new uncertainties. Most analysts agree that ideas are apt to have their greatest impact in times characterized by crisis or uncerainty. Therefore, it is particularly important to focus attention on the origins of preferences, the substance of new ideas, and how they are presented as solutions to pressing problems.

This book has argued that theories pitched at a high level of abstraction (such as neorealism) and instrumentalist/rationalist theories (such as neoliberal institutionalism) assume away interesting questions and deflect analysts' attention away from some important factors in international politics. Both types of theorizing provide useful insights into the cases presented here but paint an incomplete and distorted picture. Insofar as these theories treat interests as exogenous, they neglect the questions of where interests come from, how interests are defined, and how they change over time. The analysis presented here has emphasized interests as endogenous and focused on how the actors themselves interpret their circumstances. I contend that actors in international politics have the power to choose and the power to change. States do not respond in identical ways to similar constraints or opportunities.

By combining explanations pitched at the systemic level with those incorporating domestic politics, this book has provided insights into the source and substance of national interests and the role of ideas. Particular economic ideas were enormously important in the formation of a "Third World" identity, developing countries' national and regional legislation, negotiating bloc, and multilateral agenda. A different set of economic ideas was influential in the United States' redefinition of its approach to antitrust. One of the more striking changes over the time period examined here was the United States' redefinition of its interests in intellectual property. Within a very short period of time, the United States began vigorously to protect patent holders rights, institutionalized them in domestic laws and practices, and effectively sought to globalize this new conception. Ideas help states redefine interests; sometimes they are the product of influential economists, sometimes they are the product of mobilized interest groups. Ideas matter when they are institutionalized in the domestic practices of states, and those practices come into conflict with those of other states.

Overall, this book has presented proximate causes for particular changes in intellectual property and antitrust attitudes and policies. Perhaps this analysis could be made compatible with structural and instrumentalist/rationalist theories. The explanations presented here might well fit into a broader Gramscian analysis, like a nested Chinese box. However, analysts seeking to extend the explanatory power of the more abstract theories would have to demonstrate causal connections between the permissive conditions or broad patterns delineated by their theories and the substantive fluctuations in ideas and interests presented here.

The cases analyzed in this study, and particularly the aftermath of the negotiations, provide a vivid example of how states have redefined their interests in international technology transfer. My analysis suggests that in order to understand past and emerging global trends in the international transfer of technology between developed and developing countries, it is necessary to examine how policymakers redefine their interests and how their new interests are manifested in response to opportunities and constraints. This requires explicit consideration of domestic politics and the role of both ideas and institutions, in conjunction with an appreciation of asymmetrical power relationships.

Notes

Introduction

1. See for example, Bernard Hoekman and Petros Mavroidis, "Competition, Competition Policy and the GATT," *The World Economy* Vol. 17, No. 2 (March 1994), pp. 121–150.

Chapter 1

1. See for example, Stephen Krasner, *Structural Conflict: The Third World Against Global Liberalism* (Berkeley: University of California Press, 1985).

2. See for example, Judith Goldstein and Robert Keohane, eds., *Ideas and Foreign Policy* (Ithaca: Cornell University Press, 1993). With the exception of Geoffrey Garrett and Barry Weingast, "Ideas, Interests, and Institutions: Constructing the European Community's Internal Market," the case studies in this volume all test the null hypothesis "that variation in policy across countries, or over time, is entirely accounted for by changes in factors *other than* ideas" (p. 6). Admittedly, the editors were interested in explaining the effects of given ideas rather than the origins of the same. However,

placing ideas *in opposition* to interests stacks the deck against revealing much independent influence of ideas. By design, then, ideas could only have a supplementary, not central, role in explanation.

3. Neorealist explanations argue that powerful states determine the rules of the game. For prominent examples, see Robert Gilpin, *War and Change in World Politics* (Princeton, NJ: Princeton University Press, 1985); Krasner (1985); and Kenneth Waltz, *Theories of International Politics* (New York: McGraw Hill, 1979). Robert Keohane, a neoliberal institutionalist, in *After Hegemony* (Princeton, NJ: Princeton University Press, 1987), parts company with the realist arguments of Gilpin and Waltz insofar as he accords a stronger role for international institutions. However, his functionalist argument, that international institutions can reduce transaction costs, monitor opportunistic behavior, and reduce the incidence of cheating, places him squarely in the rationalist camp. Both neorealists and neoliberal institutionalists treat interests as exogenous. By contrast, interpretivist analyses eschew rational choice assumptions and examine the role of norms, ideas, and nonstate actors as independent variables. According to this perspective, norms can mitigate the affects of international anarchy, and institutions can play a transformative (not merely functional) role in international politics. Examples of neoliberal interpretivist scholarship include: Ernst Haas, *When Knowledge is Power* (Berkeley: University of California Press, 1989); Emmanuel Adler, *The Power of Ideology* (Berkeley: University of California Press, 1987); Kathryn Sikkink, *Ideas and Institutions* (Ithaca: Cornell University Press, 1991); and John Ruggie, "Territoriality and Beyond," *International Organization* Vol. 47, No. 1 (Winter 1993), pp. 139–174. Additionally, Charles Lipson's *Standing Guard: Protecting Foreign Capital in the Nineteenth and Twentieth Centuries* (Berkeley: University of California Press, 1985) addresses the intersubjective dimensions of international politics. For a general discussion of the relevant differences between rationalist and interpretivist approaches to the analysis of international relations see John Ruggie and Friedrich Kratochwil, "IOs as an Art of the State: A Regime Critique," *International Organization* Vol. 40, No. 4 (Autumn 1986), pp. 753–776.

4. E. H. Carr, *The Twenty Years' Crisis: 1919–1939* (London: Macmillan, 1946).

5. Stephen Krasner, *Defending the National Interest* (Princeton: Princeton University Press, 1978), especially pp. 332–333.

6. For international relations treatments of structuration theory, see Alexander Wendt, "The Agent-Structure Problem," *International Organization* Vol. 41, No. 3 (Summer 1987), pp. 355–365. For examples of Gramscian analysis, see Craig Murphy, *International Organization and Industrial Change: Global Governance Since 1850* (New York: Oxford University Press, 1994);

and Enrico Augelli and Craig Murphy, "Gramsci and International Relations: a General Perspective with Examples from Recent US Policy Toward the Third World," in Stephen Gill, ed., *Gramsci, Historical Materialism and International Relations* (Cambridge: Cambridge University Press, 1993).

7. Robert Keohane and Joseph Nye Jr., *"Power and Interdependence Revisited," International Organization*, Vol. 41, No. 4 (Autumn 1987), p. 749.

8. This is particularly the case in my discussion of changes in U.S. policy in both intellectual property protection and antitrust.

9. For a trenchant critique of rational choice approaches, see Donald Green and Ian Shapiro, *Pathologies of Rational Choice Theory: A Critique of Applications in Political Science* (New Haven: Yale University Press, 1994).

10. Krasner (1985).

11. Arthur Stein, "Coordination and Collaboration: Regimes in an Anarchic World," in Krasner, *International Regimes* (Ithaca: Cornell University Press, 1983), p. 132, 140.

12. Robert Keohane, "The Demand for International Regimes," in Krasner (1983), p. 141.

13. Ibid., p. 154.

14. John Ruggie, "Multilateralism: The Anatomy of an Institution," in John Ruggie, ed., *Multilateralism Matters* (New York: Columbia University Press, 1993), p. 30.

15. Roger K. Smith, "Explaining the Non-Proliferation Regime: Anomalies for Contemporary International Relations Theory," *International Organization* Vol. 41, No. 2 (Spring 1987), pp. 253–281, quote at p. 276.

16. Ernst Haas, *When Knowledge Is Power* (Berkeley: University of California Press, 1989), p. 77.

17. Friedrich Kratochwil, "Norms Versus Numbers: Multilateralism and the Rationalist and Reflexivist Approaches to Institutions—A Unilateral Plea for Communicative Rationality," in Ruggie (1993), p. 444.

18. The "debate" between neorealism and neoliberal institutionalism has dominated American international relations scholarship in recent years. See, for example, David Baldwin, *Neorealism and Neoliberalism: The Contemporary Debate* (New York: Columbia University Press, 1993). Yet in fact, the two perspectives share many of the same assumptions. The differences between them are not large, especially as compared to the "debate" between realism and utopianism highlighted by E. H. Carr's *The Twenty Years' Crisis* (1946). Steve Smith, commenting on the debate between neorealism and neoliberal institutionalism, states: "in an important sense they are part of a specific view of international politics rather than two alternatives that together define the space within which the debate about international theory

takes place. If this is where the action is, it takes place within a very narrow space" (Smith, "The Self-Images of a Discipline: A Genealogy of International Relations Theory," in Ken Booth and Steve Smith, eds., *International Relations Theory Today* [University Park, PA: The Pennsylvania State University Press, 1995], p. 24).

19. James Caporaso, "International Relations Theory and Multilateralism: The Search for Foundations," in Ruggie, (1993), pp. 80–81.

20. Keohane and Nye (1987), p. 752.

21. On this point see, Alexander Wendt and David Friedheim, "Hierarchy under Anarchy: Informal Empire and the East German State," *International Organization*, Vol. 49, No. 4 (Autumn 1995), pp. 689–721, especially at p. 692.

22. Ernst Haas, "Words Can Hurt You: Or Who Said What to Whom about Regimes," in Krasner, (1983), p. 58.

23. Audie Klotz, "Reconstituting Interests: Interpretive Analysis of Norms in International Relations," unpublished manuscript, revised draft (November 1992), p. 11.

24. Goldstein and Keohane (1993).

25. The lone exception to this positing of ideas versus interests is the chapter by Geoffrey Garrett and Barry Weingast, "Ideas, Interests, and Institutions: Constructing the European Community's Internal Market," in Goldstein and Keohane (1993), pp. 173–206. As Garrett and Weingast state, "we wish to integrate ideas and interests rather than segregate them" (p. 185).

26. As Jacobsen suggests, "economic ideas matter because they are 'clusters of ideas/interests' that define productive arrangements" (John Kurt Jacobsen, "Much Ado about Ideas: The Cognitive Factor in Economic Policy," *World Politics* Vol. 47, No. 2 [January 1995], pp. 283–310, especially at 309).

27. Ngaire Woods, "Economic Ideas and International Relations: Beyond Rational Neglect," *International Studies Quarterly* Vol. 39, No. 2 (June 1995), p. 170.

28. Jacobsen (1995), p. 307.

29. Ernst Haas, "Why Collaborate? Issue-Linkage and International Regimes," *World Politics* Vol. 32 (April 1980), pp. 367–368.

30. Ibid., pp. 386 and 390.

31. Robert Rothstein, "Consensual Knowledge and International Collaboration: Some Lessons from the Commodity Negotiations," *International Organization* Vol. 38, No. 4 (Autumn 1984) p. 736.

32. Woods (1995), p. 174.

33. Alexander Wendt, "Anarchy Is What States Make It," *International Organization* Vol. 46, No. 2 (Spring 1992), pp. 391–425.

34. Haas (1989), chapter 8.

35. Stephan Haggard and Beth Simmons, "Theories of International Regimes," *International Organization* Vol. 41, No. 3 (Summer 1987), p. 498.

36. Friedrich Kratochwil, *Rules, Norms, and Decisions* (Cambridge: Cambridge University Press, 1989), p. 12.

37. Haggard and Simmons (1987), p. 512.

38. Ibid., p. 510.

39. The Andean Pact's Decision 24 (1970); Argentine Laws 19,231 (1971) and 20,794 (1973); Brazil's Ordinance 15, "Normative Act" (1975); Mexico's "Law Governing the Registry for the Transfer of Technology and the Use and Exploitation of Patents and Trademarks" (1972), and India's Patents Act (1970).

40. Jagdish N. Bhagwati, "Rethinking Global Negotiations," in Jagdish N. Bhagwati and John Gerard Ruggie, eds., *Power, Passions, and Purpose: Prospects for North-South Negotiations* (Cambridge, MA: MIT Press, 1984), pp. 23–25.

41. Roger D. Hansen, *Beyond the North-South Stalemate* (New York: McGraw-Hill Book Company, 1979), p. 25.

42. Ibid., p. 21.

43. Ibid., p. 22.

44. Manuel Agosin and David Gold, "Recent Trends in FDI and Related Activities by TNCs," *The CTC Reporter* No. 21 (Spring 1986), p. 21.

45. Woods (1995), p. 176.

46. Thomas Biersteker, "The 'Triumph' of Neoclassical Economics in the Developing World: Policy Convergence and Bases of Governance in the International Economic Order," in James Rosenau and Ernst-Otto Czempiel, eds., *Governance without Government: Order and Change in World Politics* (New York: Cambridge University Press, 1992), pp. 102–131, especially at p. 123.

47. Nigel Harris, *The End of the Third World* (London: I. B. Tauris and Co. Ltd., 1986), pp. 165–166.

48. Woods (1995), p. 176.

Chapter 2

1. Jack Baranson and Robin Roark, "Trends in North-South Transfer of High Technology," in Nathan Rosenberg and Claudio Frischtak, eds., *International Technology Transfer: Concepts, Measures, and Comparisons* (New York: Praeger Publishers, 1985), p. 26.

2. Melvin Kranzberg, "The Technical Elements in International Technology Transfer: Historical Perspectives," in John R. McIntyre and David S.

Papp, eds., *The Political Economy of International Technology Transfer* (New York: Quorum Books, 1986), p. 32.

3. Ibid.

4. Ibid.

5. John R. McIntyre, "Critical Perspectives on International Technology Transfer," in McIntyre and Papp (1986), p. 34.

6. David Landes, quoted in William R. Kinter and Harvey Sicherman, *Technology and International Politics* (Lexington, MA: Lexington Books, D. C. Heath and Company, 1975), p. 92.

7. Kranzberg, in McIntyre and Papp (1986), p. 35.

8. Gerard Curzon, "Introduction," in Gerard Curzon and Victoria Curzon, eds., *The Multinational Enterprise in a Hostile World* (London: Macmillan Press Ltd., 1977), p. 3.

9. Ibid.

10. Ibid.

11. These terms are from Baranson and Roark, in Rosenberg and Frischtak (1985) p. 27.

12. Ibid.

13. Ibid., pp. 34–35.

14. Alexander Gerschenkron, "Economic Backwardness in Historical Perspective," in B. Hoselitz, ed., *The Progress of Underdeveloped Areas* (Chicago: University of Chicago Press, 1952), p. 8.

15. Baranson and Roark, in Rosenberg and Frischtak (1985), p. 37.

16. Nathan Rosenberg, *Inside the Black Box: Technology and Economics* (Cambridge: Cambridge University Press, 1982), chapter 6.

17. Rosenberg (1982), chapter 6.

18. Kranzberg, in McIntyre and Papp (1986), p. 35.

19. Ibid.

20. Curzon, in Curzon and Curzon (1977), p. 6.

21. John Ruggie, "Embedded Liberalism Revisited: Institutions and Progress in International Economic Relations," in Emmanuel Adler and Beverly Crawford, eds., *Progress in Postwar International Relations* (New York: Columbia University Press, 1991), pp. 201–234.

22. For a comprehensive analysis of this, see Robert Gilpin, *The Political Economy of International Relations* (Princeton, NJ: Princeton University Press, 1987).

23. Philip J. Meeks, "West-West Technology Transfer: The Dilemmas of Cooperation and Conflict," in McIntyre and Papp (1986), p. 141.

24. Joan Edelman Spero, *The Politics of International Economic Relations* (New York: St. Martin's Press, 1977), p. 91.

25. Ibid., p. 94.

26. Meeks, in McIntyre and Papp (1986), p. 148.

27. Karl P. Sauvant and Elton R. Lanier, "Host-Country Councils: Concepts and Legal Aspects," in Norbert Horn, ed., *Legal Problems of Codes of Conduct for Multinational Enterprises* (Deventer, the Netherlands: B. V. Kluwer, 1980), p. 344.

28. Rainer Hellman, "The Multinational Enterprise, the Nation State and Regional Groupings," in Curzon and Curzon (1977), p. 120.

29. This paragraph based on Meeks, in McIntyre and Papp (1986), p. 148.

30. Meeks, in McIntyre and Papp (1986), p. 148.

31. Richard R. Nelson, *High-Technology Policies: A Five Nation Comparison* (Washington, DC: American Enterprise Institute for Public Policy Research, 1984), p. 40.

32. David C. Mowrey and Nathan Rosenberg, *Technology and the Pursuit of Economic Growth* (New York: Cambridge University Press, 1991), p. 222.

33. Dennis Encarnation, *Rivals beyond Trade: America versus Japan in Global Competition* (Ithaca: Cornell University Press, 1992), p. 203.

34. Ibid., p. 70.

35. Mowrey and Rosenberg (1991), p. 223.

36. Ibid., p. 229.

37. Ibid., p. 232.

38. Stephen D. Krasner, *Structural Conflict* (Berkeley: University of California Press, 1985), p. 185.

39. C. Fred Bergsten, Thomas Horst, and Theodore H. Moran, *American Multinationals and American Interests* (Washington, DC: The Brookings Institution, 1978), pp. 371–372.

40. Ibid., p. 372.

41. Ibid.

42. Ibid., p. 370.

43. Anne O. Krueger, "Benefits and Costs of Late Development," in Patrice Higonnet, David S. Landes, and Henry Rosovsky, eds., *Favorites of Fortune: Technology, Growth, and Economic Development since the Industrial Revolution* (Cambridge: Harvard University Press, 1991), pp. 473–474.

44. Aqueil Ahmad and Arthur S. Wilke, "Technology Transfer in the New International Economic Order: Options, Obstacles, and Dilemmas," in McIntyre and Papp (1986), pp. 87–88.

45. Bergsten, Horst, and Moran (1978), p. 372, fn. 30.

46. Raymond Vernon, "The Curious Character of the International Technology Market: An Economic Perspective," in McIntyre and Papp (1986), pp. 48–49.

47. Gerschenkron (1952), p. 24.

48. Ngaire Woods, "Economic Ideas and International Relations: Beyond Rational Neglect," *International Studies Quarterly* Vol. 39, No. 2 (June 1995), pp. 161–180.

49. For an insightful history of the rise and decline of the idea of "Third Worldism," see Nigel Harris, *The End of the Third World* (London: Z. B. Tauris and Co. Ltd., 1986). Quote from page 18.

50. Robert Rothstein, *The Weak in the World of the Strong* (New York: Columbia University Press, 1977), pp. 83–84.

51. Harris (1986) p. 121.

52. Charles Oman and Ganeshan Wignaraja, *The Postwar Evolution of Development Thinking* (New York: St. Martin's Press, 1991), p. 138.

53. Harris (1986), p. 122.

54. Howard V. Perlmutter, "Perplexing Routes to M.N.E. Legitimacy: Codes of Conduct for Technology Transfer," *Stanford Journal of International Studies* Vol. XI (Spring 1976), p. 178.

55. Bergsten, Horst, and Moran (1978), p. 372.

56. Ibid., p. 373.

57. Ibid., p. 136.

58. Ibid., p. 137.

59. Krasner (1985), from table 7.3, p. 184.

60. Bergsten, Horst, and Moran (1978), p. 376.

61. Douglas Bennett and Kenneth Sharpe, *Transnational Corporations versus the State: The Political Economy of the Mexican Auto Industry* (Princeton, NJ: Princeton University Press, 1985), p. 35.

62. Van Whiting, Jr., *The Political Economy of Foreign Investment in Mexico: Nationalism, Liberalism, and Constraints on Choice* (Baltimore, MD: Johns Hopkins University Press, 1992), p. 82.

63. Bennett and Sharpe (1985), p. 36.

64. Bergsten, Horst, and Moran (1978), p. 376.

65. Bennett and Sharpe (1985), p. 196.

66. Ibid., p. 118.

67. Ibid., p. 37.

68. Bergsten, Horst, and Moran (1978), p. 377.

69. Ibid., p. 378.

70. A vast literature addresses reasons why these countries departed from the prevailing developing country "model" of ISI. Some authors emphasize unique external factors, such as these countries' strategic importance to the United States during the Cold War and the Japanese colonial legacy; others emphasize cultural aspects and internal factors that led to the adoption of export-oriented growth strategies. For a helpful review of a representative

sampling of this literature, see David Kang, "South Korean and Taiwanese Development and the New Institutional Economics," *International Organization* Vol. 49, No. 3 (Summer 1995), pp. 555–587.

71. Robert Wade, *Governing the Market: Economic Theory and the Role of Government in East Asian Industrialization* (Princeton, NJ: Princeton University Press, 1990), p. 149.

72. Ibid., p. 150.

73. Ibid.

74. D. Michael Shafer, *Winners and Losers: How Sectors Shape the Development Prospects of States* (Ithaca: Cornell University Press 1994), pp. 125–126.

75. Encarnation (1992), p. 164.

76. Shafer (1994), p. 111.

77. Bon Ho Koo, "The Role of the Newly Industrializing Economies in the Global and Pacific Economic Network," *Business in the Contemporary World* Vol. II, No. 3 (Spring 1990), p. 36.

78. David Yoffie, *Power and Protectionism* (New York: Columbia University Press, 1983)

79. Irma Adelman, "Prometheus Unbound and Developing Countries," in Higonnet, Landes, and Rosovsky (1991), p. 501.

80. Klaus-Heinrich Standke, "The Prospects and Retrospects of the United Nations Conference on Science and Technology for Development," *Technology in Society* Vol. 1 (1979), p. 357.

81. Rothstein (1977), p. 147.

82. Anila Graham, "The Transfer of Technology: A Test Case in the North-South Dialogue," *Journal of International Affairs* Vol. 33, No. 1 (Spring/ Summer 1979), p. 2.

83. Ibid., pp. 2–3.

84. Roger Hansen, *Beyond the North-South Stalemate* (New York: McGraw-Hill Book Company, 1979), pp. 20–21.

85. The Andean Pact's Decision 24 (1970); Argentine Laws 19,231 (1971) and 20,794 (1973); Brazil's Ordinance 15 ("Normative Act" of 1975); Mexico's "Law Governing the Registry for the Transfer of Technology and the Use and Exploitation of Patents and Trademarks" (1972); Indian Patents Act (1970).

86. Countess Pease Jeffries, "An Evaluation of the UNCTAD Code of Conduct," *Harvard International Law Journal* Vol. 18, No. 2 (Spring 1977), p. 319.

87. Emmanuel Adler, *The Power of Ideology: The Quest for Technological Autonomy in Argentina and Brazil* (Berkeley: University of California Press, 1987), p. 71.

88. Ibid., p. 78.

89. Ibid., p. 60.

90. Ibid., p. 69.

91. For a statement of this alarmist perspective on commodity power, see C. F. Bergsten, "The Threat from the Third World," *Foreign Policy* Vol. 11 (1973), pp. 102–104; and C. F. Bergsten, "The Threat Is Real," *Foreign Policy* Vol. 14 (1974), pp. 84–90.

92. George S. Trisciuzzi, "Multilateral Regulation of Foreign Direct Investment," in Bart S. Fisher and Jeff Turner, eds., *Regulating the Multinational Enterprise* (New York: Praeger Publishers, 1983), p. 150.

93. Spero (1977), p. 105.

94. Ibid., p. 113.

95. Phillipe Levy, "The OECD Declaration on International Investment and Multinational Enterprises," in Seymour Rubin and Gary Clyde Hufbauer, eds., *Emerging Standards of International Trade and Investment: Multinational Codes and Corporate Conduct* (Totowa, NJ: Rowman and Allanheld, 1983), p. 48.

96. Paul A. Tharp Jr., "Transnational Enterprises and International Regulation: A Survey of Various Approaches in International Organizations," *International Organization* Vol. 30, No. 1 (Winter 1976), p. 58.

97. Ibid., p. 59.

98. Ibid.

99. Levy, in Rubin and Hufbauer (1983), p. 58.

100. Ibid.

101. Stephan Coonrod, "The United Nations' Code of Conduct for Transnational Corporations," *Harvard International Law Journal*, Vol. 18, No. 2 (Spring 1977), pp. 286–287.

Chapter 3

1. Jack Baranson, *North-South Technology Transfer: Financing and Institution Building* (Mt. Airy, MD: Lomond Publications, 1981), p. 5.

2. Ibid., p. 105.

3. Carlos Correa, "Technology Transfer in Latin America: A Decade of Control," *Journal of World Trade Law* Vol. 15 (1981), p. 393.

4. Ibid.

5. Baranson (1981), p. 21.

6. Ibid., p. 152.

7. Ibid.

8. Ibid., p. 153.

9. Ibid.

10. Ibid.

11. Ibid., p. 55. On this point, also see Stephen Krasner, *Structural Conflict: The Third World against Global Liberalism* (Berkeley: University of California Press, 1985), pp. 50–58.

12. Baranson (1981), p. 57.

13. Ibid., p. 61.

14. Ibid.

15. Countess Pease-Jeffries, "An Evaluation of the UNCTAD Code of Conduct," *Harvard International Law Journal* Vol. 18, No. 2 (Spring 1977), p. 320.

16. Ibid., p. 319.

17. The Pugwash Conference on Science and World Affairs is a non-governmental forum for technical deliberations among scientists from the East and West. The first conference was held in 1955, where Bertrand Russell and Albert Einstein presented a manifesto for peace. The Pugwash group has been prominently involved in urging the development of nuclear-testing agreements between the former Soviet Union and the United States, and has been active in the disarmament movement.

18. Pugwash Conference on Science and World Affairs, "Draft Code of Conduct on the Transfer of Technology," *World Development* Vol. 2, Nos. 4 and 5 (April/May 1974), p. 77.

19. Debra Lynn Miller, "Panacea or Problem? The Proposed International Code of Conduct for Technology Transfer," *Journal of International Affairs* Vol. 33, No. 1 (Spring/Summer 1979), pp. 55–56.

20. Dennis Thompson, "The UNCTAD Code on Transfer of Technology," *Journal of World Trade Law* Vol. 16, No. 4 (July/August 1982), p. 313.

21. This paragraph is based on discussion in Miller (1979), p. 56.

22. UNCTAD, "Draft Outline for the Preparation of an International Code of Conduct on Transfer of Technology," submitted by the expert from Japan on behalf of the experts from Group B, TD/B/C.6/1/Annex II (Geneva, 1975), pp. 1–2.

23. Thompson (1982), p. 323.

24. The UNCTAD Committee on Transfer of Technology prepared a number of background studies that pertained to both the code of conduct negotiations and the Paris Convention revision conferences. These included: TD/B/C.6/AC.2/3, "The International Patent System as an Instrument of Policy for National Development"; TD/B/C.6/111, "Restructuring the Legal Environment: (b) National Laws and Regulations on the Transfer, Acquisition and Development of Technology"; and TD/B/C.6/91, "Restructuring the Legal Environment: International Transfer of Technology."

25. UNCTAD, "United Nations Conference on an International Code of Conduct on the Transfer of Technology: Background Note by the UNCTAD Secretariat," TD/Code TOT/4 (Geneva, September 6, 1978), p. 7, para. 33.

26. Ibid.

27. Ibid., p. 8, para. 34.

28. Ibid.

29. Thompson (1982), p. 323.

30. Pedro Roffe, "Transfer of Technology: UNCTAD's Draft International Code of Conduct," *International Lawyer* Vol. 19, No. 2 (Spring 1985), p. 690.

31. Correa (1981), pp. 401–402.

32. Roffe (1985), p. 700.

33. Ibid.

34. UNCTAD, "Draft International Code of Conduct on the Transfer of Technology," TD/Code TOT/47 (Geneva, June 5, 1985), pp. 8–10.

35. Miller (1979), pp. 58–59.

36. Thompson (1982), p. 333.

37. Ibid. Thompson cites the following cases in footnote 12 of page 33: *Saudi Arabia v. Arabian American Oil Company (Aramco),* 27 Intl L. Rep. (1963); and *Sapphire International Petroleum Ltd. v. National Iranian Oil Company,* 35 Intl L. Rep. (1967), p. 136.

38. Roffe (1985), p. 703.

39. UNCTAD, "Summary Record of the Eighth Meeting," TD/Code TOT/SR.8 (Geneva, February 29, 1979), p. 6, para. 27.

40. Ibid., p. 3, para. 10.

41. UNCTAD, "Summary Record of the Fourteenth Meeting," TD/Code TOT/SR.14 (Geneva, May 8, 1980), p. 4, para. 16.

42. Miller (1979), p. 45.

43. Ibid.

44. UNCTAD, "The Draft of an International Code of Conduct on the Transfer of Technology: Major Issues Outstanding," TD/Code TOT/27 (Geneva, November 17, 1980), p. 9, para. 40.

45. Author's interviews with Group of 77 delegations, Geneva, 1986.

46. Statement by Gerald B. Helman in "UNCTAD: A Declaration of United States Policy," *Journal of World Trade Law* Vol. 16, No. 5 (September/October 1982), p. 457.

47. Robert D. Hormats, "International Economic Policy Priorities," *U.S. Department of State Bulletin* Vol. 18, No. 2052 (July 1981), p. 27.

48. W. Allen Wallis, "American Policy to Promote World Development," *U.S. Department of State Bulletin* Vol. 83, No. 2077 (August 1983), p. 28.

49. Author's interview with UNCTAD personnel, Geneva, 1986.

50. Furthermore, to illustrate the group system as an impediment to further progress, after the sixth session of the conference, a privately sponsored meeting was convened in Montreaux. The participants were the negotiators themselves, and the purpose was to see if the negotiators from the regional groups could devise mutually acceptable language for resolving the

outstanding issues. They arrived at a mutually acceptable compromise on the most contentious issues. However, when they returned to Geneva, the negotiators disavowed these agreements and immediately adopted their requisite hard-line positions on the issues. This example points to problems posed by the group system; the real issues were not so much drafting problems as they were both political and bureaucratic problems.

51. Author's interview with Group of 77 delegate, Geneva, 1986.

52. Author's interview at U.S. Mission, Geneva, 1986.

53. Author's interview at U.S. Mission, Geneva, 1986.

54. Author's interview at U.S. Mission, Geneva, 1986.

55. Wallis (1983), p. 30.

56. Author's interview at U.S. Mission, Geneva, 1986.

57. Nigel Harris, *The End of the Third World* (London: I. B. Tauris, 1986), p. 168.

58. Ibid., pp. 165–166.

59. Ibid., p. 166.

60. Ibid.

61. Jorge Otamendi, "Update on Licensing in Argentina," *Les Nouvelles* Vol. XXII, No. 4 (December 1987), p. 166.

62. Ibid.

63. Harris (1986), p. 88.

64. "Andean Pact Seeks EEC Investment," *Latin American Regional Reports* (Andean Group Report), RA-87-07 (September 3, 1987), p. 4.

65. "Andean Pact: Little Substance Left," *Latin American Weekly Report*, WR-87-20 (May 28, 1987), pp. 6–7.

66. "Andean Pact Seeks EEC Investment" (1987), p. 4.

67. Ibid.

68. Ibid.

69. Harris (1986), p. 116.

70. George Shultz, "The U.S. and the Developing World: Our Joint Stake in the World Economy," *U.S. Department of State Bulletin* Vol. 83, No. 2076 (July 1983), p. 58.

71. "Latin America Isolated at UNCTAD VII," *Latin American Weekly Report*, WR-87-23 (June 18, 1987), p. 6.

72. Ibid.

73. Ibid.

Chapter 4

1. "Industrial property" was the term used for patents and industrial designs in the late nineteenth century. In recent years the term "intellectual

property" is more widely used in the context of the issues discussed herein. Intellectual property encompasses patents, trademarks, and copyrights as well, but the Paris Convention Conference focused on patents. Copyrights are covered by the Berne Convention.

2. WIPO, "First Consultative Meeting on the Revision of the Paris Convention," PR/CM/I/3 (Geneva, July 1985).

3. G. H. C. Bodenhausen, *Guide to the Application of the Paris Convention for the Protection of Industrial Property* (Geneva: United International Bureau for the Protection of Intellectual Property, 1968), p. 9.

4. Arcot Ramachandran (Secretary to the Government Department of Science and Technology, India), "Self-Reliance in Technology and the Patent System," in WIPO, "World Symposium on the Importance of the Patent System to Developing Countries," No. 638 (E) (Geneva, 1977), p. 304.

5. UNCTAD, "Proposals for Action in the Field of Technology," TD/B/C.6/42 (1978), p. 3, para. 14.

6. Ibid., pp. 3–4, para. 15.

7. Ramachandran, in WIPO (1977), p. 302.

8. Constantine Vaitsos, "Patents Revisited: Their Function in Developing Countries," *Journal of Development Studies* Vol. 9, No. 1 (October 1972), at pp. 77, 83.

9. Ibid., p. 85.

10. Large firms can secure patents throughout the world and then can agree to divide up the market. For example, a U.S. firm may be assigned the U.S. patents held by cooperating foreign firms; in exchange the U.S. firm would give its European-held patent rights to the cooperating European firm. As explained by Vernon and Wells, when patents are divided up in this way, "each firm has come to control all the monopoly rights in its own area, which otherwise would have been divided among [the firms]. No one firm can be blocked by any of the others operating in its home territory; but none can venture outside its home territory without encountering a block from another. In practice, the possession of a dominant patent position accumulated in this way leads to an effective international market division among the cooperating firms" (Raymond Vernon and Louis T. Wells, *The Economic Environment of International Business*, 2nd edition [Englewood Cliffs, NJ: Prentice-Hall, 1976], p. 234).

11. Vaitsos (1972) p. 87.

12. Alicia Puyana de Palacios, *Economic Integration Among Unequal Partners: The Case of the Andean Group* (New York: Pergammon Press, 1982), p. 164.

13. Francisco Ortega Vicuna, "The Control of Multinational Enterprises," in George Modelski, ed., *Transnational Corporations and World Order* (San Francisco: W. H. Freeman and Company, 1979), p. 301.

14. Stephen Coonrod, "The United Nations Code of Conduct for Transnational Corporations," *Harvard International Law Journal* Vol. 18, No. 2 (Spring 1977), p. 292.

15. Peter Kunz-Hallstein, "Patent Protection, Transfer of Technology and Developing Countries: A Survey of the Present Situation," *International Review of Industrial Property and Copyright Law (IIC)* Vol. 6, No. 4 (1975), p. 434, note 32.

16. Ibid., p. 437.

17. UNCTAD, "Compilation of Legal Material Dealing with the Transfer and Development of Technology," TD/B/C.6/81 (Geneva, 1982), p. 243.

18. Article 5quater of the Paris Convention states: "When a product is imported into a country of the Union where there exists a patent protecting a process of manufacture of the said product, the patentee shall have all rights, with regard to the imported product, that are accorded to him by the legislation of the country of importation, on the basis of the process patent, with respect to products manufactured in that country" (Bodenhausen [1968], p. 85).

19. It is important to note that the Andean countries (Bolivia, Colombia, Ecuador, and Venezuela) were not members of the Paris Union, nor were they parties to the convention.

20. Kunz-Hallstein (1975), pp. 436, 438. These policies stipulated that patent protection would not be offered for pharmaceutical products or drugs.

21. S. Vedaraman, "Patent law in India as a means towards accelerating industrial development." in WIPO (1977), p. 139. The Patents Enquiry Committee and Justice Rajagopola Ayyahgar conducted the expert inquiries.

22. UNCTAD, TD/B/C.6/81 (1982), pp. 81–82.

23. Ramachandran, in WIPO (1977), p. 303.

24. Vedaraman, in WIPO (1977), p. 140.

25. Ibid., p. 147.

26. Author's interview with Indian delegate, Geneva, 1986.

27. UNCTAD 1974. The role of the patent system in the transfer of technology to developing countries. TD/B/AC.11/19. (Geneva: United Nations).

28. See *World Development* Vol. 2 No. 9 (September 1974). The three authors (Surendra J. Patel, Pedro Roffe, and Peter O'Brian) were all staff members of UNCTAD at the time of publication. Despite disclaimers that the views were personal and not those of the organization, there is a striking similarity between points made in the journal and points made in the UNCTAD reports.

29. UNCTAD, "The International Patent System as an Instrument for National Development," TD/B/C.6/AC.2/3 (Geneva, 1975).

30. UNCTAD, "Report of the Group of Governmental Experts on the Role of the Industrial Property System in the Transfer of Technology," TD/B/C.6/24/Add. 1, Annex V (Geneva, 1977), p. 2, para. 2

31. Ibid., p. 5, para. 9.

32. Kunz-Hallstein (1975), pp. 427–455.

33. Axel Sell and Monika Mundowski, "Patent Protection and Economic Development," *IIC* Vol. 10, No. 5 (1979), pp. 565–572.

34. Peter Kunz-Hallstein, "The Revision of the International System of Patent Protection in the Interest of Developing Countries," *International Review of Industrial Property and Copyright Law (IIC)* Vol. 10, No. 6 (1979), pp. 649–670.

35. Ibid., p. 666.

36. Ibid., p. 670.

37. Bodenhausen (1968), p. 85.

38. Kunz-Hallstein (1979) p. 657.

39. Ibid., p. 658.

40. Klaus Pfanner, "Compulsory Licensing of Patents: Survey and Recent Trends," *Sartryck ur NIR Nordiskt Immateriellt Rattsskydd,* 1 NIR 1/85, p. 5.

41. Ibid.

42. UNCTAD, "The Role of the Patent System in the Transfer of Technology to Developing Countries," TD/B/AC.11/19 (Geneva, 1974), para. 286. While the figures have been disputed, everyone seemed to agree that a large percentage of patents in both developed and developing countries remain unexploited.

43. Bodenhausen (1968), p. 11.

44. Pfanner (1985), p. 11.

45. Ibid., p. 15.

46. Bodenhausen (1968), p. 67.

47. See WIPO, "Basic Proposals: Draft Approved or Forwarded to the Diplomatic Conference by the Preparatory Intergovernmental Committee," PR/DC/3 (Geneva, 1979), para. 109, 132–136, and Draft of 5A(8), p. 56.

48. WIPO, Final Summary Minutes of the Meetings of the Plenary and of Main Committee I held during the second session of the diplomatic conference. PR/SM.6, p. 91, para. 1243.2.

49. WIPO, "Revised Provisional Summary Minutes," PR/SM/5 (Geneva, 1982), p. 91, para. 1251.

50. Author's interview with Swiss delegate, Geneva, 1986.

51. Nairobi Text, Article 5A (8) (b), reproduced in *Patent and Trademark Review* Vol. 82, No. 11 (November 1984), p. 460.

52. Schuyler, quoted in Adrienne Catanese, "The Paris Convention, Patent Protection, and Technology Transfer," *Boston University International Law Journal* Vol. 3, No. 1 (Winter 1985), p. 222.

53. Author's interview with WIPO official, Geneva, 1986.

54. "The Paris Convention: Report on the Fourth Session of the Revision Conference," *Patent and Trademark Review* Vol. 82, No. 11 (November 1984), p. 456.

55. One developing country delegate said that the controversy over the Davila text was the only real conflict within the Group of 77 over the revision. He also said that even those initially assenting Latin American countries did not feel that the text was in their best interests, but buckled under U.S. pressure. Author's interview, Geneva 1986.

56. WIPO, "Final Summary Minutes," PR/SM/9 (Geneva, 1984), p. 23, para. 442.4.

57. Author's interview with WIPO official, Geneva, 1986.

58. WIPO, PR/SM/9 (1984), p. 26, para. 446.3.

59. Author's interview with developing country delegate, Geneva, 1986.

60. *Patent and Trademark Review* (November 1984), p. 457.

61. Bodenhausen (1968), emphasis in original. Also see Pfanner (1985).

62. Author's personal communication with developing country delegate, Geneva, 1986.

63. WIPO, "Final Summary Minutes," PR/SM/12 (Geneva, 1985), p. 78, para. 1452.2.

64. Ibid.

65. Ibid., p. 79, para. 1426.2.

66. Ibid., p. 79, para. 1427.2.

67. WIPO, "First Consultative Meeting on the Revision of the Paris Convention," PR/CM/1/3 (Geneva, July 1985).

68. Robert Whipple, "A New Era in Licensing," *Les Nouvelles* Vol. XXII, No. 3 (September 1987), p. 109.

69. Ibid.

70. Ibid.

71. Ibid., pp. 109–110.

72. Ibid., p. 110.

73. Ibid.

74. Alice T. Zalik, "Implementing the Trade-Tariff Act," *Les Nouvelles* Vol. XXI, No. 4 (December 1986), p. 199.

75. James Enyart, "A GATT Intellectual Property Code," *Les Nouvelles*, Vol. XXV, No. 2 (June 1990), p. 54.

76. Zalik (1986), p. 200.

77. Ibid.

78. Enyart (1990), p. 54.

79. Ibid.

80. Chang Jae Baik, "Politics of Super 301: The Domestic Political Basis of U.S. Foreign Economic Policy," unpublished Ph.D. dissertation, University of California at Berkeley, 1993, p. 147, note 56.

81. Zalik (1986), p. 200.

82. Ibid., p. 201.

83. Ibid., p. 200.

84. Ibid.

85. Judith Hippler Bello and Alan F. Homer, "The Heart of the 1988 Trade Act: A Legislative History of the Amendments to Section 301," *Stanford Journal of International Law* Vol. 25, No. 1 (Fall 1988), p. 1.

86. Ibid., p. 2.

87. Ibid., p. 3, note 10.

88. Ibid., p. 8.

89. Ibid., pp. 41–42.

90. U.S. Department of Commerce, International Trade Administration Memorandum, "Roger D. Severance Trip Report on Consultations with Taiwan and Singapore on Commercial Counterfeiting" (June 6, 1984), p. 2.

91. This umbrella organization consists of the following eight trade associations: American Publishers, Inc.; American Film Marketing; Data Processing Service Organizations; Computer Software and Services Industry; Business Software Alliance; Computer and Business Equipment Manufacturers; Motion Picture Association of America; National Music Publishers; and Recording Industry of America.

92. Zalik (1986), p. 201

93. Ibid.

94. Ibid.

95. Quoted in Larry Evans, "Licensing Disincentives in Brazil," *Les Nouvelles* Vol. XXI, No. 4 (December 1986), p. 183.

96. Mark F. Radcliffe, "New Intellectual Property Protection," *Les Nouvelles* Vol. XX, No. 3 (September 1985), p. 108.

97. Ibid.

98. Ibid., p. 109.

99. According to a WIPO official, the United States feared developing countries in WIPO because the United States felt it had no available retaliation for patent abuse since so few patents were held by developing countries' nationals. So the United States, like the developing countries, worried about the lack of reciprocity, but in a different way.

100. Enyart (1990), pp. 54–56.

101. See Office of the U.S. Trade Representative, *The 1994 General Agreement on Tariffs and Trade,* Annex 1(C), "Agreement on Trade-Related Aspects of Intellectual Property, Including Trade in Counterfeit Goods," Articles 3(1), 27(1), and 33 of the TRIPs Agreement (August 27, 1994).

102. Ibid., Article 31.

103. See Christopher Kent, "NAFTA, TRIPs Affect IP," *Les Nouvelles* Vol. XXVIII, No. 4 (December 1993), p. 179; and TRIPs Agreement, Article 34.

104. TRIPs Agreement, 1994.

105. Kent (1993), p. 176.

106. Ibid., pp. 176–177.

107. Ibid., p. 177.

Chapter 5

1. UNCTAD, "Report of the Third *Ad Hoc* Group of Experts on Restrictive Business Practices on Its First Session," TD/B/C.2/AC.6/4 (Geneva, December 23, 1976), p. 7, para. 9.

2. Debra L. Miller and Joel Davidow, "Antitrust at the United Nations: A Tale of Two Codes," *Stanford Journal of International Law* Vol. XVIII, No. 2 (Summer 1982), p. 351.

3. Philippe Brusick, "UN Control of Restrictive Business Practices: A Decisive First Step," *Journal of World Trade Law* Vol. 17, No. 4 (July/August 1983), p. 338.

4. Joel Davidow, "The Implementation of International Antitrust Principles," in Seymour J. Rubin and Gary Clyde Hufbauer, eds., *Emerging Standards of International Trade and Investment: Multinational Codes and Corporate Conduct* (Totowa, NJ: Rowman and Allanheld, 1983), p. 120.

5. Brusick (1983), p. 339.

6. Davidow, in Rubin and Hufbauer (1983), p. 124.

7. Ibid., p. 120.

8. Ibid., p. 124.

9. Ibid., p. 127.

10. Ibid.

11. Miller and Davidow (1982), p. 353.

12. Joel Davidow, "The United States, Developing Countries and the Issue of Intra-Enterprise Agreements," *Georgia Journal of International and Comparative Law* Vol. 7, No. 2 (1977), p. 514.

13. Brusick (1983), p. 340.

14. Ibid., pp. 340–341.

15. Thomas L. Brewer, "International Regulation of Restrictive Business Practices," *Journal of World Trade Law* Vol. 16, No. 2 (March/April 1982), p. 110.

16. Ibid.

17. Brusick (1983), p. 340.

18. UNCTAD, "Report of the Intergovernmental Group on Restrictive Business Practices on Its Second Session," TD/B/976 (Geneva, January 25, 1984), p. 6, para. 14.

19. UNCTAD, TD/B/C.2/AC.6/4 (1976), p. 8, para. 13.

20. Ibid., Annex I, Section A, pp. 1–2.

21. Ibid., p. 9, para. 13.

22. Ibid., p. 9, para. 14.

23. UNCTAD, "Recent Developments in the Control of Restrictive Business Practices in Latin America," TD/B/C.2/AC.6/17 (Geneva, June 19, 1978), p. 1, para. 3.

24. Ibid.

25. Ibid., p. 7, para. 13(h).

26. UNCTAD, TD/B/C.2/AC.6/4, Annex 1 (1976), section B, p. 2.

27. Davidow (1977), pp. 511–512.

28. Ibid., p. 512.

29. Davidow, in Rubin and Hufbauer (1983), pp. 132–133.

30. George S. Trisciuzzi, "Multilateral Regulation of Foreign Direct Investment," in Bart S. Fisher and Jeff Turner, eds., *Regulating the Multinational Enterprise: National and International Challenges* (New York: Praeger Publishers, 1983), p. 157.

31. Miller and Davidow (1982), p. 354.

32. Ibid.

33. UNCTAD, "The Set of Multilaterally Agreed Equitable Principles and Rules for the Control of Restrictive Business Practices," TD/RBP/CONF/ 10/Rev. 1 (New York, 1981), B(ii)9.

34. Ibid., C(ii)6.

35. UNCTAD, "Report of the Third *Ad Hoc* Group of Experts on Restrictive Business Practices at Its Third Session," TD/B/C.2/AC.6/10, Annex I (Geneva, December 5, 1977), p. 8, section E(ii).

36. UNCTAD "Report of the Third *Ad Hoc* Group of Experts on Restrictive Business Practices on its Fourth Session," TD/B/C.2/AC.6/13 (Geneva, May 2, 1978), pp. 15–16, para. 18.

37. UNCTAD, "Issues in Connection with the Formulation of a Set of Multilateral Agreed Equitable Principles and Rules for the Control of Restrictive Business Practices: Note by the UNCTAD Secretariat," TD/B/C.2/AC.6/ 2 (Geneva, October 25, 1976), p. 9, para. 26.

38. UNCTAD, "The Set," (1981), E(iii).

39. UNCTAD, TD/B/C.2/AC.6/2 (1976), p. 8, para. 21.

40. UNCTAD, TD/B/C.2/AC.6/13 (1978), p. 5, para. 8.

41. Ibid., p. 6, para. 8.

42. Ibid., p. 7, para. 10.

43. Ibid., p. 6, para. 10.

44. Ibid., p. 18, para. 15.

45. Ibid., p. 6, para. 8.

46. Miller and Davidow (1982), p. 355.

47. U.S. Department of State, "Voluntary Guidelines for Antitrust," *U.S. Department of State Bulletin* Vol. 82, No. 2058 (January 1982), p. 35.

48. Miller and Davidow (1982), p. 355.

49. UNCTAD, TD/RBP/CONF/10/Rev. 1 (1981), D(4).

50. U.S. Department of State (1982), p. 35.

51. Miller and Davidow (1982), p. 354.

52. Havana Charter definition of RBPs quoted in UNCTAD, Group B Proposal, TD/B/C.2/AC.6/4, Annex II, p. 1, at note 1.

53. Miller and Davidow (1982), p. 354.

54. Brewer (1982), p. 111.

55. UNCTAD, TD/B/C.2/AC.6/10, Annex I (1977), p. 13, Section G(vi) (a)(4).

56. Davidow, in Rubin and Hufbauer (1983), p. 132.

57. Ibid., p. 130.

58. UNCTAD, TD/RBP/CONF/Rev. 1 (1981), Section G(4).

59. Davidow, in Rubin and Hufbauer (1983), p. 131.

60. From letter, reproduced in *U.S. State Department Bulletin* Vol. 82, No. 2058 (January 1982), p. 34.

61. Ibid., p. 35.

62. Miller and Davidow (1982), p. 356.

63. Davidow, in Rubin and Hufbauer (1983), p. 131.

64. Marc Allen Eisner, *Antitrust and the Triumph of Economics: Institutions, Expertise, and Policy Change* (Chapel Hill: University of North Carolina Press, 1991).

65. Ibid., p. 105.

66. Ibid., pp. 106–107.

67. Ibid., p. 91.

68. Ibid., p. 148.

69. Ibid., p. 3.

70. Ibid., p. 226.

71. Paul Hoff, *Inventions in the Marketplace: Patent Licensing and the U.S. Antitrust Laws* (Washington, DC: American Enterprise Institute, 1986), p. 1.

72. UNCTAD, "Annual Report 1982: On Legislative and Other Developments in Developing Countries in the Control of Restrictive Business Practices," TD/B/RBP/11 (Geneva, August 4, 1983), p. 8, para. 20.

73. Eisner (1991), p. 198.

74. Hoff (1986), p. 19.

75. Eisner (1991), p. 221.

76. UNCTAD, TD/B/RBP/11 (1983), p. 11, para. 29.

77. McKenna, Barnes, and Cohen, cited in John H. Barton, Robert B. Dellenbach, and Paul Kuruk, "Toward a Theory of Technology Licensing,"

Stanford Journal of International Law Vol. 25, No. 1 (Fall 1988), p. 218, note 95.

78. Reich and Mankin, cited in Barton, Dellenbach, and Kuruk (1988), p. 218, note 95.

79. Ibid., p. 222.

80. Peter Cowhey and Jonathan Aronson, *Managing the World Economy: The Consequences of Corporate Alliances* (New York: Council on Foreign Relations Press, 1993), p. 79.

81. Barton, Dellenbach, and Kuruk (1988), p. 222.

82. Mark Dodgson, *Technological Collaboration in Industry* (New York: Routledge, 1993), p. 15.

83. Christopher Avery and Raymond Smilor, "Research Consortia: The Microelectronics and Computer Technology Corporation," in Frederick Williams and David V. Gibson, eds., *Technology Transfer: A Communication Perspective* (Newbury Park, CA: 1990)

84. Thomas Jorde and David Teece, "Innovation, Cooperation, and Antitrust," in Thomas Jorde and David Teece, eds., *Antitrust and Innovation* (New York: Oxford University Press, 1992), p. 57.

85. Ibid., p. 58.

86. Ibid., p. 59.

87. Wayne Sandholtz, *High-Tech Europe: The Politics of International Cooperation* (Berkeley: University of California Press, 1992), p. 302.

88. Barton, Dellenbach, and Kuruk (1988), p. 229.

89. UNCTAD, TD/B/RBP/11 (1983), p. 3, para. 3.

90. Ibid., p. 4, para. 3.

91. Ibid., p. 10, para. 27.

92. UNCTAD, "Annual Report 1983–1984," TD/B/RBP/29 (Geneva, June 17,1985), p. 1, para. 13.

93. Author's interview with Brusick, Geneva, April 25, 1986.

94. UNCTAD, TD/RBP/CONF/Rev. 1 (1981), F(6).

95. Brusick (1983), p. 349.

96. UNCTAD, TD/B/976 (1984) p. 7, para. 19.

97. Ibid., p. 61, para. 279.

98. Ibid., p. 36, para. 161.

99. Ibid., pp. 37–38, para. 166.

100. Ibid., p. 42, para. 189.

101. Ibid., p. 36, para. 160.

102. Ibid., p. 10, para. 39.

103. Ibid., p. 48, para. 222.

104. Ibid., p. 49, para. 226.

105. Ibid.

106. Ibid.
107. Ibid.
108. Ibid., p. 49, para. 223.
109. Ibid., p. 51, para. 243.
110. Ibid., p. 52, para. 244.
111. Ibid., p. 26, para. 121.
112. Ibid., p. 9, para. 13.
113. Ibid., p. 52, para. 245.
114. Ibid., p. 51, para. 242.
115. Ibid., p. 53, para. 249.
116. Author's interview with Brusick, Geneva, April 25, 1986.
117. UNCTAD, TD/B/976 (1984) p. 35, para. 155.
118. UNCTAD, TD/B/RBP/29 (1985), p. 2, para. 3.
119. Author's interviews with Brusick, April 25, 1986, and Greenhill, May 5, 1986, Geneva.

Chapter 6

1. G. John Ikenberry and Charles Kupchan, "Socialization and Hegemonic Power," *International Organization* Vol. 44, No. 3 (Summer 1990), p. 285, fn. 3.

2. Phrase adapted from comments from Marshall Alcorn, at the seminar "The Rhetoric of Disciplined Inquiry," George Washington University, October 9, 1993.

3. See Clive Gray, "Antitrust as a Component of Policy Reform: What Role for Developing Countries?" in Dwight Perkins and Michael Roemer, eds., *Reforming Economic Systems in Developing Countries* (Cambridge, MA: Harvard Institute for International Development, 1991), pp. 403–440; World Bank, *Korea: Managing the Industrial Transition Volume I: The Conduct of Industrial Policy* (Washington, DC: The World Bank, 1987), p. 74; and World Bank, *Korea: Managing the Industrial Transition Volume II: Selected Topics and Case Studies* (Washington, DC: The World Bank, 1987), pp. 34, 80, 88.

4. As Lisa Martin argues in *Coercive Cooperation* (Princeton, NJ: Princeton University Press 1992), such incentives may be supplied by either hegemonic power or institutions. However, in the intellectual property case, international institutions played a minimal role in providing incentives for developing countries to change their policies of lax protection. Indeed, the United States chose to bypass the World Intellectual Property Organization as early as 1986 in favor of bilateralism and the General Agreement on Trade and Tariffs. In short, the United States pursued the two avenues that provided it the strongest leverage.

5. Particularly in South Korea and Taiwan, antitrust policies have become a potent political weapon in the hands of democratic reformers. See Susan K. Sell, "Antitrust in Korea and Taiwan: The Link Between Politics and Money in the Context of Democratization," prepared for the 1994 American Political Science Association Convention, New York.

6. Industry associations in service, investment, high-technology, agricultural chemical, pharmaceutical, and entertainment sectors lobbied Congress for more effective intellectual property protection abroad. Among the most active groups were the associations of the Pharmaceutical Manufacturers; the Chemical Manufacturers; the Semiconductor Industry; and the International Intellectual Property Alliance (an umbrella organization of eight trade associations: American Publishers, Inc.; American Film Marketing; Data Processing and Service Organizations; Computer Software and Services Industry; Business Software Alliance; Computer and Business Equipment Manufacturers; National Music Publishers; the Recording Industry of America; and Motion Picture Association of America).

7. Alan O. Sykes, "Constructive Unilateral Threats in International Commercial Relations: The Limited Case for Section 301," *Law and Policy in International Business* Vol. 23, No. 2 (1992), p. 282.

8. The private sector began to see the GSP as an attractive trump card to force recipient countries to strengthen their intellectual property protection. Gerald Mossinghoff, former U.S. Commissioner of Patents and Trademarks (and in 1985 the president of the Pharmaceutical Manufacturers Associations of America); Jack Valenti, president of the Motion Picture Association of America; and Vico Henriques, spokesman for the International Intellectual Property Alliance all testified before Congress and urged the government to suspend GSP benefits for pirating countries.

9. Sykes (1992), p. 313.

10. Gerald J. Mossinghoff, "For Better International Protection," *Les Nouvelles* Vol. XXVI, No. 2 (June 1991), p. 76.

11. Michael P. Ryan, "Strategy and Compliance with Bilateral Trade and Dispute Settlement Agreements: USTR's Section 301 Experience in the Pacific Basin," *Michigan Journal of International Law* Vol. 12 (Summer 1991), p. 824.

12. "Software Piracy: Self-Defense the Best Choice for Victims," *Business International* Vol. XXIV (July 20, 1992), p. 250.

13. Fred M. Greguras and Moon Sung Lee, "Software Licensing in Korea," *Les Nouvelles* Vol. XXVII, No. 4 (December 1992), p. 217.

14. "Differences over Code on Patents," *Latin American Regional Reports—Brazil* RB-91-04 (2 May 1991), p. 4.

15. Mossinghoff (1991), p. 77.

16. John Pearson, "The Patent Pirates Are Finally Walking the Plank," *Business Week* No. 3253, Industrial/Technology Edition (February 17, 1992), p. 127.

17. William Neuman, "IPR Protection Improves, but Reforms Not Uniform," *Business Latin America* (April 20, 1992), p. 127.

18. Scott Studebaker, "Brazil: Constitutional Revision Session Floundering," *Latin American Law and Business Report* Vol. 2 (April 1994), p. 12.

19. "Market Notes," *Latin American Law and Business Report* Vol. 1 (August 1993), p. 32

20. Helen J. Simon, "Unfair Practices in the Spotlight," *Business Latin America* (January 25, 1993), pp. 6–7.

21. Mossinghoff (1991) p. 76.

22. Chris Shore, "The Thai Copyright Case and Possible Limitations of Extraterritorial Jursidiction in Actions Taken under Section 301 of the Trade Act of 1974," *Law and Policy in International Business* Vol. 23, No. 3 (1992), p. 729.

23. "Thai-U.S. Trade Relations Skate on Thin Ice over IP Rights Inaction," *Business Asia* Vol. 13 (November 1989), p. 371.

24. Ibid., p. 372.

25. Shore (1992), p. 747, note 108.

26. Hamish McDonald, "The Late Convert: India Wins Reprieve in Patent Row with U.S.," *Far Eastern Economic Review* Vol. 154 (December 5, 1991), p. 65.

27. U.S. Bureau of the Census, *Statistical Abstract of the United States: 1993*, 113th edition (Washington, DC, 1993), table No. 1351, p. 813.

28. Philip Shenon, "Chinese Accused of Pirating Disks," *The New York Times* (August 18, 1994), p. D1.

29. Ibid., p. D17.

30. Ibid.

31. Smith, quoted in Martha Hamilton and Steven Mufson, "Clinton Hails Accord with China on Trade," *The Washington Post* (February 27, 1995), p. A16.

32. Paul Blustein, "Accord Won't Resolve Frictions with China, Trade Experts Say," *The Washington Post* (June 18, 1996), C4.

33. Quoted in Steve Mufson, "In Fight for Intellectual Rights in China, Pirates Still Winning," *The Washington Post* (February 18, 1996), A29.

34. "Market Notes," *Latin American Business and Law Report* Vol. 2, No. 1 (January 1994), p. 31.

35. Figures for both the Mexican and Thai cases from Mossinghoff (1991), p. 76.

36. Traditionally, developing countries have favored the use of exclusive compulsory licenses in cases in which the patentee fails to exploit commercially the patent in the developing country. Under exclusive compulsory licenses, the patent rights are transferred to local parties. As Klaus Pfanner points out, "when an exclusive license is granted, the patent owner is excluded from using his own invention" (Klaus Pfanner, "Compulsory Licensing of Patents: Survey and Current Trends," *Sartryck ur NIR Nordiskt Immateriellt Rattsskydd*, 1 NIR 1/85, p. 5).

37. Summarized from Oscar Becerril, "Mexico's New Law Liberalizes Technology Transfer," *Les Nouvelles* Vol. XXVII, No. 1 (March 1992), pp. 4–5.

38. Quoted in Neuman (1992), p. 127.

39. Julia Preston, "As Piracy Grows in Mexico, U.S. Companies Shout Foul," *The New York Times* (April 20, 1996), p. A1.

40. Ibid., p. A34.

41. Thomas Biersteker, "The 'Triumph' of Liberal Economic Ideas in the Developing World," in Barbara Stallings, ed., *Global Change, Regional Response: The New International Context of Development* (Cambridge: Cambridge University Press, 1995), p. 186.

42. In the early 1980s the East Asian "miracles" were inaccurately held up as paragons of free market economics. Much of the subsequent East Asian scholarship has exposed this fallacy and demonstrated the importance of extensive state intervention in these countries' development policies. On the demonstration effect, see G. John Ikenberry, "The International Spread of Privatization Policies: Inducements, Learning, and 'Policy Bandwagoning,' " in Ezra Suleiman and John Waterbury, *The Political Economy of Public Sector Reform and Privatization* (Boulder: Westview Press, 1990), pp. 88–110.

43. In fiscal year 1988 the following twenty-six countries accounted for 85 percent of World Bank lending geared to reforming industrial and trade policies: Argentina, Brazil, Chile, China, Colombia, Ecuador, Egypt, Greece, Hong Kong, Hungary, India, Indonesia, Malaysia, Mexico, Morocco, Nigeria, Pakistan, Peru, Philippines, Poland, Republic of Korea, Singapore, Thailand, Turkey, Venezuela, and Yugoslavia (Claudio R. Frischtak, "Competition Policies for Industrializing Countries," Policy and Research Series #7 [Washington, DC: World Bank, 1989], p. 25, fns. 3, 4).

44. Vinod Aggarwal suggested this in his comments on an earlier draft of this paper, presented at the American Political Science Association meeting in September 1993.

45. UNCTAD, "Report of the Second United Nations Conference to Review All Aspects of the Multilaterally Agreed Equitable Principles and Rules for the Control of Restrictive Business Practices," TD/RBP/CONF.3/9 (February 11, 1991), p. 1, para. 3.

46. Ibid., p. 2, para. 7.

47. Ibid., p. 15, para. 46.

48. Stanley P. Wagner, "Antitrust, the Korean Experience 1981–1985," *The Antitrust Bulletin* (Summer 1987), p. 500.

49. Roger Alan Boner and Reinald Krueger, "The Basics of Antitrust Policy," World Bank Technical Paper Number 160 (Washington, DC: World Bank, 1991), p. 43, fn. 92.

50. Wagner (1987) p. 505.

51. Ibid., p. 516.

52. UNCTAD, "Draft Report of the Intergovernmental Working Group of Experts on Restrictive Business Practices on Its Eleventh Session," TD/B/RBP/L.58/Add. 1 (November 26, 1992), p. 9, para. 40.

53. "Hyundai Founder Sentenced for Violating Election Laws," *The New York Times* (November 2, 1993), p. A10.

54. Bruce Cheeseman, "Hyundai Probe Turns Up Heat on Big Business," *South China Morning Post* (December 13, 1992), p. 2.

55. John Burton, "South Korea to Probe Chaebol Power," *Financial Times* (April 7, 1993), p. 7.

56. Ibid.

57. UNCTAD, TD/B/RBP/CONF.3/9 (1991), p. 16, para. 49.

58. "Management Alert," *Business Latin America* (August 3, 1992), p. 268.

59. Thomas Hughes, "Venezuela: Recent Developments," *Latin American Law and Business Report* Vol. 2 (February 1994), p. 23.

60. Thomas Hughes, "Venezuela: Recent Developments," *Latin American Law and Business Report* Vol. 1 (August 1993), pp. 27–28.

61. Thomas Hughes, "Venezuela: Recent Developments," *Latin American Law and Business Report* Vol. 1 (September 1993), pp. 32–33.

62. Thomas Hughes, "Venezuela: Recent Developments," *Latin American Law and Business Report* Vol. 1 (November 1993), p. 26.

63. The Chilean government had adopted neoclassical economic reforms in the early 1970s after the takeover by Pinochet. For a discussion of this earlier period see Alejandro Foxley, *Latin American Experiments in Neoconservative Economics* (Berkeley: University of California Press, 1983).

64. UNCTAD, TD/B/RBP/CONF.3/9 (1991), p. 26, para. 91.

65. Ibid.

66. This paragraph is based on Pinheiro Neto-Advogados, "Investigation of Pharmaceutical Industry for Abuse of Economic Power," *Latin American Law and Business Report* Vol. 1 (April 1993), pp. 23–24.

67. This paragraph based on Scott Studebaker, "Brazil—Economic Plan, Privatization, Status of Constitutional Congress and Other Recent

Developments," *Latin American Law and Business Report* Vol. 2 (February 1994), p. 8.

68. Natalia Delgado and Steven Martin, "Mexico: The New Law of Economic Competition," *Latin American Law and Business Report* Vol. 1 (June 1993), p. 27.

69. Jeffrey Lang and Laura Brank, "A Step in the Right Direction: Unlocking the Mexican Energy Market," *Latin American Law and Business Report* Vol. 1 (August 1993), p. 14.

70. See "Market Notes: Mexico's SECOFI Implements Competition Law," *Latin American Law and Business Report* Vol. 1 (May 1993) pp. 34–35.

71. "Tata Timken Shows India's Monopolies Law Is Losing Its Teeth," *Business Asia* Vol. 4 (September 1989), p. 292.

72. Ibid.

73. Ibid., p. 293.

74. Suman Dubey, "India Clears Some Foreign Investments, Sending Bullish Signal on Reform Drive," *The Wall Street Journal* (June 24, 1993), p. A6.

75. "Indian Economy, Pepsi Generation," *The Economist*, Vol. 315, (June 6, 1990), p. 40.

76. Jayanta Sarkar, "Back in Charge: India's Reforms Entice Foreign Firms to Raise Their Profile," *Far Eastern Economic Review* (July 8, 1993), pp. 49–50.

77. Ibid.

78. An anonymous reviewer for *International Organization* suggested this example to me.

79. UNCTAD, TD/B/RBP/CONF.3/9 (1991), p. 17, paras. 56–57.

80. Based on Sally Bowen, "Peru Opens Up Economy with Deluge of Laws," *Financial Times* (November 20, 1991), p. 8, quoted in Pierre Guislain, "Divestiture of State Enterprises: An Overview of the Legal Framework," World Bank Technical Paper Number 186 (Washington, DC: World Bank, 1992), p. 10, fn. 27.

81. UNCTAD, TD/B/RBP/CONF.3/9 (1991), p. 18, para. 58.

82. Ibid., p. 38, para. 144.

83. UNCTAD, TD/B/RBP/L.58/Add.1 (1992), p. 10, para. 43.

84. UNCTAD, "Review of the Operation of and Experience Arising from the Application and Implementation of the Set of Multilateral Agreed Equitable Principles and Rules for the Control of Restrictive Business Practices," TD/B/RBP/89/Add.1 (September 30, 1992), p. 2, paras. 4–9.

85. UNCTAD, TD/B/RBP/CONF.3/9 (1991), p. 29, para. 104.

86. UNCTAD, "Adoption of the Agenda and Organization of Work," TD/B/RBP/86 (July 21, 1992).

87. Ibid., p. 2.

88. UNCTAD, TD/B/RBP/CONF.3/9 (1991), pp. 20, 21, paras. 70, 71.

89. Ikenberry and Kupchan (1990) p. 290.

90. Ibid., p. 291.

91. Robert M. Sherwood, "New Theory of Conductivity in Licensing," *Les Nouvelles* Vol. XXIV, No. 4 (December 1989), p. 187.

92. Ibid., p. 187.

93. Robert Merges, "Battle of the Lateralisms: Intellectual Property and Trade," *Boston University International Law Journal* 8 (Fall 1990), p. 246.

94. Robert Mallott, "1990s Issue: Intellectual Property Rights," *Les Nouvelles* Vol. XXIV, No. 4 (December 1989), p. 152.

95. An anonymous reviewer for *International Organization* provided me with this example.

96. Paul Liu, "A Review of Intellectual Property Laws in Taiwan: Proposals to Curb Piracy and Counterfeiting in a Developing Country," *Brigham Young University Law Review* Vol. 1988 (1988) p. 630.

97. Ibid.

98. Ibid.

99. In the recently concluded Uruguay Round the provisions of the Trade-Related Aspects of Intellectual Property Rights (TRIPs) include important exemptions for developing countries. As Christopher Kent points out, developing countries "obtained a major concession, which would allow them to continue to pursue conscious policies of drug patent exemption" (Kent, "NAFTA, TRIPs Affect IP," *Les Nouvelles* Vol. XXVIII, No. 4 [December 1993], p. 176).

100. Lowell Fleischer, "Round of Presidential Elections Will Determine Whether Region Will Continue Economic and Political Reform," *Latin American Law and Business Report* Vol. 2 (January 1994), p. 2.

Chapter 7

1. David Mowrey and Nathan Rosenberg, *Technology and the Pursuit of Economic Growth* (Cambridge: Cambridge University Press, 1989), p. 278.

2. Sir Leon Brittan, as EC vice president, has been a strong proponent of this. For a circumspect analysis of the merits of incorporating competition policy into GATT, see Bernard Hoekman and Petros Mavroidis, "Competition, Competition Policy and the GATT," *The World Economy* Vol. 17, No. 2 (March 1994), pp. 121–150.

3. For a discussion of intellectual property protection's potentially negative effects on technological innovation, see R. C. Levin, A. K. Levorick,

R. R. Nelson, and S. G. Winter, "Appropriating the Returns from Industrial Research and Development," Brookings Papers on Economic Activity, 3 (1987), pp. 783–820, especially p. 788.

4. Jeroen van Wijk and Gerd Junne, *Intellectual Property Protection of Advanced Technology: Changes in the Global Technology System: Implications and Options for Developing Countries,* Contract No. 91/026 (Maastricht, the Netherlands: United Nations University, Institute for New Technologies, October 1992), p. 63.

5. Levin et al. (1987), p. 788.

6. Donal O'Connor, "TRIPS: Licensing Challenge," *Les Nouvelles* Vol. XXX, No. 1 (March 1995), p. 17.

7. Surendra Patel, "Intellectual Property Rights in the Uruguay Round: A Disaster for the South?" *Economic and Political Weekly* (May 6, 1989), pp. 983–984.

8. Dorothy Shrader, *Intellectual Property Provisions of the GATT 1994: The TRIPs Agreement,* Congressional Research Service Report for Congress, Report No. 94-302 A (Washington, DC: The Library of Congress, March 16, 1994), p. 13.

9. H.R. 5110, quoted in Sylvia Morrison, *How Will the Uruguay Round of GATT Affect the U.S. Computer Industry?* Congressional Research Service Report for Congress, Report No. 94-840-E (Washington, DC: The Library of Congress, November 3, 1994), p. 3.

10. Shrader (1994), p. 13.

11. Business Software Alliance, "Fact Sheet: International Policies Governing the Software Industry," (Washington, DC: May 5, 1995), p. 4.

12. Edwin Einstein, "NAFTA: Little Protection For Technology," *Les Nouvelles* Vol. XXX, No. 1 (March 1995), p. 29.

13. On the issues of gray-market goods and border enforcement, see Shrader (1994).

14. Marc Eisner, *Antitrust and the Triumph of Economics* (Chapel Hill: University of North Carolina Press, 1991), p. 230.

15. Michelle Lee and Mavis Lee, "High-Technology Consortia: A Panacea for America's Technological Competitiveness Problems?" *High Technology Law Journal* Vol. 6, No. 2 (Summer 1991), p. 357.

16. Thomas Jorde and David Teece, eds., *Antitrust and Innovation* (New York: Oxford University Press, 1992).

17. Deborah Wince-Smith, "Challenge of Technological Competitiveness," *Les Nouvelles* Vol. XXVIII, No. 1 (March 1993), p. 4.

18. Lee and Lee (1991), pp. 339–340.

19. Anne Bingaman, "Innovation and Antitrust: Competition and the World Community," speech delivered before the Commonwealth Club of

California, San Francisco, CA, July 29, 1994, reprinted in *Vital Speeches of the Day* (September 1994), pp. 712–713.

20. James Rill, "Competition Policy: A Force for Open Markets," *Antitrust Law Journal* Vol. 61 (1993), p. 649.

21. Joseph Griffin, "Antitrust Law," *The National Law Journal* (August 29, 1994), p. B5.

22. Ibid.

23. Bingaman (1994), p. 714.

24. Bingaman, quoted in Griffin (1994), p. B6.

25. Peter Cowhey and Jonathan Aronson, *Managing the World Economy: The Consequences of Corporate Alliances* (New York: Council on Foreign Relations Press, 1993), p. 5.

26. Brian N. Smith, "Reflecting on a Changing Business World," *Les Nouvelles*, Vol. XXIII, No. 1 (March 1988), p. 3

27. Peter L. Waite, "Profit and Technology Transfer," *Les Nouvelles* Vol. XXII, No. 4 (December 1987), p. 134.

28. Mowrey and Rosenberg (1989), p. 213.

29. Waite (1987), pp. 134–135.

30. Ibid.

31. Mowrey and Rosenberg (1989), pp. 249–250.

32. Cowhey and Aronson (1993), p. 4.

Abbreviations

ACAST	Advisory Committee for the Application of Science and Technology for Development
ANCOM	Andean Common Market
CADE	Administrative Council for Economic Defense (Brazil)
CONACYT	National Council of Scientific and Technological Research (Mexico)
CPPA	Computer Program Protection Act (South Korea)
DSU	Dispute Settlement Understanding
ECLA	Economic Commission for Latin America
ECOSOC	Economic and Social Council
FCC	Federal Competition Commission (Mexico)
FDI	Foreign Direct Investment
FTC	Fair Trade Commission
GATT	General Agreement on Tariffs and Trade
GSP	Generalized System of Preferences

263

IGE	Intergovernmental Group of Experts
IMF	International Monetary Fund
INPI	National Institute for Industrial Property (Brazil)
IPC	Intellectual Property Committee
ISI	Import Substituting Industrialization
LDC	Less Developed Country
MITI	Ministry of Trade and Industry (Japan)
MNC	Multinational Corporation
MRTP	Monopolies and Restrictive Trade Practices Act (India)
NAFTA	North American Free Trade Agreement
NIC	Newly Industrializing Country
NIEO	New International Economic Order
OECD	Organization for Economic Cooperation and Development
OEEC	Organization for European Economic Cooperation
OPEC	Organization of Petroleum Exporting Countries
R & D	Research and Development
RBP	Restrictive Business Practices
TNC	Transnational Corporation
TNE	Transnational Enterprise
TOT	Transfer of Technology
TRIPs	Trade-Related Aspects of Intellectual Property, Including Trade in Counterfeit Goods
UNCTAD	United Nations Conference on Trade and Development
USTR	United States Trade Representative
WIPO	World Intellectual Property Organization

Selected Bibliography

Adler, Emmanuel. 1987. *The Power of Ideology: The Quest for Technological Autonomy in Argentina and Brazil.* Berkeley: University of California Press.

———— and Beverly Crawford, eds. 1991. *Progress in Postwar International Relations.* New York: Columbia University Press.

Agosin, Manuel, and David Gold. 1986. "Recent Trends in FDI and Related Activities by TNCs." *The CTC Reporter* 21 (Spring), 21–24.

Andean pact seeks EEC investment. *Latin American Regional Reports* (Andean Group Report) RA-87-07 (September 3, 1987), p. 4.

Andean pact: Little substance left. *Latin American Weekly Report,* WR-87-20 (May 28, 1987) pp. 6–7.

Augelli, Enrico and Craig Murphy. 1993. Gramsci and international relations: A general perspective with examples from recent US policy toward the third world, in Stephen Gill (ed.), *Gramsci, historical materialism and international relations.* Cambridge: Cambridge University Press.

Avery, Christopher, and Raymond Smilor. 1990. "Research Consortia: The Microelectronics and Computer Technology Corporation." In Frederick Williams and David Gibson, eds. *Technology Transfer: A Communication Perspective.* Newbury Park, CA: Sage Publications.

Baik, Chang Jae. 1993. *Politics of Super 301: The Domestic Political Basis of U.S. Foreign Economic Policy.* Unpublished Ph.D. dissertation, University of California at Berkeley.

Baldwin, David, ed. 1993. *Neorealism and Neoliberalism: The Contemporary Debate*. New York: Columbia University Press.

Baranson, Jack. 1981. *North-South Technology Transfer: Financing and Institution Building*. Mt. Airy, MD: Lomond Publications.

Barton, John H., Robert B. Dellenbach, and Paul Kuruk. 1988. "Toward a Theory of Technology Licensing." *Stanford Journal of International Law* 25 (1), 195–230.

Becerril, Oscar. 1992. "Mexico's New Law Liberalizes Technology Transfer." *Les Nouvelles* XXVII, (1), 1–5.

Bello, Judith Hippler, and Alan F. Holmer. 1988. "The Heart of the 1988 Trade Act: A Legislative History of the Amendments to Section 301." *Stanford Journal of International Law* 25 (1), 1–44.

Bennett, Douglas, and Kenneth Sharpe. 1985. *Transnational Corporations versus the State: The Political Economy of the Mexican Auto Industry*. Baltimore: The Johns Hopkins University Press.

Bergsten, C. Fred. 1973. "The Threat from the Third World." *Foreign Policy* 11, 102–124.

———. 1974. "The Threat Is Real." *Foreign Policy* 14, 84–90.

———, Thomas Horst, and Theodore Moran. 1978. *American Multinationals and American Interests*. Washington, DC: The Brookings Institution.

Bhagwati, Jagdish, and John Ruggie, eds. 1984. *Power, Passions, and Purpose: Prospects for North-South Negotiations*. Cambridge, MA: MIT Press.

Biersteker, Thomas. 1992. "The 'Triumph' of Neoclassical Economics in the Developing World: Policy Convergence and Bases of Governance in the International Economic Order." In James Rosenau and Ernst-Otto Czempiel, eds. *Governance without Government: Order and Change in World Politics*. New York: Cambridge University Press.

———. 1995. "The 'Triumph' of Liberal Economic Ideas in the Developing World." In Barbara Stallings, ed. *Global Change, Regional Response: The New International Context of Development*. Cambridge: Cambridge University Press.

Bingaman, Anne. 1994. "Innovation and Antitrust: Competition and the World Community." *Vital Speeches of the Day* 60 (23), 712–716.

Blustein, Paul. Accord won't resolve frictions with China, trade experts say. *The Washington Post*. June 18, 1996, C4.

Bodenhausen, G. H. C. 1968. *Guide to the Application of the Paris Convention for the Protection of Industrial Property*. Geneva: United International Bureau for the Protection of Intellectual Property.

Boner, Roger Alan, and Reinald Krueger. 1991. *The Basics of Antitrust Policy*. World Bank Technical Paper Number 160. Washington, DC: World Bank.

Booth, Ken, and Steve Smith, eds. 1995. *International Relations Theory Today.* University Park: The Pennsylvania State University Press.

Bowen, Sally. Peru opens up economy with deluge of laws. *Financial Times.* (November 20, 1991), p. 8.

Brewer, Thomas. 1982. "International Regulation of Restrictive Business Practices." *Journal of World Trade Law* 16 (2), 108–118.

Brusick, Philippe. 1983. "UN Control of Restrictive Business Practices: A Decisive First Step." *Journal of World Trade Law* 17 (4), 337–351.

Burton, John. South Korea to probe chaebol power. *Financial Times.* April 7, 1993, p. 7.

Business Software Alliance. Fact sheet: International policies governing the software industry. Washington, D.C. (May 5, 1995), pp. 1–5.

Carr, Edward H. 1946. *The Twenty Years' Crisis: 1919–1939.* London: Macmillian.

Catanese, Adrienne. 1985. "The Paris Convention, Patent Protection, and Technology Transfer." *Boston University International Law Journal* 3 (1), 209–227.

Cheeseman, Bruce. Hyundai probe turns up heat on big business. *South China Morning Post.* December 13, 1992, p. 2.

Coonrod, Stephan. 1977. "The United Nations' Code of Conduct for Transnational Corporations." *Harvard International Law Journal* 18 (2), 273–307.

Correa, Carlos. 1981. "Technology Transfer in Latin America: A Decade of Control." *Journal of World Trade Law* 15, 388–409.

Cowhey, Peter, and Jonathan Aronson. 1993. *Managing the World Economy: The Consequences of Strategic Corporate Alliances.* New York: Council on Foreign Relations Press.

Curzon, Gerard, and Victoria Curzon, eds. 1977. *The Multinational Enterprise in a Hostile World.* London: Macmillan.

Davidow, Joel. 1977. "The United States, Developing Countries and the Issue of Intra-Enterprise Agreements." *Georgia Journal of International and Comparative Law* 7 (2), 507–514.

Delgado, Natalia, and Steven Martin. 1993. "Mexico: The New Law of Economic Competition." *Latin American Law and Business Report.* 1 (June), 27–28.

Differences over code on patents. *Latin American Regional Reports— Brazil,* RB-91-04 (May 2, 1991): 4.

Dodgson, Mark. 1993. *Technological Collaboration in Industry.* New York: Routledge.

Dubey, Suman. India clears some foreign investments, sending bullish signal on reform drive. *The Wall Street Journal,* June 24, 1993, p. A6.

Einstein, Edwin. 1995. "NAFTA: Little Protection for Technology." *Les Nouvelles*. XXX (1), 28–30.

Eisner, Marc Allen. 1991. *Antitrust and the Triumph of Economics: Institutions, Expertise, and Policy Change*. Chapel Hill: University of North Carolina Press.

Encarnation, Dennis. 1992. *Rivals beyond Trade: America Versus Japan in Global Competition*. Ithaca: Cornell University Press.

Enyart, James. 1990. "A GATT Intellectual Property Code." *Les Nouvelles* XXV (2), 53–56.

Evans, Larry. 1986. "Licensing Disincentives in Brazil." *Les Nouvelles* XXI (4), 180–183.

Fisher, Bart S. and Jeff Turner, eds. 1983. *Regulating the Multinational Enterprise: National and International Challenges*. New York: Praeger Publishers.

Fleischer, Lowell. 1994. "Round of Presidential Elections Will Determine Whether Region Will Continue Economic and Political Reform." *Latin American Law and Business Report* 2 (January), 2 and 30.

Foxley, Alejandro. 1983. *Latin American Experiments in Neoconservative Economics*. Berkeley: University of California Press.

Frischtak, Claudio. 1989. *Competition Policies for Industrializing Countries*. Policy and Research Series No. 7. Washington, DC: World Bank.

Gerschenkron, Alexander. 1952. "Economic Backwardness in Historical Perspective." In B. Hoselitz, ed. *The Progress of Underdeveloped Areas*. Chicago: University of Chicago Press.

Gill, Stephen. (ed.). 1993. *Gramsci, historical materialism and international relations*. Cambridge: Cambridge University Press.

Gilpin, Robert. 1985. *War and Change in World Politics*. Princeton: Princeton University Press.

———. 1987. *The Political Economy of International Relations*. Princeton: Princeton University Press.

Goldstein, Judith, and Robert Keohane, eds. 1993. *Ideas and Foreign Policy*. Ithaca: Cornell University Press.

Graham, Anila. 1979. "The Transfer of Technology: A Test Case in the North-South Dialogue." *Journal of International Affairs* 33 (1), 1–17.

Green, Donald, and Ian Shapiro. 1994. *Pathologies of Rational Choice Theory: A Critique of Applications in Political Science*. New Haven: Yale University Press.

Greguras, Fred, and Moon Sung Lee. 1992. "Software Licensing in Korea." *Les Nouvelles* XXVII (4), 215–219.

Griffin, Joseph. 1994. "Antitrust Law." *The National Law Journal*. (August 29), 135–136.

Guislain, Pierre. 1992. *Divestiture of State Enterprises: An Overview of the Legal Framework*. Technical Paper Number 186. Washington, DC: World Bank.

Haas, Ernst. 1980. "Why Collaborate? Issue-Linkage and International Regimes." *World Politics* 32 (April), 357–405.

———. 1989. *When Knowledge Is Power*. Berkeley: University of California Press.

Haggard, Stephan, and Beth Simmons. 1987. "Theories of International Regimes." *International Organization* 41 (3), 491–517.

Hamilton, Martha and Steve Mufson. Clinton hails accord with China on trade. *The Washington Post*. February 27, 1995, A16.

Hansen, Roger. 1979. *Beyond the North-South Stalemate*. New York: McGraw-Hill.

Harris, Nigel. 1986. *The End of the Third World*. London: I. B. Tauris and Co. Ltd.

Helman, Gerald. 1982. "UNCTAD: A Declaration of United States Policy." *Journal of World Trade Law* 16 (5), 455–460.

Higonnet, Patrice, David Landes, and Henry Rosovsky, eds. 1991. *Favorites of Fortune: Technology, Growth, and Economic Development since the Industrial Revolution*. Cambridge: Harvard University Press.

Hoekman, Bernard, and Petros Mavroidis. 1994. "Competition, Competition Policy and the GATT." *The World Economy* 17 (2), 121–150.

Hoff, Paul. 1986. *Inventions in the Marketplace: Patent Licensing and the U.S. Antitrust Laws*. Washington, DC: American Enterprise Institute.

Horn, Norbert, ed. 1980. *Legal Problems of Codes of Conduct for Multinational Enterprises*. Deventer, the Netherlands: B. V. Kluwer.

Hormats, Robert. 1981. "International Economic Policy Priorities." *U.S. Department of State Bulletin* 81 (2052), 24–27.

Hoselitz, B., ed. 1952. *The Progress of Underdeveloped Areas*. Chicago: University of Chicago Press.

Hughes, Thomas. 1993. Venezuela: recent developments. *Latin American Law and Business Report*. Vol. 1, (August), pp. 27–28.

———. 1993. Venezuela: recent developments. *Latin American Law and Business Report*. Vol. 1, (September), pp. 32–33.

———. 1993. Venezuela: recent developments. *Latin American Law and Business Report*. Vol. 1, (November), p. 26.

———. 1994. Venezuela: recent developments. *Latin American Law and Business Report*. Vol. 1, (February), p. 23.

Ikenberry, G. John, and Charles Kupchan. 1990. "Socialization and Hegemonic Power." *International Organization* 44 (3), 283–315.

Indian economy, Pepsi generation. *The Economist*, Vol. 315 (June 6, 1990), p. 40.

International Monetary Fund. 1993. *International Financial Statistics Yearbook*. Vol. 46, Washington, D.C.: International Monetary Fund, pp. 136–137.

Jacobsen, John Kurt. 1995. "Much Ado about Ideas: The Cognitive Factor in Economic Policy." *World Politics* 47 (2), 283–310.

Jorde, Thomas, and David Teece, eds. 1992. *Antitrust and Innovation*. New York: Oxford University Press.

Kang, David. 1995. "South Korean and Taiwanese Development and the New Institutional Economics." *International Organization* 49 (3), 555–587.

Kent, Christopher. 1993. "NAFTA, TRIPS Affect IP." *Les Nouvelles* XXVIII (4), 176–181.

Keohane, Robert. 1987. *After Hegemony*. Princeton: Princeton University Press.

———, and Joseph Nye Jr. 1987. "*Power and Interdependence* Revisited." *International Organization* 41 (4), 725–753.

Kinter, William R., and Harvey Sicherman. 1975. *Technology and International Politics*. Lexington, MA: Lexington Books, D. C. Heath and Company.

Klotz, Audie. 1992. "Reconstituting Interests: Interpretive Analysis of Norms in International Relations." Unpublished manuscript, revised draft.

Koo, Bon Ho. 1990. "The Role of the Newly Industrializing Economies in the Global and Pacific Economic Network." *Business in the Contemporary World* II (3), 34–42.

Krasner, Stephen. 1974. "Oil is the Exception." Foreign Policy (13), 68–84.

———. 1978. *Defending the national interest*. Princeton: Princeton University Press.

———. (ed.) 1983. *International Regimes*. Ithaca: Cornell University Press.

———. 1985. *Structural Conflict: The Third World against Global Liberalism*. Berkeley: University of California Press.

Kratochwil, Friedrich. 1989. *Rules, Norms, and Decisions*. Cambridge: Cambridge University Press.

Kunz-Hallstein, Peter. 1975. "Patent Protection, Transfer of Technology and Developing Countries: A Survey of the Present Situation." *International Review of Industrial Property and Copyright Law (IIC)* 6 (4), 427–455.

———. 1979. "The Revision of the International System of Patent Protection in the Interest of Developing Countries." *International Review of Industrial Property and Copyright Law (IIC)* 10 (6), 649–670.

Lang, Jeffrey, and Laura Brank. 1993. "A Step in the Right Direction: Unlocking the Mexican Energy Market." *Latin American Law and Business Report* 1 (August), 12–15.

Latin America isolated at UNCTAD VII. *Latin American Weekly Report.* WR-87-23, (June 18, 1987), p. 6.

Lee, Michelle, and Mavis Lee. 1991. "High-Technology Consortia: A Panacea for America's Technological Competitiveness Problems?" *High Technology Law Journal* 6 (2), 335–362.

Levin, R. C., A. K. Levorick, R. R. Nelson, and S. G. Winter. 1987. "Appropriating Returns from Industrial Research and Development." Brookings Papers on Economic Activity, 3. Washington, DC: The Brookings Institution.

Lipson, Charles. 1985. *Standing Guard: Protecting Foreign Capital in the Nineteenth and Twentieth Centuries.* Berkeley: University of California Press.

Liu, Paul. 1988. "A Review of Intellectual Property Laws in Taiwan: Proposals to Curb Piracy and Counterfeiting in a Developing Country." *Brigham Young University Law Review*, 619–642.

Mallott, Robert. 1989. "1990s Issue: Intellectual Property Rights." *Les Nouvelles* XXIV (4), 149–153.

Management alert. *Business Latin America.* (August 3, 1992), p. 268.

Market notes. *Latin American Law and Business Report.* Vol. 1 (August 1993), p. 32.

Market notes: Mexico's SECOFI implements competition law. *Latin American Law and Business Report.* (May 1993), pp. 34–35.

Market notes. *Latin American Law and Business Report.* Vol. 2, No. 1 (January 1994), p. 31.

Martin, Lisa. 1992. *Coercive Cooperation.* Princeton: Princeton University Press.

McDonald, Hamish. 1991. The late convert: India wins reprieve in patent row with U.S. *Far Eastern Economic Review,* Vol. 154 (December 5), p. 65.

McIntyre, John R., and David S. Papp, eds. 1986. *The Political Economy of International Technology Transfer.* New York: Quorum.

Merges, Robert. 1990. "Battle of the Lateralisms: Intellectual Property and Trade." *Boston University International Law Journal* 8, (Fall), 239–246.

Miller, Debra L. 1979. "Panacea or Problem? The Proposed International Code of Conduct for Technology Transfer." *Journal of International Affairs* 33 (1), 43–62.

Miller, Debra L., and Joel Davidow. 1982. "Antitrust at the United Nations: A Tale of Two Codes." *Stanford Journal of International Law* XVIII (2), 347–375.

Modelski, George, ed. 1979. *Transnational Corporations and World Order.* San Francsico: W. H. Freeman and Company.

Morrison, Sylvia. 1994. *How Will the Uruguay Round of GATT Affect the U.S. Computer Industry?* Congressional Research Service Report for Congress. Report No. 94-804-E. Washington, DC: The Library of Congress.

Mossinghoff, Gerald. 1991. "For Better International Protection." *Les Nouvelles* XXVI (2), 75–79.

Mowrey, David C., and Nathan Rosenberg. 1989. *Technology and the Pursuit of Economic Growth.* New York: Cambridge University Press.

Mufson, Steve. In fight for intellectual rights in China, pirates still winning. *The Washington Post.* February 18, 1996, A29.

Murphy, Craig. 1994. *International Organization and Industrial Change: Global Governance since 1850.* New York: Oxford University Press.

Nelson, Richard. 1984. *High-Technology Policies: A Five Nation Comparison.* Washington, DC: American Enterprise Institute for Public Policy Research.

Neto-Advogados, Pinheiro. 1993. "Investigation of Pharmaceutical Industry for Abuse of Economic Power." *Latin American Law and Business Report.* 1 (April), 23–24.

Neuman, William. IPR protection improves, but reforms not uniform. *Business Latin America* (April 20, 1992), p. 127.

O'Connor, Donal. 1995. "TRIPs: Licensing Challenge." *Les Nouvelles* 16–18.

Office of the U.S. Trade Representative. 1994. *The 1994 General Agreement on Tariffs and Trade,* Annex 1(C), "Agreement on Trade-Related Aspects of Intellectual Property, Including Trade in Counterfeit Goods." August 27.

Oman, Charles, and Ganeshan Wignaraja. 1991. *The Postwar Evolution of Development Thinking.* New York: St. Martin's Press.

Otamendi, Jorge. 1987. Update on licensing in Argentina. *Les Nouvelles.* Vol. XXII, No. 4 (December): 166–168.

de Palacios, Alicia Puyana. 1982. *Economic Integration among Unequal Partners: The Case of the Andean Pact.* New York: Pergammon Press.

The Paris Convention: Report on the fourth session of the revision conference. *Patent and Trademark Review.* Vol. 82, No. 11 (November 1984), pp. 456–457.

Patel, Surendra. 1989. "Intellectual Property Rights in the Uruguay Round: A Disaster for the South?" *Economic and Political Weekly* (May 6), 978–993.

Pearson, John. 1992. "The Patent Pirates are Finally Walking the Plank." *Business Week* (3253, Industrial/Technology Edition) (Feb. 17), 125–127.

Pease Jeffries, Countess. 1977. "An Evaluation of the UNCTAD Code of Conduct." *Harvard International Law Journal* 18 (2), 309–342.

Perkins, Dwight, and Michael Roemer, eds. 1991. *Reforming Economic Systems in Developing Countries.* Cambridge, MA: Harvard Institute for International Development.

Perlmutter, Howard. 1976. "Perplexing Routes to M.N.E. Legitimacy: Codes of Conduct for Technology Transfer." *Stanford Journal of International Studies* XI (Spring), 169–199.

Pfanner, Klaus. 1985. "Compulsory Licensing of Patents: Survey and Recent Trends." *Sartryck ur NIR Nordiskt Immateriellt Rattsskydd* 1 (NIR 1/ 85), 1–29.

Preston, Julia. As piracy grows in Mexico, U.S. companies shout foul. *The New York Times,* April 20, 1996, p. A1 and A34.

Pugwash Conference on Science and World Affairs. 1974. "Draft Code of Conduct on the Transfer of Technology." *World Development* 2 (4 and 5), 77–82.

Radcliffe, Mark F. 1985. "New Intellectual Property Protection." *Les Nouvelles* XX (3), 105–109.

Ramachandran, Arcot. 1977. Self-reliance in technology and the patent system, in WIPO, *World symposium on the importance of the patent system to developing countries.* No. 638 (E) (Geneva), 293–318.

Rill, James. 1993. "Competition Policy: A Force for Open Markets." *Antitrust Law Journal* 61, 639–650.

Roffe, Pedro. 1985. "Transfer of Technology: UNCTAD's Draft International Code of Conduct." *International Lawyer* 19 (2), 689–707.

Rosenau, James, and Ernst-Otto Czempiel, eds. 1992. *Governance without Government: Order and Change in World Politics.* New York: Cambridge University Press.

Rosenberg, Nathan. 1982. *Inside the Black Box: Technology and Economics.* Cambridge: Cambridge University Press.

———, and Claudio Frischtak, eds. 1985. *International Technology Transfer: Concepts, Measures, and Comparisons.* New York: Praeger.

Rothstein, Robert. 1977. *The Weak in the World of the Strong.* New York: Columbia University Press.

———. 1984. "Consensual Knowledge and International Collaboration: Some Lessons from the Commodity Negotiations." *International Organization* 38 (4), 733–762.

Rubin, Seymour, and Gary Clyde Hufbauer, eds. 1983. *Emerging Standards of International Trade and Investment: Multinational Codes and Corporate Conduct.* Totowa, NJ: Rowman and Allanheld.

Ruggie, John, ed. 1993. *Multilateralism Matters.* New York: Columbia University Press.

———. 1993. "Territoriality and Beyond: Problematizing Modernity in International Relations," *International Organization* 47 (1), 139–174.

————, and Friedrich Kratochwil. 1986. "IOs as an Art of the State: A Regime Critique." *International Organization* 40 (4), 753–775.

Ryan, Michael. 1991. "Strategy and Compliance with Bilateral Trade and Dispute Settlement Agreements: USTR's Section 301 Experience in the Pacific Basin." *Michigan Journal of International Law* 12 (Summer), 799–827.

Sandholtz, Wayne. 1992. *High-Tech Europe: The Politics of International Cooperation.* Berkeley: University of California Press.

Sarkar, Jayanta. Back in charge: India's reforms entice foreign firms to raise their profile. *Far Eastern Economic Review.* (July 8, 1993), pp. 49–50.

Sauvant, Karl, and Elton Lanier. 1980. "Host-Country Councils: Concepts and Legal Aspects." In Norbert Horn, ed. *Legal Problems of Codes of Conduct for Multinational Enterprises.* Deventer, the Netherlands: B. V. Kluwer.

Sell, Axel, and Monika Mundowski. 1979. "Patent Protection and Economic Development." *International Review of Industrial Property and Copyright Law (IIC)* 10 (5), 565–572.

Sell, Susan K. 1994. Antitrust in Korea and Taiwan: The Link Between Politics and Money in the Context of Democratization. Prepared for the 1994 American Political Science Associations Convention, New York.

————. 1995. The Origins of a trade-based approach to intellectual property protection: The role of industry associations. *Science Communication* Vol. 17, No. 2 (December), 163–185.

Shafer, D. Michael. 1994. *Winners and Losers: How Sectors Shape the Developmental Prospects of States.* Ithaca: Cornell University Press.

Shenon, Philip. Chinese accused of pirating disks. *The New York Times,* August 18, 1994, p. D1.

Sherwood, Robert. 1989. "New Theory of Conductivity in Licensing." *Les Nouvelles* XXIV (4), 186–189.

Shore, Chris. 1992. "The Thai Copyright Case and Possible Limitations of Extraterritorial Jurisdiction in Actions Taken under Section 301 of the Trade Act of 1974." *Law and Policy in International Business* 23 (3). 725–748.

Shrader, Dorothy. 1994. *Enforcement of Intellectual Property Rights Under the GATT 1994 TRIPs Agreement.* Congressional Research Service Report for Congress. Report No. 94-228-A. Washington, DC: The Library of Congress.

————. 1994. *Intellectual Property Provisions of the GATT 1994: The TRIPs Agreement.* Congressional Research Service Report for Congress. Report 94-302-A. Washington, DC: The Library of Congress.

Shultz, George. 1983. "The U.S. and the Developing World: Our Joint Stake in the World Economy." *U.S. Department of State Bulletin* 83 (2076), 57–61.

Sikkink, Kathryn. 1991. *Ideas and Institutions.* Ithaca: Cornell University Press.

Simon, Helen. Unfair practices in the spotlight. *Business Latin America,* (January 25, 1993), pp. 6–7.

Smith, Roger K. 1987. "Explaining the Non-Proliferation Refime: Anomalies for Contemporary International Relations Theory." *International Organization* 41 (2), 253–281.

Smith, Brian. 1988. "Reflecting on a Changing Business World." *Les Nouvelles* XXIII (1), 1–3.

Software piracy: Self-defense the best choice for victims, *Business International.* Vol. XXIV (July 20, 1992), p. 250.

Spero, Joan Edelman. 1977. *The Politics of International Economic Relations.* New York: St. Martin's Press.

Standke, Klaus-Heinrich. 1979. "The Prospects and Retrospects of the United Nations Conference on Science and Technology for Development." *Technology in Society* 1, 353–386.

Studebaker, Scott. 1994. "Brazil: Constitutional Revision Session Floundering." *Latin American Law and Business Report* 2. (April), 11–13.

———. 1994. "Brazil—Economic Plan, Privatization, Status of Constitutional Congress and Other Recent Developments." *Latin American Law and Business Report* 2 (February), 7–9.

Suleiman, Ezra, and John Waterbury. 1990. *The Political Economy of Public Sector Reform and Privatization.* Boulder, CO: Westview Press.

Sykes, Alan O. 1992. "Constructive Unilateral Threats in International Commercial Relations: The Limited Case for Section 301." *Law and Policy in International Business* 23 (2), 263–330.

Tata Timken shows India's monopolies law is losing its teeth. *Business Asia,* Vol. 4 (September 1989), pp. 292–293.

Tharp, Paul. 1976. "Transnational Enterprises and International Regulation: A Survey of Various Approaches in International Organization." *International Organization* 30 (1), 47–73.

Thompson, Dennis. 1982. "The UNCTAD Code on Transfer of Technology." *Journal of World Trade Law* 16 (4), 311–338.

United Nations Conference on Trade and Development (UNCTAD). 1974. "The Role of the Patent System in the Transfer of Technology to Developing Countries." TD/B/AC.11/19. Geneva: United Nations.

———. 1975. "Draft Outline for the Preparation of an International Code of Conduct on Transfer of Technology." TD/B/C.6/1/Annex II. Geneva: United Nations.

———. 1975. "The International Patent System as an Instrument for National Development." TD/B/C.6/AC.2/3. Geneva: United Nations.

———. 1976. "Issues in Connection with the Formulation of a Set of Multilateral Agreed Equitable Principles and Rules for the Control of Restrictive Business Practices: Note by the UNCTAD Secretariat." TD/B/C.2/AC.6/2. Geneva: United Nations.

———. 1976. "Report of the Third *Ad Hoc* Group of Experts on Restrictive Business Practices on Its First Session." TD/B/C.2/AC.6/4. Geneva: United Nations.

———. 1977. "Report of the Group of Governmental Experts on the Role of the Industrial Property System in the Transfer of Technology." TD/B/C.6/24/Add. 1, Annex V. Geneva: United Nations.

———. 1977. "Report of the Third *Ad Hoc* Group of Experts on Restrictive Business Practices on its Third Session." TD/B/C.2/AC.6/10. Geneva: United Nations.

———. 1978. "Proposals for Action in the Field of Technology." TD/B/C.6/42. Geneva: United Nations.

———. 1978. "Recent Developments in the Control of Restrictive Business Practices in Latin America." TD/B/C.2/AC.6/17. Geneva: United Nations.

———. 1978. "Report of the Third *Ad Hoc* Group of Experts on Restrictive Business Practices on its Fourth Session." TD/B/C.2/AC.6/13. Geneva: United Nations.

———. 1978. "United Nations Conference on an International Code of Conduct on the Transfer of Technology: Background Note by the UNCTAD Secretariat." TD/Code TOT/4. Geneva: United Nations.

———. 1979. "Summary Record of the Eighth Meeting." TD/Code TOT/SR.8. Geneva: United Nations.

———. 1980. "The Draft of an International Code of Conduct on the Transfer of Technology: Major Issues Outstanding." TD/Code TOT/27. Geneva: United Nations.

———. 1980. "Summary Record of the Fourteenth Meeting." TD/Code TOT/SR.14. Geneva: United Nations.

———. 1981. "The Set of Multilaterally Agreed Equitable Principles and Rules for the Control of Restrictive Business Practices." TD/RBP/CONF/10/Rev. 1. New York: United Nations.

———. 1982. "Compilation of Legal Material Dealing with the Transfer and Development of Technology." TD/B/C.6/81. Geneva: United Nations.

———. 1983. "Annual Report 1982: On Legislative and Other Developments in Developing Countries in the Control of Restrictive Business Practices." TD/B/RBP/11. Geneva: United Nations.

———. 1984. "Report of the Intergovernmental Group on Restrictive Business Practices on Its Second Session." TD/B/976. Geneva: United Nations.

————. 1985. "Annual Report 1983–1984: On Legislative and Other Developments in Developing Countries in the Control of Restrictive Business Practices." TD/B/RBP/29. Geneva: United Nations.

————. 1985. "Draft International Code of Conduct on the Transfer of Technology." TD/Code TOT/47. Geneva: United Nations.

————. 1991. "Activities Relating to Specific Provisions of the Set: Technical Assistance, Advisory and Training Programs on Restrictive Business Practices." TD/B/RBP/83. Geneva: United Nations.

————. 1991. "Report of the Second United Nations Conference to Review All Aspects of the Multilaterally Agreed Equitable Principles and Rules for the Control of Restrictive Business Practices." TD/RBP/CONF.3/9. Geneva: United Nations.

————. 1992. "Activities Relating to Specific Provisions of the Set: Technical Assistance, Advisory and Training Programs on Restrictive Business Practices." TD/B/RBP/90. Geneva: United Nations.

————. 1992. "Adoption of Agenda and Organization of Work." TD/B/RBP/86. Geneva: United Nations.

————. 1992. "Draft Report of the Intergovernmental Working Group of Experts on Restrictive Business Practices on Its Eleventh Session." TD/B/RBP/L.58/Add. 1. Geneva: United Nations.

————. 1992. "Review of the Operation of and Experience Arising from the Application and Implementation of the Set of Multilateral Agreed Equitable Principles and Rules for the Control of Restrictive Business Practices." TD/B/RBP/89. Geneva: United Nations.

————. 1993. *1991 International Trade Statistics Yearbook,* Vol. 1, *Trade by Country,* New York: United Nations).

U.S. Bureau of the Census. 1993. *Statistical Abstract of the United States.* 113th edition. Washington, DC: U.S. Bureau of the Census.

U.S. Department of Commerce. 1984. Roger Severance trip report on consultations with Taiwan and Singapore on commercial counterfeiting. International Trade Administration, U.S. Department of Commerce. Washington, D.C. Memorandum, June 6.

U.S. Department of State. 1982. "Voluntary Guidelines for Antitrust." *U.S. Department of State Bulletin* 82 (2058).

Vaitsos, Constantine. 1972. "Patents Revisited: Their Function in Developing Countries." *Journal of Development Studies* 9 (1), 71–98.

Vedaraman, S. 1977. Patent law in India as a means towards accelerating industrial development, in WIPO, *World symposium on the important of the patent system to developing countries.* No. 638 (E), (Geneva), pp. 137–147.

Vernon, Raymond, and Louis T. Wells. 1976. *The Economic Environment of International Business.* 2nd edition. Englewood Cliffs, NJ: Prentice-Hall.

Vicuna, Francisco Ortega. 1979. "The Control of Multinational Enterprises." In George Modelski, ed. *Transnational Corporations and World Order.* San Francisco: W. H. Freeman and Company.

Wade, Robert. 1990. *Governing the Market: Economic Theory and the Role of Government in East Asian Industrialization.* Princeton: Princeton University Press.

Wagner, Stanley. 1987. "Antitrust: the Korean Experience 1981–1985." *The Antitrust Bulletin* (Summer), 471–522.

Waite, Peter. 1987. "Profit and Technology Transfer." *Les Nouvelles* XXII (4), 133–139.

Wallis, W. Allen. 1983. "American Policy to Promote World Development." *U.S. Department of State Bulletin* 83 (2077), (August) 27–30.

Waltz, Kenneth. 1979. *Theories of International Politics.* New York: McGraw-Hill.

Wendt, Alexander. 1987. "The Agent-Structure Problem." *International Organization* 41 (3), 335–370.

———. 1992. "Anarchy Is What States Make of It." *International Organization* 46 (2), 391–425.

———, and David Friedheim. 1995. "Hierarchy under Anarchy: Informal Empire and the East German State." *International Organization* 49 (4), 689–721.

Whipple, Robert. 1987. "A New Era in Licensing." *Les Nouvelles* XXII (3), 109–110.

Whiting, Van. 1991. *The Political Economy of Foreign Investment in Mexico: Nationalism, Liberalism, and Constraints on Choice.* Baltimore: Johns Hopkins University Press.

Wijk, van Jeroen and Gerd Junne. 1992. *Intellectual Property Protection of Advanced Technology: Changes in the Global Technology System: Implications and Options for Developing Countries.* Contract No. 91/026. Maastricht, the Netherlands: United Nations University, Institute for New Technologies.

Wince-Smith, Deborah. 1993. "Challenge of Technological Competitiveness." *Les Nouvelles* XXVIII (1), 1–4.

Woods, Ngaire. 1995. "Economic Ideas and International Relations: Beyond Rational Neglect." *International Studies Quarterly* 39 (2), 161-180.

World Bank. 1987. *Korea: Managing the Industrial Transition Volume I: The Conduct of Industrial Policy.* Washington, DC: World Bank.

————. 1987. *Korea: Managing the Industrial Transition Volume II: Selected Topics and Case Studies.* Washington, DC: World Bank.

World Intellectual Property Organization (WIPO). 1979. "Basic Proposals: Draft Approved or Forwarded to the Diplomatic Conference by the Preparatory Intergovernmental Committee." PR/DC/3. Geneva: WIPO.

————. 1982. "Revised Provisional Summary Minutes." PR/SM/5. Geneva: WIPO.

————. 1983. Final summary minutes of the meetings of the plenary and of main committee I held during the second session of the diplomatic conference. PR/SM/6 (December 23) (Geneva: WIPO).

————. 1984. "Final Summary Minutes." PR/SM/9. Geneva: WIPO.

————. 1985. "Final Summary Minutes." PR/SM/12. Geneva: WIPO.

————. 1985. "First Consultative Meeting on the Revision of the Paris Convention." PR/CM/1/3. Geneva: WIPO.

Yoffie, David. 1983. *Power and Protectionism.* New York: Columbia University Press.

Zalik, Alice. 1986. "Implementing the Trade-Tariff Act." *Les Nouvelles* XXI (4), 199–202.

Index

Activist developing countries, 69–70, 80, 86, 107, 219, and economic liberalization, 103. *See also* Andean Pact countries; Argentina; Brazil; India; Mexico

African countries, 106; and antitrust, 210

Algeria, 69, 95

American Metal Climax, 62

Anaconda, 55

Andean Pact countries, and antitrust, 209; and economic liberalization, 103, 104–105; and import-substituting industrialization, 10; legislation, 29, 69–70, 80–82; Decision 24, 81–82, 104, 112; Resolution 85, 112–113; Investment Code, 82; and the Paris Convention, 109–110, 115; and intellectual property 112–113, 115; technocrats, 112; Treaty of Cartagena, 11, 112. *See also* Chile; Colombia; Peru

Anglo-American Corporation of South Africa, 62

Antitrust policy, 4, 6, 37, 38, 92–94, 149; benefits of, 180; and the Chicago School, 38, 158–159, 224; and developing countries, 177–178, 179, 198–201, 204–212, 218, 220; domestic incentives for, 180; in the EEC, 160, 161–162, 224; and mergers, 159–160, 224; and the "rule of reason," 93, 154, 168; in the U.S., 224; U.S. enforcement, 225–226; U.S.-European antitrust cooperation agreement of 1991, 225. *See also* Restrictive business practices; restrictive business practices code

Arbitration, 94–96

Argentina, and import-substituting industrialization, 10; legislation, 29, 69, 80–81, 82–83; local content requirements, 63; investment laws, 103–104; pharmaceutical patents, 191–192; Section 301 action against, 191–192